ERNLE BRADFORD

CLEOPATRA

HARCOURT BRACE JOVANOVICH INC

NEW YORK 1972

THIS BOOK WAS DESIGNED AND PRODUCED BY

GEORGE RAINBIRD LIMITED
MARBLE ARCH HOUSE
44 EDGWARE ROAD
LONDON W2

FILMSET IN MONOPHOTO BEMBO
BY JOLLY AND BARBER, RUGBY
PRINTED BY VAN LEER, N.V.,
BOUND BY VAN RIJMENAM, N.V.
PRINTED AND BOUND IN THE NETHERLANDS

HOUSE EDITOR: CAROLINE LIGHTBURN
PICTURE RESEARCH: JOCELYN SELSON
DESIGNER: JUDITH ALLAN
INDEXER: SANDRA RAPHAEL

ISBN 0-15-118140-3

LIBRARY OF CONGRESS
CATALOG CARD NUMBER: 73-153683

FRONTISPIECE REVERSE: *gold snake bracelet, 1st century* B.C./A.D., *actual size.*

FRONTISPIECE: *sandstone relief from the corridor of the Great Temple of Horus at Edfu, showing Ptolemy VIII Euergetes II, in the traditional style of an Egyptian pharaoh, with the goddess Hathor; 2nd century* B.C.

FOR MARIE BLANCHE

Haec . . . scripsi . . . non otii abundantia sed amoris erga te.

I HAVE WRITTEN THESE THINGS OUT OF THE ABUNDANCE,
NOT OF MY LEISURE, BUT OF MY LOVE TOWARDS YOU.

CICERO. EP., BOOK 7, I.

CONTENTS

COLOR PLATES

QUEEN OF EGYPT

Cleopatra was a queen. It is the failure to take this into consideration that has prompted so many misjudgments and false analyses of her character. She was, as her handmaiden Charmion reminded the Romans who broke into the mausoleum where she lay dead, 'the descendant of so many kings'. The whole of her life was devoted to her country, Egypt, and to the attempt to preserve its national sovereignty under the rule of the Ptolemaic dynasty to which she belonged. She was the seventh Egyptian queen of her name, but it is doubtful if she had any Egyptian blood in her veins. She was a Macedonian Greek. She was also the first of her line who had troubled to learn the language of the country over which she ruled.

The reputation that she has commonly had in later centuries – of the arch-seductress, the guileful and sensual woman – is almost entirely a product of Roman propaganda against her. Those who are defeated rarely have the opportunity of writing their own version of history, since it is usually written by the victors. As with Carthage, so with Cleopatra: the biased accounts we possess were written by the conquering Romans. That she was finally defeated in her attempt to keep Egypt free from Roman rule is recorded by the poets and historians who lived under the Roman Emperors, the first of whom was the Octavian/Augustus who achieved her ruin. In those days of imperial patronage it was inevitable that writers should be sycophants, and in extolling the virtues of Augustus it was natural that they should portray the woman who had tried to prevent Rome from dominating the Mediter-ranean as evil, treacherous, and given to sexual excess.

In another context, writing on the view of the Etruscan people that we get from Roman authors, D. H. Lawrence put it as follows: 'The Etruscans were vicious. We know it, because their enemies and exterminators said so. . . . However, those pure, clean-living, sweet-souled Romans, who smashed nation after nation and crushed the free soul in people after people, and were ruled by Messalina and Heliogabalus and such-like snowdrops, they said the Etruscans were vicious.' Cleopatra was capable of ruthlessness and even murder in defence of her throne and her kingdom, but her actions were as nothing compared with those of the Roman leaders who were fighting among themselves for the mastery of the world.

Sandstone relief on the outside south wall of the temple of Hathor at Denderah. Caesarion, depicted as an Egyptian pharaoh, with Cleopatra behind, offers incense.

She was eighteen when she ascended the throne of Egypt in 51 B.C. Cleopatra VII was formally married to her elder brother Ptolemy XIII, who was only a boy of ten at the time. It is unlikely, even at a later date when Ptolemy had reached puberty, that this marriage was ever consummated. It would not have been unusual if it had been, for the Ptolemies had adopted the ancient dynastic incest of Egypt among the other trappings of the Pharaohs whom they had succeeded. That the Ptolemies took lovers and that the children who succeeded them were often not the product of brother and sister union cannot be disputed. The fact remains that, in order to maintain their hold over the Egyptian people and the still powerful priesthood, they had to conform to the traditions of ancient Egypt. Their claim to be the successors of the divine Pharaohs had to be maintained by such a stratagem. This royal incest had originated in ancient times in Egypt, when the law of female succession had made the monarch's eldest daughter the heiress of the kingdom. The matrilineal system most probably derived from the simple fact that paternity was a matter of inference while maternity was a matter of observation.

If the Pharaohs and their successors were indeed, as was claimed for them, gods on earth, then it was essential that they should only mate with each other (or, at any rate, for it to appear so). The son selected by his father to succeed to the throne obtained his right to it by marriage with the heiress. Naturally there must have been occasions when no heiress existed, and in this case the rule must have been waived. The real trouble arose because there were usually several brothers and sisters, and the ones who failed to succeed often felt that they were stronger or cleverer than the elected rulers. The result was that there were blood-thirsty fights between brothers and sisters, with rebellion and murder as the weapons. The dynastic history of the Ptolemies was stained time and time again with such conflicts between the children of the ruling house. The life of Cleopatra, the last sovereign ruler of Egypt, was, in this respect at least, to follow the familiar pattern.

Of her appearance we know little except from coins and descriptions in ancient writers, for no portrait busts that can be fully authenticated have yet been discovered although one or two have been ascribed to Cleopatra VII. A copper coin from Alexandria, which shows Cleopatra when young, depicts her wearing the diadem of monarchy, and with her hair arranged in a bun at the nape of her neck. The neck itself is strong, long and graceful. The general appearance of her features is of neatness and delicacy, with fine large eyes. The famous nose is not as long as it appears in some other coin portraits, but is definitely more Semitic than classical Greek. Her mouth is rather large and beautifully formed, with well chiselled lips. Her chin is prominent, but not excessively. The overall impression one gets from this, and other coins at later stages of her life, is of a good-looking, but not pretty, woman. The eyes, the height of the brow, the clarity of the features, the nose and chin, all suggest a woman of intellect and power – which indeed she was. Although she was a consummate actress, this is not the face of any of the actresses who have subsequently portrayed her. This is a face of great dignity: the face of a queen.

Coins of Cleopatra VII

Cleopatra did indeed inherit the intellectual capacities of some of the early Ptolemies, capacities which had been sadly lacking in most of her recent predecessors – including her father, Ptolemy XII, nicknamed by his people Auletes (The Fluteplayer). He was in most respects a weak and pathetic figure, saved only from complete ridicule by his fondness for music. His daughter, on the other hand, was a brilliant linguist who, as Plutarch remarked, 'easily turned her tongue to any language that she wished. It was very rare that she had need of an interpreter, for she dealt with most matters by herself, talking with Ethiopians, Troglodytes, Jews, Arabs, Syrians, Medes and Parthians. It is said that she knew the languages of many other peoples, although her royal predecessors had not even bothered to learn the Egyptian language, and some of them still spoke the Macedonian dialect of Greek. . . .'

Cleopatra, one must infer from this, had learned from her professors in the Mouseion the Athenian Attic (considered like the Spanish of Castile to be the purest and best). She was also a fluent and expressive Latin speaker, for she would hardly have interested or amused a man like Julius Caesar solely on the basis of her physical charms, or even the financial potential of her kingdom. It is true that both Caesar and Antony had political and financial reasons enough to wish to become the husband of Egypt's Queen, but this can hardly be the whole story. Caesar was a military, political and even literary giant (as well as being one of the outstanding bisexual philanderers of all time). Antony, who had only a fraction of his abilities, was nevertheless a brave and fine soldier, built like a bull, and – with his aggressive qualities and his hard-drinking, hail-fellow-well-met outlook – the very image of the classic extrovert. Both men had had innumerable sexual affairs, and it can hardly have been entirely on the basis of Cleopatra's body that they became so deeply involved with her.

She was a woman of powerful intelligence, wit and considerable political ability. Plutarch commented that, 'To know her was to be touched with an irresistible

13

Cosmetics had virtually been invented in ancient Egypt. ABOVE: *toilet box belonging to a man from Thebes, c. 1790 B.C.;* *8 inches high.* OPPOSITE: *Tutankhamen pours perfumed water; from a small gold-covered wooden shrine in his tomb.*

charm. Her form, coupled with the persuasiveness of her conversation, and her delightful style of behaviour – all these produced a blend of magic. Her delightful manner of speaking was such as to win the heart. Her voice was like a lyre. . . .' The Roman historian Dio Cassius also said of her that 'her delightful way of speaking was such that she captured all who listened to her'. Clearly she was one of those women who have far more powerful weapons in their armoury than their sisters who are merely beautiful. Also it is true, as Byron remarked, that,

> The Devil hath not, in all his quiver's choice,
> An arrow for the heart like a sweet voice.

This information about her face, voice and intelligence is well substantiated, but we have little further knowledge of her physical appearance. Dio Cassius (who lived long after her, but who was careful and selective in his use of authorities) says that she was wonderful both to hear and to look at, and capable of inspiring love in the hearts of young and old. Plutarch, who said that Antony's wife Octavia surpassed her in beauty, adds that the Egyptian Queen had a fascination rarely to be found in the world. Neither the writers nor the coins tell us whether she was blonde or brunette, fair-skinned or dark. (Macedonians can be white-skinned, blonde and blue-eyed.) The coins, however, do suggest an Eastern Mediterranean type, and it would be reasonable to infer that Cleopatra was dark-haired with a pale olive skin. It is likely that her skin colour will have been an inherited characteristic rather than due to exposure to the sun, for aristocratic ladies in this part of the world made every effort to keep out of the sun (peasants are dark-skinned). Cosmetics had virtually been invented in ancient Egypt, and

14

Cleopatra in this respect will have had a far greater knowledge of their usage than any Roman woman of the period. Similarly, the Alexandrians were famous for their skill in the concoction of perfumes and incense, due to their trade with the East. All of these artificial but stimulating aids to glamour will have been used by Egypt's Queen. After her death a treatise entitled 'Cosmetics' was widely circulated in Mediterranean cities, purporting to have been written by Cleopatra. Although it is improbable that she had any hand in this work (the author using the name of the famous Queen to arouse interest), there is no doubt that she would have been capable of writing a book on the subject.

The coins suggest a delicacy of features, and it is likely that she was also fine boned and well proportioned. The famous occasion when she was rolled up in some bedding, or a carpet, and carried over her attendant's shoulder into the palace to see Caesar, suggests that she was small and slim. This incident, with its courage and sense of humour, confirm what we know from other sources, that Cleopatra amalgamated with her regal nature and her cleverness an immense fund of high spirits and impulsiveness. She was not all things to all men like a courtesan, but there was an immense variety in her character. To Caesar, apart from being his mistress, she undoubtedly showed those aspects of her character that would have appealed to him: her political and intellectual skills, and her mastery of language. To Antony, on the other hand, who conceived of himself as the New Dionysus, she was Aphrodite, Queen of Love: an Aphrodite who could evolve more elaborate

ABOVE: *detail from a painted scene in the tomb of Nakht, Thebes, representing a banquet; New Kingdom, c. 1400* B.C.
OPPOSITE: *bronze statuette of Aphrodite, 5th–4th century* B.C.; *9¾ inches high.*

pageants and banquets than the simple Roman; and who would light-heartedly join him in pranks and escapades on the streets of Alexandria.

She fought like a tigress for her child by Caesar, and her children by Antony. A large part of her life may be seen as a struggle to try to ensure that her children should inherit her empire and her throne. Nothing should be allowed to stand in her way if their interests were threatened. As far as is known, there were only two men in her life, Caesar and Antony. In view of her age at the time when she met Caesar (as well as his notorious reputation sexually) it is far more likely that he seduced her than the reverse. Josephus, who in any case was writing over a century later, described her as 'a slave to her lusts'. He was doing no more than reflect the current bias against the woman who had seemed such a threat to Rome. (Josephus became a friend of Nero and his wife Poppaea, neither of whom could be called 'clean-living, sweet-souled Romans'.) She was indeed adept in the arts of luxurious entertainment – with which she bedazzled even the cynic Caesar, as well as the rough sensualist Antony. Her sex was certainly an important weapon in her armoury, with which she intended to make herself Caesar's wife and mistress of the

16

world, and which did make her Antony's wife and Queen of the Eastern Empire. More than most other women in history she knew how to use her sexuality politically. This is hardly the achievement of someone who is 'a slave to her lusts', but rather of a woman whose head is in command of her instincts.

As her life will show, she had immense courage – even the courage to die as befitting a queen when all was lost. Apart from her talent for languages she seems to have had considerable interest in the arts and sciences. When Antony was master of the East she induced him to give to Alexandria the famous library of Pergamum, which is said to have contained nearly a quarter of a million volumes. Among the numerous other learned men of the Alexandrian Mouseion, who were acquaintances or friends of the Queen, was the famous astronomer Sosigenes. It is almost certain that it was Cleopatra who introduced him to Caesar, and it was he who reformed the Roman calendar which was in a hopeless confusion. (The new, or Julian, calendar was to last until the sixteenth century when it was once again reformed by Pope Gregory.)

The last Macedonian Queen of Egypt, the last of the Ptolemy Pharaohs, was no ordinary woman. The Western World, in which we live, is based largely upon the shattered fragments of the Roman Empire; and many of our weaknesses as well as strengths still derive from that Empire's concepts. This Macedonian Queen of Egypt was the last person seriously to challenge the creation of a 'Roman Mediterranean'. It was not as an 'Egyptian' that she challenged the Romans, but as a civilized Greek – who must have regarded them as semi-barbarians. Had she succeeded, a Greco-Roman monarchy would have been established; the influence of Hellenism upon the Roman world would have been extended; and Alexandria – not Rome – might well have become the capital of this empire. Cleopatra still casts a long shadow over history.

THE EARLY PTOLEMIES

The Ptolemaic dynasty was founded in the fourth century B.C. by Ptolemy I, the son of Lagos, a Macedonian nobleman. Ptolemy was one of Alexander's most able and trusted companions, as well as being one of his best generals. He was also, unlike some of the others, not only a good soldier, but a brilliant politician and indeed more than that, a statesman. On the death of Alexander and the division of the empire that he had carved out of Asia and the East, only one man managed to assure himself and his descendants a dynasty that really worked, and a kingdom that was economically sound. This was Ptolemy.

As A. R. Burn writes in his *Alexander the Great*: '"Alexander dead?" said Demades at Athens. "Impossible! The whole world would stink!" Yet it was even so; and now men must accustom themselves to the fact that had so many times been prematurely reported.'

Immediately after his death – in Babylon, 323 B.C. – the inevitable fight broke out between his battle-hardened generals for the inheritance of his conquered kingdoms. Some hoped to win all, and others (the more prudent) set themselves limited objectives. Ptolemy was one of these.

By setting himself this limited objective Ptolemy succeeded where most of the others ultimately failed. In choosing Egypt he had chosen one of the richest countries (and one of the main granaries) of the ancient world. Syria, Persia, Asia Minor, all these might on the surface appear to have more attractions, but they also had greater problems – hostile tribesmen and hostile neighbours among them. Egypt, on the other hand, was – and had always been – something of an isolationist country. Its basic wealth lay in the valley of the Nile. Every summer the river overflowed its banks, and the inundated land proved in autumn to be perfect for man's necessary cereals, such as barley and wheat. The land had in its further mountains rich metal-deposits and semi-precious stones. The people themselves were accustomed over thousands of years to autocratic rule and were unlikely to make any trouble – intellectual or political. There were yet other advantages: Egypt was difficult to attack and difficult of access. The only ways by which an enemy could approach it were either from the north, across the sea, or across the desert from the east. To the west also lay desert land, and the first of the Ptolemies was astute enough to

From ancient Mauretania, a marble head of a veiled woman, persuasively argued on the evidence of the coin portraits to be Cleopatra VII, whose daughter by Antony, Cleopatra Selene, married Juba II of Mauritania

seize and garrison this area (Cyrenaica) so that his left flank was secure, while his right, or eastern, flank could only be approached by the coast road which was commanded by the garrison town of Pelusium.

'Everything fears Time, but Time fears the pyramids!' The Ptolemies, like the Pharaohs before them, had the immense conservatism of the Egyptian people on their side. They would continue to toil and work the delta, and adore their ancient gods, so long as the new rulers also appeared to be god-descended. This was a most important factor in the life of Cleopatra's ancestors, and in assessing her character we must remember that she saw herself not only as a queen, but of divine descent.

This concept, which the Ptolemies had inherited from their predecessors and, to some extent, from Alexander himself, is incomprehensible to us. But the patterns of thought two thousand years ago were very different from today. As Professor J. A. K. Thomson put it in the context of the Homeric world:

> The limits of human and superhuman were but dimly realized. There was something in common between gods and men and the beasts of the field and all growing things, and a pathway between the living and the dead. . . . Every stream and oak and mountain was the habitation of a spiritual being whose nature was on the borderland between the human and the divine and partook of both. And so weak was the sense of identity, that with a touch of magic it was felt the barrier might be passed, and a man might become a wolf or a serpent or a hoopoe or a purple lily. He might renew his youth; he might be raised from the dead. With the waving of a branch and sprinkled waterdrops the wizard might bring a rain-shower down the sides of Lykaios. Like Melampous he might understand the language of all living creatures, even the woodworms in the decaying rafters, and say with Alkman 'I know the songs of all the birds'.

Ptolemy I added to the authenticity, as it were, of his kingship of Egypt by securing the body of Alexander the Great – to the fury of the other claimants – and by having it taken to Memphis. The High Priest, so the legend goes, was unwilling that the world conqueror should lie there, saying: 'Take him to the new city he has built at Rhakotis; for wherever his body lies, the place will be uneasy, and troubled with wars and battles.' So Alexander came down the Nile and was interred in a splendid tomb in the very centre of the city that he had founded. Certainly the High Priest's prophecy was proved true in terms of both Alexandria and the lives of the Ptolemies.

A large part of Ptolemy I's reign was occupied with wars with the other Macedonian chiefs who were dividing up Alexander's empire. Having secured his western flank by seizing Cyrenaica, it was his ambition to do the same to the east and the north, by annexing Palestine and Cyprus. Although at various times he managed to occupy Palestine he was ultimately defeated by Antigonus, another general of Alexander's who claimed dominion over all Asia, and who founded the Antigonid

Bronze statuette of Isis, 2nd century A.D., modelled in a mixed Greek and Egyptian style, with the ends of the mantle tied between the breasts in a magical knot; 10⅝ inches high.

dynasty. With Cyprus, however, Ptolemy was more fortunate, and he managed to establish an Egyptian protectorate over the petty kings in that warm and fertile island.

Ptolemy had three wives and several mistresses, by all of whom he seems to have had children. Among his mistresses was the famous courtesan Thais, who had accompanied Alexander on his Asiatic campaign, and who is said, though on doubtful authority, to have persuaded the conqueror to set fire to the city of Persepolis. It is Berenice, Ptolemy's third wife, who is of importance in the history of the dynasty, for it was her son, Ptolemy Philadelphus, who was decreed heir to the kingdom by his father. Berenice may possibly have been a daughter of Lagos, and therefore Ptolemy I's sister or half-sister. She was a woman of considerable intellect and ability, and exerted a great deal of influence over him and the whole pattern of the court. These two founders of the Ptolemaic dynasty were equally remarkable for their strength of character and their talents. Ptolemy himself was not only a fine soldier; he and Berenice between them set the pattern for the future Ptolemaic patronage of the arts. Liberal and full of bonhomie, he attracted to his city and his cause many Macedonian and other Greeks, as well as securing peace and prosperity in Egypt for the native people. He is perhaps best remembered in history for his foundation of the great library of Alexandria, which was to prove an inspiration to scholarship in the Mediterranean world. On his death at the age of eighty-two, after half a century or more of soldiering and statecraft, he left behind for his son by Berenice a secure and well ordered inheritance.

Ptolemy II, later known as Philadelphus, was a very different man from his father though in his way as distinguished. He was no Macedonian warrior-general but an intellectual, who nevertheless managed to maintain his kingdom during the wars that were then ravaging the Mediterranean, and created in Alexandria one of the most splendid courts in history. During his reign Egypt became the dominant naval power in the eastern Mediterranean, and a large part of the Aegean Sea, including the Cycladic islands, as well as many of the ports and coastal towns of Asia Minor, came within the Ptolemaic sphere of influence. After an unsuccessful campaign against Antiochus II, the descendant of another of Alexander's generals who ruled the Syrian area, Ptolemy managed to secure a successful peace by marrying his daughter to his former enemy. At home in Alexandria he was an outstanding patron of the arts and sciences and is said to have increased the contents of the library founded by his father from two hundred thousand volumes to four hundred thousand. He set the style which many other Ptolemies were to emulate, but few to equal, for magnificent displays and pageants, for the elaboration of public buildings, and for a whole way of life that was as un-Greek as it was un-Egyptian. In him the West and the East were curiously mingled, and it was he, even more than his father, who first evolved what can only be called the 'Alexandrian Mode'. It has been rightly said of him that his court was 'magnificent and dissolute, intellectual and artificial'. It has been compared with the Versailles of Louis XIV.

His first wife was Arsinoë, daughter of the King of Thrace and Macedonia, who

Marble head of Ptolemy I Soter, 304–282 B.C., said to be from El-Faiyum; 9¾ inches high

may also have been his half-sister; for Ptolemy I had married his daughter to her father. (The couplings of the Ptolemaic dynasty are incredibly complicated.) Arsinoë was to become the mother of his successor Ptolemy III although he later repudiated her and married his genuine, full sister, yet another Arsinoë. The latter seems to have been indeed the love of his life. Their marriage was celebrated in the Egyptian style as the union of two deities, Isis and Osiris. These were two of the principal Egyptian divinities: the goddess of the moon and the great father–god (who were also supposed to have been brother and sister).

It was during the reign of this second Ptolemy that so much of the intellectual and artistic vitality of his city flourished with poets like Theocritus and Callimachus and innumerable lesser poets, authors, scholars and scientists all engaged in perpetuating the image of the King and his court. On the death of his second wife Ptolemy II was grief-stricken. He did all that he could to perpetuate her memory, having her declared a goddess, and worshipped as such in the Egyptian temples, as well as erecting buildings and statues to her. He never married again, but we are familiar with the names of some of his successive mistresses – Agathoclea, Didyma, an Egyptian, Myrtion, an actress, and so on – all of whom seem to have been women of intellect as well as beauty. Once again there is a parallel with the Sun King's court at Versailles.

23

Bas-relief of Ptolemy II

It was during the reigns of these first two Ptolemies that the Egyptian economy and agriculture were, for the first time, properly systematized. Surveys were conducted throughout the kingdom to determine which areas were best for particular crops. The finest land was declared the personal property of the ruler and this was leased for cultivation to Egyptian natives – who thus became crown peasants. The grain was carefully measured at the time of the harvest and the rent due to the King was then determined. The whole of Egypt was now run and regulated by a carefully organized bureaucracy, at the head of which was the government in Alexandria, where the King's chief minister or *dioiketes* resided. A series of papyri exists containing correspondence between this minister and one of his subordinates during the reign of Ptolemy II. They show how the Greek genius in the alien land of Egypt was applied with scientific precision to furthering and improving the return of the fertile land. Foreign strains of wheat and vines were imported, a careful system of rotation of crops was introduced – with the result that the land was soon made to yield two harvests a year. Throughout all the great estates (which were given by the King to his nobles in reward for their services) the same type of scientific farming became the rule.

The nobles themselves were mainly absentee landlords. They had their country houses but Alexandria was the hub of the world; for where Ptolemy was, there was the power and the influence. Besides, Egypt itself can have had little attraction for these Greeks. Only in Alexandria, with its theatre, gymnasium, library, law courts and palaces, was anything like the Greek 'way of life' to be found. But it was not really that, not at least as it had been understood in, say, Periclean Athens. These Greeks of the Hellenistic period were not the same men as their ancestors, except in their insatiable curiosity and their capacity for intrigue. The ancient virtues –

24

which few of their ancestors followed, but many had aspired to – were gone. They had become orientalized.

Centuries later Renaissance Italians would say of Englishmen who learned their language, and aped their fashions and manners: '*Inglese Italianato, Diavolo incarnato*' ('An Englishman Italianate, Devil incarnate'). The same might, in a sense, have been said of the Greeks of Alexandria and indeed of the other eastern states. They retained a courage, vitality and capacity to do mischief far greater than the peoples they had conquered, but they had also absorbed the devious approach, the sensual tastes and the corrupting luxury of the East. Herodotus tells the story of how, several centuries before, the great Persian King Cyrus was approached by some of his most influential citizens, who suggested that, since Persia was now the most powerful country in the world, it would be a good thing if they were to emigrate from their own poor and mountainous country and settle in the rich lowlands. Cyrus thought the matter over carefully and then made his judgement: 'You may do so, if you wish. But, *if you do*, you must be prepared no longer to be the rulers, but to live under the rule of other men. Soft countries breed soft people. It is not in the law of nature that a land which produces fine crops will also produce fine fighting-men.' Egypt was a soft country.

The third Ptolemy, known as Euergetes (The Benefactor), was the son of the first Arsinoë, but had been adopted by her successor and proclaimed the legitimate heir. His name 'The Benefactor' derived from the fact that, early in his reign, he had made an immense raid into the eastern provinces of what had been Alexander's empire, advancing as far as Babylon and Susa. He had brought back with him not only a vast amount of treasure but also all the statues of Egyptian deities which had been captured long ago by the Persians, and he restored them to their respective temples. Little of the territory that he had 'conquered' remained in his hands for long, saving only a part of Syria. His fleets, however, carried on the expansion that had been begun by his father, and nearly all the eastern Mediterranean now fell under the dominance of the Ptolemies. Euergetes was equally remarkable in his patronage of the arts and science; among other things attempting to discover the source of the Nile (a task in which he failed). This third Ptolemy combined most of the virtues – as well as the vices – of his predecessors. But there can be no doubt that he consolidated their work, and Egypt was at the height of its power when he died at the end of 222 or early in 221 B.C. The predominant civilization in the eastern Mediterranean – just as it had been centuries before in the days of the Pharaohs – the Land of the Pyramids was flourishing and prosperous and, in Alexandria at least, more cultured than anywhere else. All was soon to change.

In-breeding, as any horse-racing stud-book can show, has its benefits. Stamina, intelligence and courage can be transmitted through it. But after a comparatively short length of time out-breeding becomes essential in order to retain the 'bone' and other necessary physical qualities. The decline of the Ptolemies began with the fourth of the line. The stock went steadily from bad to worse.

DECLINE OF A DYNASTY

Ptolemy IV, who is said to have murdered his father to attain the throne, set the dismal pattern that was henceforth to characterize nearly all the dynasty. Anyone who looked as if he or she might be even a remote threat to his position was immediately eliminated – his uncle, his younger brother, his mother. Even Nero, whose name has become synonymous with cruelty and lust, could hardly compete with this monarch, whose private life was as contemptible as his public life was murderous. He married his sister, Arsinoë III, but was in fact more or less governed by his mistress Agathoclea, the sister of his male favourite, Agathocles. Like many of the Ptolemies who were to follow him, he was bisexual and surrounded himself with a court of male and female favourites. Again, however, like many of his successors, he was a patron of the arts, built a temple to Homer, and himself composed a tragedy.

The characteristics of this and the successive Ptolemies have been described by Mahaffy as follows: 'Great power and wealth, which makes an alliance with them imply the command of large resources in men and money; mutual hatred; disregard of all ties of family and affection; the dearest object-fratricide – such pictures of depravity as make any reasonable man pause and ask whether human nature had deserted these women and the Hyrcanian tiger of the poet taken its place.' For in the subsequent history of the dynasty the women played the major part. While the men through their in-breeding declined into more or less negligible ciphers, the women of the line emerged as the real rulers, and formidable killers into the bargain.

Ptolemy V was like his father, dissolute and cruel, while Ptolemy VII is described by Polybius as 'riotous'. Ptolemy VIII murdered his nephew, the rightful heir to the throne, and married the boy's mother, Cleopatra II. He later married his niece, who in her turn, on being widowed, murdered her predecessor. She was then murdered by her son. Over and over again the pattern of incest and family violence repeats itself, as if to prove that the ancient Greek warnings against incest, as contained for instance in the Oedipus legend, were not without validity. The Roman historian Justin (who of course had no reason to write well of the Ptolemies)

From the open court of Kom Ombo temple, c. 30 B.C., a relief of a goddess with offerings representing the plentitude of Egypt

nevertheless based his work on an earlier history of the Macedonian monarchy written in the reign of Augustus. He describes how Ptolemy VIII, having murdered his sister's child by Ptolemy VI, was then received into the Queen's bed with his hands still red with the blood of her own child. The women seem to have resembled the praying mantis, devouring their mates once they had produced an heir or heirs. Cleopatra III, having driven her elder son from the throne, installed her younger son Ptolemy X, since she felt that he would be more amenable to her discipline. In this case, however, the lady had miscalculated – she was murdered by him for her pains. He was described thus: 'This King of Egypt, who was hated by his people, but worshipped by his immediate circle, spent his days in revelry, and could walk only when supported by two of his boon companions. But at the Bacchanalia, when he grew excited, he would spring from his couch, and in his bare feet dance more wildly than the professional dancers. . . .'

In this atmosphere of corruption and moral decay, the arts and sciences nevertheless continued to flourish in Alexandria. If there is little good to be said of the later Ptolemies, yet they did still try to emulate their predecessors as patrons. In all other respects, however, their kingdom presented an abject picture of decline. Throughout the first century B.C., while these dissolute and murderous kings and queens were frittering away their inheritance, the shadow of Rome lengthened over the East. It was inevitable that as Rome changed from a republic to an empire her new rulers should turn their eyes to Egypt – the richest country in the Mediterranean and a granary that could feed the Roman people.

The father of Cleopatra VII, Ptolemy XII, was most probably not a member of the Lagidae dynasty. He and his brother (who became ruler of Cyprus) were generally assumed to be illegitimate. Ptolemy XII was, however, the eldest male descendant of the line, even if his mother was not the regnant queen at the time of his birth. He ascended the throne and took the religious-political title of *Neos Dionysos* – The New Dionysus, the God of Wine. This was all part of the ruler-cult which had been enforced on the Ptolemies from the very beginning, and which they had adopted as an essential part of their hold over the Egyptian people. As Sir William Tarn put it:

> To the King, it was a political measure which gave him a footing in Greek cities and ensured the continuing validity of his acts after death; and it was rendered possible by the general disbelief of the educated classes, for the Olympian religion was spiritually dead, and when king-worship was established nothing else had yet taken its place. . . . The Olympians conferred no personal salvation, no hope of immortality, little spirituality; and as guardians of the higher morality they were mostly sad misfits. And one had to take so much on trust; one might believe in the power and splendour of Zeus, but one

Giza: the Sphinx, obscuring the Chephren pyramid, with the pyramid of Mycerinus in the distance. OVERLEAF: *the Chephren pyramid and, without apex, the pyramid of Cheops. All Old Kingdom, c. 2500 B.C.*

could see the power and splendour of Ptolemy. The local god could not feed you in a famine; but the King did.

Ptolemy XII, this 'New Dionysus', was a strange and tragi-comic figure. He came to the throne at a time when Rome had become involved in the affairs of Egypt because of the increasing collapse of the Greek government. As early as 139 B.C. the great Scipio, the conqueror of Carthage, had visited Alexandria, where he had been received by Ptolemy VIII, commonly known as Physkon, 'The Bloated'. The latter, clad in a diaphanous robe of purple, had personally conducted Scipio round the city and throughout the palaces, puffing at the unaccustomed exercise. The Roman is said to have remarked, in an aside to a friend, that he had at least brought one benefit to the Alexandrians – they had actually seen their sovereign walk! Other visiting Romans from time to time confirmed the evidence obtained from Scipio's official visit: that the country was immensely fertile and rich – and in need of better government. There could be no doubt at that moment in history where the better government would come from.

Ptolemy XII's immediate predecessor, his cousin Ptolemy XI, had been a protégé of the Roman dictator Sulla. Indeed it was only with Roman support that he had acquired the throne. He married his step-mother, Berenice, who had been ruling the country since her husband's death, and had her murdered. This was too much even for the Alexandrians – who, in any case, did not like seeing a Pharaoh installed by the might of the Roman legions. They dragged the King from his palace and killed him. When Cleopatra's father succeeded him it was only to discover that his predecessor, who owed his throne to the Dictator Sulla, had made a will appointing the Roman Republic his heir. This act, surprising though it sounds, was not entirely unknown, and had already occurred in several other places including Cyrene.

The New Dionysus Ptolemy XII, or Auletes, 'The Flute Player', as he was commonly called, had therefore inherited a throne that was disputably not his. Even if the will were challenged, the fact remained that he was ruler of Egypt only so long as it suited the convenience of the Romans. To this sad end had come the Hellenistic kingdom of Egypt which, for at least a century, had been the dominant power in the Eastern Mediterranean and the leading cultural influence.

Although Rome did not officially recognize the new ruler there were a number of reasons why the Republic did not challenge him directly and seize the kingdom. The principal of these was that a large party both in the Senate and outside was against Roman involvement in colonial expansion, particularly in the direction of the East. The great wealth of Egypt (which was acknowledged to be the second

Palm trees reflected in the water near Memphis, with an upturned block bearing the cartouche of Ramases II, c. 1304–1237 B.C.

33

Sandstone relief, c. 135 B.C., from Kom Ombo temple showing Ptolemy VIII Euergetes II receiving a scimitar from Haroeris. Behind are Cleopatra II and Cleopatra III.

power in the Mediterranean), while a distinct attraction, also presented a danger. If the country was made a Roman province, into whose hands as Governor should it be assigned? Many feared that Egypt, together with Cyprus (and possibly other dependencies), might develop into an eastern empire – a rival and a threat to Rome itself.

Ptolemy Auletes did not inherit the great violence and malevolence of his predecessors on the throne of the Pharaohs. All that he really asked was to be left in peace. He was a weak, self-indulgent man, a drunkard and a music-lover. There is little else to be said of him. He married his sister Cleopatra by whom he appears to have had two children, Cleopatra VI and Berenice. It is just possible that the famous Cleopatra, Cleopatra VII, was the third and last child of this union. Equally, she may have been the first child of her father's second marriage. Unfortunately history does not record the name of his second wife by whom he had three more children – Cleopatra's younger sister Arsinoë and two brothers, Ptolemy XIII and

34

XIV. Of one thing it is possible to be certain – that Cleopatra VII was the child of the regnant Queen of Egypt. Had she been illegitimate it is inconceivable that this fact would not have been used against her in the spate of hostile propaganda to which she was later subjected. Among all the insults that were hurled at her by Latin writers there is never a suggestion that she was not the legitimate Queen of her country.

Cleopatra grew up in a hard school where deviousness was second nature and where the Greek dynasty of the Ptolemies was constantly threatened with extinction. First of all her father had to contend with the might of Rome and the fact that technically he appeared to have no right to the throne. And he had to maintain his position by placating the powerful Romans of the time. This was far from easy because of the struggle in Rome as to who was to rule the Mediterranean world. The Republic was rapidly disintegrating, and all the birth-pangs of the impending Empire were racking the city and the state. Ptolemy the Flute-Player knew well enough that the forces at his disposal could never compete against the strength of the Roman legions, which were enjoying immense success on almost all fronts. They were, in fact, in the process of creating the Empire that would ultimately destroy the old Republic. There was only one way by which Cleopatra's father could retain his throne and secure his dynasty – bribery.

In 63 B.C. when the great Pompey was marching from victory to victory in the East, at the moment he was engaged in Judaea, Ptolemy – seeing him as 'the Roman most likely to succeed' – sent him a large gold crown and offered to provide him with a cavalry force of eight thousand men. At the same time he invited Pompey to come to Egypt on a friendly visit. The King thought that the presence of this triumphant Roman – together with some of his legions – would serve to quieten his kingdom, which was becoming restive through excessive taxation and a general run-down of efficiency in the bureaucracy. Pompey took the bribe but declined the visit. Ptolemy, however, could still be happy in the knowledge that Pompey had now, as it were, become his patron and under the Roman system a patron would not desert his client in times of need.

The three dominant Romans of this period were Julius Caesar, Crassus and Pompey. All had to be placated, as their differing ambitions drove them violently around the Mediterranean world. Caesar was always short of money. This was something that Ptolemy had become vividly aware of when, two years before his accommodation with Pompey, he had found out that Caesar and Crassus together had proposed that Egypt should be incorporated into the Roman Empire. The Ptolemaic dynasty was only saved on this occasion by the fact that the republican and conservative Cicero foiled the plan of these potentially dictatorial masters, and disclosed what they were intending to do. (Caesar and Crassus, of course, had been hoping to blackmail Ptolemy into paying them a large cash sum in return for an official recognition of his right to the throne.) As Theodor Mommsen put it: 'In Rome men had forgotten what honesty was. A person who refused a bribe was regarded not as an upright man, but as a personal foe. . . .' Finally in 58 B.C. Ptolemy the Flute-Player realized he had no option but to secure an official Roman acknowledgment of his kingship of Egypt. He went to Rome in person and, in return for an immense bribe of six thousand talents (several million pounds in modern money), secured the necessary recognition. Julius Caesar, who was nearly bankrupt at the time, moved a resolution in the Senate (the so-called 'Julian Law concerning the King of Egypt'), whereby Ptolemy was confirmed on his throne and acknowledged as 'The friend and ally of the Roman people'. Ptolemy no doubt heaved a sigh of relief, and set sail for Alexandria and the pleasures of his palace.

If he thought that his troubles were at an end, he did not know the Romans. The very next year disaster struck in Cyprus. This was the last overseas possession of what had once been the considerable Ptolemaic empire. The island was now ruled by Ptolemy's younger brother, and the Romans did not feel that they were under any obligation to keep him on his throne, although they had done a deal with his brother in Egypt. Publius Clodius, a politician who – even by the standards then prevailing in Rome – was exceptional for his vicious chicanery, proposed that the island of Cyprus should be annexed to the Empire. He had a personal grudge against the ruler and he also wished to get the younger Cato, who was an opponent of his, out of Rome for a time. Cato was accordingly despatched to take Cyprus, and the unfortunate King, rather than be banished from his island, took poison. His personal treasure, said to have been worth seven thousand talents, was seized by the Romans and paraded in a triumph through the Forum. Oskar von Wertheimer accurately commented: 'We who today are filled with admiration of the Roman conquests which introduced Latin culture into countries inhabited by barbarians ought not to forget that the people thus favoured regarded the matter very differently. All they saw of Latin culture were the legionaries who threatened their existence, the tax-farmers who extorted money from them, and the officials who enriched themselves without scruple.' Cyprus had long been in the sphere of Greek culture. It was the Romans who were the barbarians.

LEFT: *Ptolemy Auletes, Cleopatra's father.* RIGHT: *Ptolemy XIII*

In Alexandria the seizure of the island was seen as the writing on the wall. It was clear that if the Romans were prepared to annex Cyprus without any legitimate grounds for doing so, the time was not far distant when it would be Egypt's turn. That Ptolemy XII had failed his brother in his hour of need – had done nothing – was also seen by the people as clear evidence that as a king he was a total failure. In addition there was mounting indignation at the weight of taxation (much of which had been applied to secure the bribe-money for Ptolemy to retain the throne). There was a general rebellion, and the Flute-Player was forced to flee his own country and seek safety in the very city that most threatened his interests – Rome.

On his way, having heard that the conqueror of Cyprus, the younger Cato, was in Rhodes, Ptolemy broke his voyage at the island in order to secure his patronage. It is difficult to conceive of such debasement: that a king should be willing to try to curry favour with the man who had been responsible for the death of his brother, and who had taken away from Ptolemaic control the rich island of Cyprus. But the Flute-Player had no dignity and no shame. He did, however, attempt for a brief moment to indicate that he was indeed a king – sending a message to Cato that the King of Egypt would like the latter to call on him. Cato sent back a reply that he was suffering from a bilious attack, and that if Ptolemy wanted to see him he had better come himself. Ptolemy (who in some respects reminds one of the late King Farouk of Egypt) tottered corpulently into Cato's house. The Roman did not bother to rise, but indicated a chair to his guest. He then gave him some straightforward advice: telling him bluntly that he was wasting his time going to Rome; that he would be fleeced as he had been fleeced before, and that he should not trust the promises of anyone. Better, he suggested, for the King to go back to his country and come to terms with his people. (Cato knew well enough that sooner or later Egypt was bound to fall like a ripe plum into Roman hands.) The Flute-Player hesitated, but did not heed the warning.

While Ptolemy pursued his voyage to Rome his daughter, Berenice IV, had seized the throne as Queen of Egypt. (His eldest daughter Cleopatra VI, who had originally been instated, had died.) Cleopatra VII was at this time a child about eleven years old. In the nurseries of the later Ptolemies one learned early the realities of life, the hardships of power and the devious windings of statecraft. Because of the steady deterioration that had marked the affairs of Egypt the people were increasingly restive, the economy was on the decline, and even the efficient agricultural methods that had been introduced earlier were being forgotten. Necessary canals, as well as irrigation waterways, had been abandoned. Peasants had left their lands rather than pay the increased taxes, and had fled to desolate areas like the marshlands and the fringes of the desert. The currency had been devalued: silver coins had replaced gold; copper coins replaced silver, and there had been a steep rise in the cost of living. All in all, the country presented what has subsequently become a familiar spectacle – the collapse of an organized community and the arrival of anarchy.

Bust of Cato

There is no substitute in human societies for wise, strong and firm government. There is no such thing as a 'permissive' society. It is a contradiction in terms. And the Ptolemies and their fellow Greeks who ruled the Delta had been permissive for far too long.

Ptolemy in Rome was now spending his time in efforts to persuade influential senators and others that, as he held his throne under a guarantee from Rome, they should fulfil their side of the bargain and have him reinstated. Naturally, once again, he needed large sums of bribe-money to secure Roman co-operation. But on this occasion he was no longer in a position to secure it by squeezing his people, so he had to go to some of the richest money-lenders in the city and give them promissory notes against the day when he was restored as ruler of Egypt. Whether Pompey was one of those whom he bribed is uncertain, but it is known that the Flute-Player stayed in Rome at Pompey's villa in the Alban district, and that it was Pompey who urged his case for restoration. Ptolemy had become his client, and Pompey now acted as his patron. There can be little doubt that Pompey saw that the King owing his throne to Pompey's favour would be a very useful source of income.

The Alexandrians, getting wind of what was going on in Rome, thought that the best way of preventing the restoration of their detested monarch would be to send a delegation to Rome and argue their case. In this they were certainly naive, for the only way of arguing was the way Ptolemy was doing it. The delegation, consisting of a hundred citizens led by the philosopher Dion, arrived in the port of Puteoli (modern Pozzuoli) on the bay of Naples. Puteoli was the principal port for Roman trade with Alexandria and the East, and accordingly the delegates were housed in their embassy. But before they could even get to Rome or begin any discussions Ptolemy hired a group of assassins and had them attacked. During this affray many of the delegates were killed, and the others terrified or bribed into silence. Dion, who managed to escape to Rome, was poisoned on Ptolemy's orders. The Flute-Player was a weak and dissolute man with hardly a virtue, but he was determined to return to his palace in Alexandria.

This whole incident was a little too much even for the climate of Rome and, despite the fact that he still had powerful friends and patrons, Ptolemy decided that it would be better if he absented himself for a while. Leaving an agent behind him to keep an eye on things and promote his interests, he now moved to Ephesus, where he bided his time, waiting to see which way the political wind would blow. For three years 'the Alexandrian Question' was one of the principal debating and feuding points in Rome, some being openly hostile to any further involvement in eastern affairs, and others, like Pompey, quietly working for their own ends to restore the degenerate monarch. Pompey in particular, being jealous of Julius Caesar's re-sounding successes in Gaul, was eager to open up for himself a new sphere of influence in the rich land of Egypt. It is more than likely that the other member of the triumvirate then dominating Roman affairs, Licinius Crassus, did all he could to block Pompey's promotion of the Flute-Player's cause. Crassus, of whom it has been said that 'his ruling passion was love of money', was almost certainly interested in the wealth of Egypt – for himself.

In 57 B.C. the Senate came to the conclusion that the interests of Rome would best be served by Ptolemy's restoration, for they saw (as Pompey had seen for himself all along) that an Egyptian monarch who owed his throne to Roman arms, and who would have to be maintained there by Roman legions, would also have to pay heavily for such a favour. Furthermore, there must have been many who looked ahead to the day when, with the Flute-Player dead, it would be easy to deny the succession to any of his heirs and quietly take over Egypt as a province. The corn and grain on which the citizens of Rome depended would then be theirs at a cheap price, and all the rich trade of Alexandria would also come under Roman control. The consul in office, Lentulus Spinther, who was to become governor of Cilicia in the following year, was accordingly entrusted, upon taking up his governorship, with the task of restoring the King.

Early in 56 B.C., however, just as Ptolemy, secure in Ephesus, must have felt that he would soon be lounging in Alexandria once more, there occurred one of those portents so common in the ancient world, often (one suspects) heavily contrived: the great statue of Jupiter on the Alban Mount had been struck by a thunderbolt. In such an emergency there was only one thing to do – consult the Sibylline books. These repositories of ancient wisdom and oracles had supposedly been bought by one of the early kings of Rome, Tarquinius Superbus, from the last of the Sibyls or prophetesses. They were kept in the temple of Jupiter Capitolinus, and in any great crisis the Senate would order them to be consulted – in much the same manner as in later, Christian times, people would open the Bible at random and take the necessary advice from the first section that met their eye.

In this case what the books produced, while it may have pleased some, must have disappointed a number of others: 'If an Egyptian king should come asking for help, do not refuse him friendship; but do not go to his aid with force, for if you do you will meet with dangers and difficulties'. Certainly the conservatives and republicans like Cato and Cicero must have welcomed the advice. (It is surely no coincidence that the keepers of the Sibylline books were inevitably men of a conservative stamp?) The message was quite plain – no Roman military involvement in Egypt!

The Senate began a turbulent debate about how best to act in accord with the advice of the sacred books. Clearly, a mission should be sent to Egypt to demand the abdication of Ptolemy's daughter, Berenice. But who should lead it? As well as Lentulus, who had originally been entrusted with Ptolemy's restoration, the names of Pompey and Crassus were now mooted. Everyone knew that what was ultimately at stake was the rich prize of Egypt. Finally Crassus, who was backed by Clodius, managed to move the whole matter out of the Senate and into the public Forum. Here, in a scene of hysteria and abuse (arranged by his supporters), Crassus managed to ensure that whoever went to Egypt it would not be Pompey.

Lentulus, meanwhile, had taken up his governorship of Cilicia. So he was out of the way, as far as the other contestants were concerned. Only one man, Cicero, wrote advising him to take action for Ptolemy's return to his kingdom. Lawyers, orators and writers – because of the very nature of their trades – often tend to be specious men. Cicero was all three. In a letter to Lentulus he managed to find a way around the Sibylline injunction against employing force to restore the Flute-Player.

ABOVE: *gold jewelry of 1st century* B.C. – *dove ear-rings; Aphrodite-head medallion; Serapis, Harpocrates and Isis finger-ring.* BELOW: *gold ear-rings set with pendants in the form of cocks, 1st century* A.D.

Why Cicero, who theoretically was against imperialist expansion, changed his mind is difficult to say. Possibly he had concluded that Egypt would inevitably come under the rule of Rome. He was therefore determined that the Roman who took the country should not be Pompey, Caesar or Crassus.

In the end all the schemings, contrivings and discussions came to nothing. None of the main contestants for the rich prize of restoring Ptolemy managed to get the job. The Flute-Player, acting on his own behalf and with the connivance of Pompey, bribed the Roman proconsul of Syria, Aulus Gabinius, with the promise of the vast sum of ten thousand talents if he was restored. The reason that Gabinius chose to ignore the Sibylline warnings and act in direct defiance of the Senate was that he himself was completely bankrupt and needed the money. He probably concluded that once the matter was a *fait accompli* Rome would not only accept but welcome his action. He knew Pompey's reasoning on the ultimate future of Egypt.

The Alexandrians in the meantime had arranged a marriage between Berenice IV and a certain Archelaus of Cappadocia. The reason Berenice was not married to her brother was that he was still only a child. Aulus Gabinius now sought for an excuse for his invasion, and found the pretext that the Egyptians were encouraging pirates on their coasts, who were interfering with the trade of Rome. He also maintained that they were building a large fleet which would threaten Rome's naval supremacy. Accordingly he declared war on Archelaus and Berenice, and set out with his legions across the desert from Gaza to Pelusium. In command of the cavalry, which swept ahead of the legions and played a major part in the capture of Pelusium, was a brilliant young soldier, the twenty-seven-year-old Mark Antony. With the fall of the fortress the road into Egypt lay open, and Gabinius escorted Ptolemy into his capital. There was only a minor skirmish outside the city, in which Archelaus was killed. The palace soldiers now deserted and joined the Romans. At long last, after so much scheming and the expenditure of many millions of pounds, the Flute-Player was back. It was just as well for Archelaus that he died in the fighting. Ptolemy would have killed him anyway, for he immediately had Berenice executed, as well as many in the court circle who had supported her.

Cleopatra was now fourteen years old. By the death of her sister Berenice she automatically became heir to the throne. It seems that Mark Antony remained for a short time in the city, and it was later said that the young princess's beauty and wit made an immediate impression upon him. It is strange to think that they first met this way – the young princess who had all her life lived in a network of intrigue, and the dashing cavalry officer who had been responsible for restoring her father to his throne. Antony's future seemed to lie all golden before him. It was then that he saw for the first time the palace where one day he would live, the beautiful harbour, the gracious gardens and the elegant but disturbing city of Alexandria.

Sarcophagus chamber of the catacomb of Kom esh-Shougafa, one of the few remains of early Alexandria, with architectural features and reliefs in a mixed Egyptian-Greek style, 2nd or 3rd centuries A.D.

THE CITY

Alexandria, the capital of Egypt, the burial place of Alexander the Great, was one of the most extraordinary creations of that far from ordinary man. Its site, selected by Alexander himself, was probably chosen because it was detached from Egypt proper. It was built upon a narrow peninsula that had the Mediterranean Sea to the north and the lake of Mareotis to the south. It was distinguished from the rest of Egypt by being known simply as 'The City'.

Alexandria was the lynch-pin in the life of Cleopatra and in the whole development of the Roman Empire. The city was founded upon a limestone spur, which jutted out into the sea from a long line of indistinguishable desert sands. To the north of this, and largely parallel with it, other outcrops of limestone combined to form a series of reefs. It was these which, by breaking the force of the seas induced by prevailing northerly winds, enabled the harbour to come into being. Clearly on so inhospitable a coast this strange promontory, affording such excellent shelter, must have attracted mariners from earliest times. Remains of a prehistoric harbour have been found off the tip of what is now called Ras el Tin (Headland of the Figs).

The first known reference to the area occurs in Homer's *Odyssey*, where he speaks of 'an island called Pharos in the surging seas off the Nile's mouth. . . . Here is a good harbour where shipmen can find water.' Here Menelaus encountered the Old Man of the Sea, Proteus, the divine King of the island. An Egyptian papyrus equates 'Prouti' with 'Pharaoh', so one may possibly conclude that Proteus, the magic Old Man of the Sea, was in fact the 'Pharaoh' or ruler of this area. Within recorded history there was a small Egyptian settlement here known as Rhakotis, founded about 1,300 B.C. Pharos itself was indeed a limestone island, lying off, as Homer describes it, until the channel between it and the mainland became silted up in later centuries. Similar siltings connecting off-shore islands with the mainland have occurred elsewhere in the Mediterranean: at Tyre for instance; Monte Circeo in western Italy, and, at the far end of the sea, Gibraltar. The promontory on which Alexandria was founded, however, is different from these other outcrops of limestone rock, for it projects from the flat desert-land of Egypt. Inevitably on this

---

Idealized statue of Alexander, found at Magnesia at the foot of Mount Sipylus, and probably the work of an artist of Pergamum; 6 feet high.

undistinguished coastline it acquired an importance out of all proportion to its size.

In the winter of 332–1 B.C. Alexander, having destroyed Tyre and captured Syria and Palestine, rode unopposed into Egypt and accepted the surrender of the kingdom. One of his first concerns was to found a capital that would be Greek, that would be outward-looking, and that would above all be a 'Mediterranean' city. Egypt, it must be remembered, had never desired much contact with the Mediterranean world, being self-sufficient, and having over the centuries found that most of its troubles came either from Persia and the East or from across the water. Alexander on the other hand, with his world-view of a Greek Mediterranean, wanted to turn introspective Egypt into an extrovert. Being a Greek, even if a Macedonian highlander, he knew that it is the sea and seaports which effect this change in a country, and he looked for a place on the Egyptian coastline that might prove suitable for a major city. There was a port already in existence some miles to the east of Pharos, situated on the banks of the Canopic mouth of the Nile, called Naucratis. There had long been a Greek colony here and it was the only place in Egypt where Greeks had been permitted to settle and trade. The situation, however, was unsuitable for the size of the city that Alexander had in mind, so he looked elsewhere. The settlement of Rhakotis and the island of Pharos, as we have seen, had been known to the Greeks since the days of Homer, and had become a haunt of both Greek and Phoenician sea-rovers during their voyages along the North African coast. It is tempting to speculate that it was one such leathery veteran who suggested to the great conqueror that he knew just the place for the new foundation. 'It has,' he might have said, 'a deep-water anchorage, an excellent fresh-water supply, and it is agreeably near the Nile Delta. It is also well sited on the western side of the Delta, directly below the Aegean, so that the northerly winds of summer will speed the trading vessels down to it.'

Alexander arrived and saw at once that this was what he had been looking for. He appointed a well known architect, Deinocrates, to lay out the town plan. The latter did this on lines which had been familiar in Greece since the fifth century B.C., when the originator of 'town planning', Hippodamus of Miletus, laid out Peiraeus, the port of Athens, on the system of broad straight streets cutting one another at right angles. Arrian says that it was the great conqueror himself who indicated where he wished the main square to lie, what temples were to be built (to the gods of Egypt as well as of Greece), and where the great walled perimeter was to be set. The soothsayers said that the town would undoubtedly prosper and that chief among its blessings would be the fruits of the earth. Alexander then moved on. He was a young man of twenty-five and in a hurry to achieve all his ambitions. He can hardly have foreseen that he would soon be ferried back down the Nile, wrapped in gold, and laid in a coffin of alabaster in the very centre of Alexandria.

The city which 'rose thus so strangely beside the waters is expressive of what in the ways of a thousand years men had come to desire. . . .' The first thing that the mariner, coasting down from Greece and the north, saw of Alexandria was the great lighthouse, the Pharos: a pillar of fire by night and a pillar of marble by day. Regarded as one of the wonders of the world, the Pharos had been designed by the architect Sostratus during the reign of Ptolemy II Philadelphus, in the third century B.C. It stood on the eastern arm of the island and was over four hundred feet high (six hundred according to some accounts). Surrounded by a colonnaded courtyard this masterpiece of engineering contained every known device for the protection of shipping, as well as acting as a weather-information centre. One statue on the top turned throughout the day following the passage of the sun; another pointed in the direction of the wind; yet another called out the hours of the day. A fourth is said to have shouted the alarm if ever a hostile fleet was sighted. None of these mechanical toys was beyond the capability of Alexandrian craftsmen and technicians.

The crew of the lighthouse were all housed in the square bottom storey, which is said to have contained three hundred rooms. The great beacon on the top was wood-fuelled and hydraulic machinery on the ground floor kept hoisting a constant supply up to the men maintaining the fire. The light of this was reflected seaward by vast mirrors, possibly made of glass, although more probably of polished metal. Also housed within the upper framework was a kind of giant periscope, whereby a watchman could descry the approach of ships when they were still out of sight below the horizon. The light of the Pharos, according to Josephus, could be seen three hundred stadia, thirty-four miles, from out at sea.

The island was joined to the city by a great embankment, known as the Heptastadion. This also performed the useful function of breaking the strong currents and creating two separate harbours: the Great Harbour to the east; and the Eunostos, or Happy Return, to the west. At either end of the embankment there were bridged-over waterways connecting one harbour with another, through which small boats could pass. In case of necessity these bridges could be raised up in the manner of medieval drawbridges. 'As for the Great Harbour,' writes Strabo, 'in addition to its being beautifully enclosed by both the embankment and by nature, it is not only so deep, close to the shore, that the largest ship can be moored at the steps, but also it is cut up into several minor harbours.' Alexandria, washed by water on both sides, was above all a city of the sea; a Hellenistic Venice.

The main street of Alexandria, known as the Canopic, was one hundred feet wide and ran for more than three miles right through the heart of the city. Starting at the Gate of the Necropolis at the western end, behind the harbour of Eunostos, it ended at the Gate of Canopus south of the Lochias Promontory. To the north of it lay the Mouseion, the Palaces, the tomb of Alexander (where the Ptolemies were also buried) and the gardens. South of it lay a number of temples and public buildings, as well as the courts of justice and the magnificent gymnasium. South too lay a most fascinating part of the city's planned 'landscape', the Panaeum. This, as we learn from Strabo, was an artificial mound 'in the shape of a fir-cone, looking rather like a pile of rock, to the top of which one can ascend by a spiral path, and from whose summit one can see the whole city spread out around one's feet'.

Bronze drachma piece with representation of the Pharos lighthouse, built by Sostratus in the reign of Ptolemy II Philadelphus; 2¾ inches diameter. RIGHT: *reconstruction of the lighthouse*

In this first century B.C., when Cleopatra was on the throne, the city was the unrivalled queen of the eastern Mediterranean. It is doubtful whether Rome could at that time in any way compare with the grandeur and the sense of history and destiny that infused the very air of Alexandria. Far more than Rome, which was *nouveau riche*, martial and still unplanned, Alexandria was a city of culture. Here Euclid had systematized geometry and founded the great Alexandrian school of mathematics during the reign of the first Ptolemy. It was in response to Ptolemy's query, whether geometry could not be made easier, that Euclid gave the famous answer: 'There is no royal road'. It was in Alexandria, too, during the third century B.C., that Eratosthenes became the first man ever to measure the circumference of the earth. He had been informed that at Aswan, in midsummer, the sun shone direct to the bottom of a dry well, thus indicating that the sun was vertically overhead, and that Aswan was therefore on the tropic. Accordingly, at the next summer solstice, Eratosthenes erected a vertical pole at Alexandria and measured the shadow which it cast. By this simple but ingenious means, he found the angle subtended between the two cities. This corresponded to one-fiftieth of a great circle, and it was on this basis that he calculated the circumference of the earth. It was also at Alexandria, during this same century, that the mathematician and astronomer Aristarchus had evolved the epoch-making theory that the sun – and not the earth – was the centre of the universe.

The two great institutions founded by the Ptolemies, which set the whole character of Alexandria, were the Mouseion (from which our word museum

48

derives) and the Palace. The latter, which stood on the Lochias promontory to the east of the Great Harbour, was surrounded by gardens, filled with the sound of the sea, and cooled in summer by the prevailing northerly winds. No Latin ruler, gasping for air in the hot Roman summer, had nearly as attractive a situation as these Greek rulers of the Egyptian people. The palace had its own private small-boat harbour, and it was also directly connected to the Mouseion. 'It was,' as E. M. Forster wrote, 'in this area, among gardens and colonnades, that the culture of Alexandria came into being. The Palace provided the finances and called the tune; the Mouseion responded with imagination or knowledge.'

The Ptolemaic patronage of the arts was not so unusual, for many previous Greek rulers or 'tyrants' (such as Hiero of Syracuse in the fifth century B.C.) had been munificent towards art and science. Yet, in the sense that the Mouseion was a special place devoted to these subjects, it was unique. Here, in an atmosphere remote from the ordinary concourse of the world, men of proven ability were enabled to live out their lives, their only concern that they should make a contribution to the glory and distinction of the Ptolemies and their city, Alexandria. It was, however, in this very dependence upon the patronage of the rulers that there lay a flaw.

During the centuries of the Ptolemies the great contributions made to human life were – except for the mathematical ones – essentially scholarly and non-creative. Periclean Athens, during a brief fifty years, enriched the human spirit far more. To quote E. M. Forster again: 'Victory odes, Funeral dirges, Marriage-hymns, genealogical trees, medical prescriptions, mechanical toys, maps, engines of war: whatever the Palace required it had only to inform the Mouseion, and the subsidized staff set to work. . . .' Just as in modern Soviet Russia all depends on the state (and the artist must therefore conform) so in Ptolemaic Alexandria there was little scope for individual thinking. The artists and savants who inhabited the Mouseion knew which side their bread was buttered, and acted accordingly. It is hardly surprising that such a situation should have produced a great deal of excellent work – but more of it second- than first-rate.

Despite this criticism it must be conceded that the role which Alexandria played in the history of world culture during these centuries was a very considerable one. In the great library the scholars classified and codified the literature of Greece. They worked carefully at emending manuscripts, and preserved for posterity innumerable works of literature and scholarship that otherwise would have been lost. (It was the desire of the Ptolemies to own at least one copy of every work of value that had been written in Greek.) It was in the library, for instance, that the first definitive texts of Homer were put together: and it was in the library that works of literature were first divided into 'volumes'. This particular division was simply determined by the length of a papyrus roll; papyrus being the paper-reed cultivated in Upper Egypt and the only ancient writing material. Without the papyrus, communications, organization and bureaucracy would have been impossible. It is on record that at one time during the reign of the Emperor Tiberius the plant was afflicted by a disease, and the year's supply failed. The organization of the Roman Empire very nearly ground to a halt.

The literature that flourished in the comfortable but artificial atmosphere of the Mouseion was almost inevitably of a somewhat artificial nature. As in the court of the Sun King centuries later, little was allowed to emerge that could displease the royal ear. We can trace at least one epic, *The Voyage of the Argo* by Apollonius, to Alexandria, and this is a very conscious product. It has none of the robust genius of Homer, upon whose work it was modelled. A typical Alexandrian poet was Callimachus. He is remembered for his aphorism 'A big book is a bad thing', and also (by English-speakers) for one of his poems translated by the Victorian schoolmaster, William Cory:

> They told me, Heraclitus, they told me you were dead,
> They brought me bitter news to hear and bitter tears to shed.
> I wept as I remembered how often you and I
> Had tired the sun with talking and sent him down the sky.
> And now that thou art lying, my dear old Carian guest,
> A handful of grey ashes, long, long ago at rest,
> Still are thy pleasant voices, thy nightingales awake:
> For Death, he taketh all away, but these he cannot take.

This has the true Alexandrian ring: charm, resignation, and elegance. The real sadness in these words stems from the fact that 'the nightingales' of Heraclitus were his poems, which his friend hoped would preserve his immortality. Not one of them has survived. A more important poet than either, however, and one who benefited by his stay in Alexandria, was the Sicilian-born Theocritus. His idylls brought into the hot air of Egypt something of a true island freshness, and he also gave the city its voice. His poems in themselves were very Alexandrian and contrived. He created an artificial world of nymphs and shepherds that was to be copied, again at Versailles and by writers including the English poet A. E. Housman:

> Oh stay at home, my lad, and plough
> The land and not the sea,
> And leave the soldiers at their drill,
> And all about the idle hill
> Shepherd your sheep with me.

Although the Alexandria of which Theocritus wrote was two centuries before that of Cleopatra, one of his mimes gives something of the essence of life as it was lived in the city. Gorgo is calling on her friend Praxinoe, whom she has not seen for some time:

ABOVE: *painted terracotta figurines of Alexandrian ladies, c. 30 B.C.; taller figure 9 inches high.* OPPOSITE: *ancient Egyptian necklace of gold and carnelian beads, New Kingdom, c. 1400 B.C.*

GORGO: My nerves are all in pieces, Praxinoe. Really, I hardly got here alive. The crowds and the people! And the carriages! And then, all the soldiers with their boots and swaggering uniforms. The street, too, it seems endless. You really live too far away!

PRAXINOE: That's the fault of my crazy husband. Total jealousy – as usual. We took this house – at the end of the earth – just so that we shouldn't have neighbours.

GORGO: My dear, better not talk about your husband while the little boy is here. Look, he's staring at you. (*Addresses the child*) That's my sweet, everything's all right. Your mummy isn't talking about papa. . . .'

Alexandria was more than a great port, it was also one of the major industrial centres of the world. Quite apart from the manufacture of papyrus, the city was a great glass-making centre. Egyptian glass-makers had been famous for centuries for the quality of their work. The beds of vitreous sand in Egypt had early been used for making the most beautiful glass, and Alexandrian glass was particularly prized throughout the Greco-Roman world. The city was also a great centre of the gem trade, and emeralds, amethysts, topaz and onyx (all of which were found in Egypt) were here converted into superb works of art in the shape of cameos and intaglios and small carved ornaments. The textile trade – much of it inherited from ancient Tyre – was very prosperous, and the quick-witted Alexandrians had even anticipated modern mass-production. The tastes of different nations were carefully catered for, as Professor Oertel has pointed out, 'Barbarian cloth was specially made for Axum, the Sabaeans and the natives of the Somaliland coast, while a particular

51

type of ready-made sleeved garment was worked up at Arsinoë [near modern Suez]'. Linens and fabrics woven out of cotton from India and silk from China were as famous in their day as the products of Parisian couturiers in later centuries. Commercial dyes and medicinal drugs were among the other exports which gave the city its wealth, its marble temples, its great theatre, its library and all those advantages of civilization that are only made possible by the exercise of intelligence and industry.

Edward Gibbon summarized the city as follows:

> The beautiful and regular form of that great city, second only to Rome itself, comprehended a circumference of fifteen miles; it was peopled by three hundred thousand free inhabitants, besides at least an equal number of slaves. The lucrative trade of Arabia and India flowed through the port of Alexandria to the capital [Rome] and the provinces of the empire. . . . Some were employed in blowing glass, others in weaving linen, others again manufacturing the papyrus. Either sex, every age, was engaged in the pursuits of industry, nor did even the blind or the lame want occupation. But the people of Alexandria, a various mixture of nations, united the vanity and inconstancy of the Greeks with the superstition of the Egyptians.

There was some truth in the great historian's comment that there was to be found in the people of cosmopolitan Alexandria a strange amalgam of the virtues and vices of its conflicting races. It was not only the Egyptians themselves, nor the Greeks, but the Jews, Syrians and traders from all over North Africa, who made this city an uneasy one in which to live. Cleopatra, who knew most of their tongues, was – although Greek by blood – a compendium of this world.

Selection of core-made polychrome glass cosmetic jars from Egypt, c. 1400 B.C.; tallest vessel 6½ inches high. Egypt was not a prominent glass manufacturer again until the foundation of Alexandria.

BATTLE FOR THE WORLD

The restoration of Ptolemy Auletes to the throne of Egypt inevitably meant that his Roman creditors gathered round demanding payment of the immense sums he had promised them. Principal of these was an immensely rich and powerful financier, Rabirius Postumus. Ptolemy's solution to the problem was typical of his weak but crafty nature – make Rabirius his financial minister or Dioiketes. The Roman could squeeze the Egyptian people, but it would be he who would incur their hatred for the increases in taxation, and not Ptolemy.

Rabirius, who was now virtually in control of the country, proceeded to re-imburse himself handsomely. He had almost a monopoly of the important glass and papyrus trade and he made good use of it as well as sending ships back to Rome laden with the gold and gems of Egypt. It was not surprising that before very long the economic condition of the country, the increased taxation and the knowledge that all this was due to the return of the sovereign whom they had been so eager to get rid of, brought on a wave of protest. It was not only the Greeks, Jews and other inhabitants of Alexandria who started to give trouble, but even the peasants in the remote country districts began to desert their fields. There can be little doubt that but for the presence of Roman soldiers the people would once again have deprived the Flute-Player of his throne. But, as Ptolemy had foreseen, the real hatred of the Alexandrians fell upon Rabirius. The King was obliged to put him in jail in order to save him from a murderous mob. Next, Ptolemy contrived to allow him to escape by ship to Rome. He had finally achieved his objective. The Romans were paid off – and he was King. Gabinius, who had restored him to the throne, and Rabirius were both brought to trial in Rome – the one for having acted against the decree of the Senate, as well as the voice of the Sibylline books, and the other for having held an administrative post under a foreign king.

Ptolemy now made a will, one copy of which was lodged in Alexandria, and the other in Rome with his powerful patron Pompey. In it he asked that the succession to the throne of Egypt should go to his eldest daughter, Cleopatra VII, who was to reign in conjunction with her brother Ptolemy XIII, his eldest son. Possibly in order to avoid the scorpion-like fight that so often broke out among Ptolemaic heirs on the death of the ruler, he begged the Roman people to see that his wishes as to the succession were duly carried out. He knew that Cleopatra and her sister Berenice did not get on together. But later evidence shows that she and the brother destined to be her husband were also incompatible. The root cause of so many of

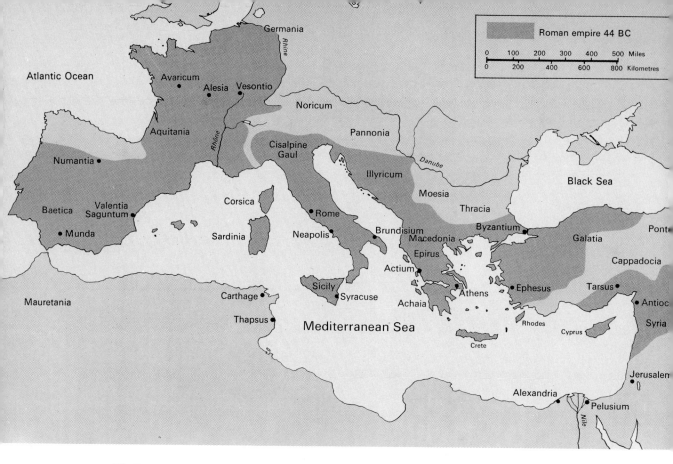

The Roman Empire, 44 B.C.

the troubles surrounding the Ptolemaic dynasty stemmed from their incestuous unions. Brothers and sisters are often prone to quarrel over the contents of an ordinary will – let alone one concerning a throne – and they are usually unlikely to make compatible partners, sexually or emotionally.

Ptolemy XII, having done all he could to ensure the succession, was now able to appreciate his palace and gardens for his few remaining years, his music and – in his capacity as the New Dionysus – the enjoyment of wine and revelry. What he had done by having himself restored and maintained on his throne by the might of the Roman legions, was to make his country a client state of Rome. And client states had a habit of ending up as part of the steadily expanding Roman Empire. This was what Cleopatra was to spend all her years as Queen trying to prevent.

In the spring of 51 B.C. Ptolemy the Flute-Player died. He was succeeded by Cleopatra, who was then eighteen, and her brother Ptolemy XIII, who was ten. There can be little doubt that they were now formally married, as was the custom. Since Ptolemy was a minor, a board of guardians was appointed to look after his interests and, in the corrupt and scheming court of Alexandria, these guardians were inevitably looking after their own. One of them was Achillas, commander of

54

the army; another a Greek rhetorician Theodotus who was to supervise the young King's education; and the third a eunuch, Pothinus, a typically devious palace intriguer, who was minister of finance. These three quickly saw that it would be to their advantage to attach the boy-King to their interests, and if possible get rid of Cleopatra.

It seems that from the very first she displayed the strength of character and political intelligence which were to be so evident throughout her life. A clear instance of this occurred in 55 B.C., when the Roman Governor of Syria sent his two sons to Alexandria requesting that the legions stationed in the city should be released, to aid him in a campaign against the ever troublesome Parthians. (The 'Alexandrian Question' was, after all, theoretically resolved once the daughter and son nominated by Ptolemy the Flute-Player were installed on the throne.) However, the troops (many of whom were Gauls and Germans) had settled down happily among the comforts of the city. They had taken wives and mistresses, and they had no wish to march north and fight against the toughest enemies of the Roman people. They not only mutinied, but proceeded to murder the Syrian Governor's sons. Cleopatra immediately ordered the arrest of the mutineers, and had the ring-leaders despatched to Syria. She knew from the beginning that her position depended upon her friendship with Rome.

But the fact that the young Queen showed an independence of action was not at all to the liking of the triumvirate surrounding her brother. They wanted an amenable monarch, and it was clear that Cleopatra had her own thoughts and judgments. Better, Pothinus and the other two must have thought, that they continue to mould Ptolemy to their ways, and marry him off to his sister Berenice. A typical court intrigue now developed. Cleopatra (warned by her advisers as well as her own instincts) managed to avoid the fate that befell unsuccessful Ptolemies, and fled the country. The year was 48 B.C., and she was twenty-one; her whole life had been lived in a spider's web of intrigue, corruption, bribery and murder.

Cleopatra made her way to Syria where her political act in sending the mutineers back no doubt secured her a favourable reception. Pothinus and his friends, for their part, must have been delighted, since they now seemed to have the whole situation under control. Achillas, the army commander, became in effect governor of Egypt, and the others must have felt secure in the knowledge that they had got rid of the young woman who had seemed the only potential threat to their dominance of the country. They had reckoned without Cleopatra's resource and determination.

While Cleopatra was busy rallying her supporters, and gathering together an army in Syria, momentous events had been taking place on the far side of the Mediterranean. The coalition between the three predominant Romans of the era, Caesar, Pompey and Crassus, had already broken up, largely because their individual ambitions were too great to tolerate any rival. Crassus was removed from the scene when in 53 B.C. he decided to take Roman arms into Parthia. He was jealous of both

Pompey's and Caesar's military renown, and wished to achieve a military victory on his own account – as well, perhaps, as laying his hands on the wealth of the East. His army was completely destroyed at the battle of Carrhae, and Crassus was killed. It was one of the most disastrous defeats in Roman history, and was never to be forgotten. But the major effect of Carrhae was to leave only Caesar and Pompey in the dispute for power. It was inevitable that the great struggle for supreme authority should now take place.

Julius Caesar, most of whose great achievements had been in Gaul and the far north-west, meant relatively little or nothing to the Alexandrians. Pompey the Great, on the other hand, had been their patron, the friend of Egypt, and its protector. It was natural that they should favour his cause. Indeed before her flight to Syria Cleopatra had received Pompey's son in the city and, in response to an appeal from his father, had despatched a number of merchant ships laden with corn to help to feed his troops in the civil war raging between him and Caesar. When, only a year later, the news reached Egypt of Pompey's utter defeat on the battlefield of Pharsalia in Thessaly, there must have been consternation. They had backed the wrong horse. What would now be the attitude of the all-powerful Julius Caesar to Egypt and Egyptian affairs? Would he descend with his triumphant legions and seize the country – just as Alexander, nearly three centuries before, had seized it from the Persians?

After fleeing from the scene of his defeat, Pompey made his way to Cyprus. He still had hopes that there might be a second round in this battle for the world. He learned that Cato had managed to rally a considerable number of the Pompeian forces, and that his fleet, one of the mainstays of his strength, was still loyal and willing to fight for his cause. What he really needed was money, grain for his troops, and further military support. It was natural that immediately he should think of Egypt. After all, it was through his influence that Ptolemy Auletes had been restored, and it was the Flute-Player's son who now sat upon the throne. He would go to Alexandria, and claim some visible return for his earlier help and patronage. Pompey and his wife Cornelia accordingly embarked in a large galley, and prepared to make the easy down-wind crossing to Egypt.

Cleopatra in the meantime, showing so early the courageous and indeed pugnacious side of her nature, had raised an army in Syria and was preparing to invade her kingdom. Her troops stood on the borders of Syria and Egypt, while moving up to oppose her came the Egyptian army commanded by Achillas. It was at this juncture, when civil war between brother and sister was just about to break out, that Pompey arrived near Pelusium where the Egyptian army was encamped. He dropped anchor off the small harbour and waited to see what emissaries would come out to him. As soon as the presence of the great Pompey became known there was an immediate and agitated discussion. In this, one may presume, the young Ptolemy can have had little share. Between the three councillors, Achillas, Theodotus and the eunuch Pothinus, the debate raged as to what kind of

56

reception they should accord this defeated Roman, who had once seemed to them the future master of the world. As Plutarch remarks: 'It was a tragic situation that the fate of Pompey the Great should have been determined by three such men; and that he, riding at anchor off the shore, should have been forced to wait on the decision of such a tribunal.'

The argument went roughly as follows. Since he had been Egypt's patron in his days of power it was only right to accord him asylum. Besides, was there not always the chance that he might prove the ultimate victor? Set against this went their recently acquired knowledge that Caesar was undoubtedly the greatest soldier of his time. Perhaps, they reasoned, they might suggest that he took asylum in another country. But then, the thought must certainly have crossed their minds,

Column of polished Aswan granite erected in honour of the Emperor Diocletian c. A.D. 300 at or near the Serapeum, traditionally though unverifiably known as Pompey's pillar

suppose that country was Syria? With Pompey's formidable military abilities behind her, Cleopatra might drive Ptolemy from the throne. It was Theodotus who, with a lawyer's guile, proposed the ultimate solution. They should lure Pompey ashore – and then make away with him. In this way they would not only prevent any possibility of his talents going to assist Cleopatra, but they would also find favour with Caesar. They would put an end to this contest in the Roman world, and lay the victorious Caesar under an obligation. Once they had defeated Cleopatra they would ensure that Egypt – theoretically ruled by the young Ptolemy – would remain in their hands. 'And besides,' concluded Theodotus, 'dead men don't bite.'

It was natural that Achillas, as commander of the army, should be the one selected to meet this Roman who had been one of the greatest generals and admirals of his time. He took with him, to give further authenticity to the military nature of the reception, Septimius, a Roman officer who had once held command under Pompey, together with a Roman centurion. The three of them were rowed out in a small boat to bring the great Pompey ashore. Arriving at the galley, Achillas invited Pompey to step aboard, saying that it was the only way, since his galley had too deep a draught to enter the harbour. Pompey's wife, Cornelia, was immediately suspicious, and cautioned her husband not to go. But Pompey, who had already noticed that a number of Egyptian warships were active off the shore, realized that, as Caesar had remarked when he crossed the Rubicon to begin the Civil War, 'the die was cast'. As he went down to the boat, in company with a freedman called Philip, he quoted in farewell to Cornelia the lines of Sophocles:

> He that once enters at a tyrant's door
> Becomes a slave, even if free before. . . .

There was a curious silence in the boat, and Pompey, prompted to break it, looked at Septimius the Roman officer, and said: 'Surely I recognize you? Did you not at one time serve under me?' The latter nodded, but made no reply. Disconcerted, Pompey took out a small book and continued to read until they reached the beach. Then, as the boat grounded, he got to his feet and made ready to step ashore. At this moment Septimius drew his sword and stabbed him in the back. His action was immediately followed by Achillas and the centurion. Pompey drew his robe over his head (as his enemy Caesar was one day to do) and fell dying in the bottom of the vessel. Cornelia, watching from the galley, witnessed the whole scene and raised a great cry that was heard by all those on shore. The galley's crew and Pompey's supporters immediately urged the captain to up-anchor, or they would all be killed. Before the Egyptian warships could get under way, the galley bearing the widowed Cornelia was headed out for the open sea.

The murderers cut Pompey's head from his body and held it aloft in triumph.

Glass beaker showing the top of the Pharos lighthouse surmounted by a divine or heroic figure holding an oar. Probably Alexandrian workmanship c. the end of the 1st century B.C.; found at Begram, Afghanistan.

They intended to have tangible proof for Caesar, when he arrived, that his great rival was dead. They left the body itself lying on the foreshore, and Pompey's loyal freedman, whom they had not molested, was allowed to make a funeral pyre and reduce his remains to ashes. (These were later sent by Caesar to Pompey's widow, who had buried them in the grounds of his Alban villa – the very villa where Pompey had once given sanctuary and hospitality to Auletes. The life of Pompey the Great, the man who had cleared the Mediterranean of pirates, one of the outstanding generals of his time, was over. The whole Mediterranean was Caesar's.

While Cleopatra's and Ptolemy's armies still lay confronting one another Caesar and some four thousand men were crossing the Mediterranean in thirty-five galleys, headed for Alexandria. Caesar knew that Pompey had fled to Egypt, and he wanted to secure his victory of Pharsalia before Pompey could once again rally his forces. Upon his arrival on 2 October, (in reality 27 July, so much had the Roman Calendar got out of line until Caesar reformed it) he disembarked his legionaries and cavalry in 'The City'. It was a small enough force with which to meet a potential enemy and possibly subdue a country. But Caesar, like his great predecessor Alexander, was a man with an instinct for the moment, and had no hesitation in acting when he felt that his star directed him. He was, after all, from a family who believed themselves to be descendants of the goddess Venus – and to the gods, or demi-gods, all things are possible.

Caesar's object at this moment was most probably to effect a reconciliation between the warring brother and sister – as well as to track down Pompey and his supporters. It can only have been a matter of moments after his landing in Alexandria that he heard of his enemy's death. His troubles were at an end. But when, a few days later, the instigator of the whole plot, the cynical Theodotus, came back from Pelusium bearing the head and signet ring of Pompey, and proudly showed them to Caesar, the latter is said to have burst into tears. To have killed Pompey on the battlefield would have been one thing; or to have had him make an end of his life in the old Roman way; but to know that he had been treacherously murdered by degenerate Egyptians and Greeks was another thing altogether. To the amazement of Theodotus, who was undoubtedly expecting some reward, Caesar dismissed him from his presence with the contempt that would normally have been reserved for a slave.

To the Alexandrian, used to all the deviousness and cruelty of local politics, the whole incident must have seemed incomprehensible. These 'barbarian' Romans seemed to have an extraordinary set of standards! Pompey had been Caesar's enemy; the latter, had he met Pompey on the battlefield, would undoubtedly have killed him; and in that case what more could he desire than the head of his enemy? Shortly afterwards Theodotus, realizing that he had incurred the hatred and scorn of Caesar, fled from the city and became a wandering refugee in Syria

Papyrus growing at Giza

Head of Pompey the Great

and Asia Minor. Some years later Brutus found the rhetorician and had him crucified. The Romans of this period were violent and cruel, but they still retained a little of the old Republican code of ethics. The murder of a man seeking sanctuary – and a man, moreover, who had formerly been one's patron – was unacceptable.

To the consternation of the Alexandrians, Caesar had all of Pompey's followers (whom the 'loyal' citizens had had imprisoned) released from jail and pardoned. Caesar was a hard and ruthlessly ambitious man, but he had always known that the best policy towards the defeated – provided that they were 'little men' and not leaders – was magnanimity. By being magnanimous he intended to attach to his own cause men who had formerly been his enemies. It was a policy that would one day rebound on his own head, for there are some men who can never forgive the favours that are done to them.

CAESAR IN EGYPT

While the armies of brother and sister, Ptolemy XIII and Cleopatra VII, still lay encamped against each other at Pelusium, the victor of Pharsalia nonchalantly moved himself into the royal palace on Lochias promontory. It was typical of Caesar that he automatically appropriated the finest place in Alexandria: the marble palace with its sumptuous furniture, its gardens, flowers and fountains. Caesar, like Napoleon after him, knew himself to be a king by right of achievement and, unlike Napoleon, he was indeed of noble blood. There can be little doubt that, as a Roman, he felt himself superior in every way to these degenerate Macedonian Ptolemies. After all the campaigning of the Civil War he was tired to his very bones. The knowledge that he must soon go back to Rome and put the house of Italy in order must have inspired him with the desire to take a rest, however brief. He was, moreover, as the leading representative of the Roman people, responsible for the execution of the Flute-Player's will; and in accordance with this Caesar was determined to check this civil war and bring Ptolemy and Cleopatra to terms. He had another important interest in Egypt – the repayment of the loan he had made to their father, when the Flute-Player had been in Rome. As usual, Caesar was short of money.

The man who now took up his residence in the royal palace, home of the two younger Ptolemies, was in his early fifties. The conqueror of half the world, the greatest soldier since Alexander, Julius Caesar was at this moment the master of the Mediterranean. As Arthur Weigall said of him:

> He was an extremely active soldier, a clever, graceful swordsman, a powerful swimmer and an excellent athlete. In battle he had proved himself brave, gallant and cool-headed; and in his earlier years he had been regarded as a dashing young officer. . . . Already at the age of twenty-one he had won the Civic Crown, the Victoria Cross of that period, for saving a soldier's life at the storming of Mytilene. In action he exposed himself bareheaded amongst his men, cheering them and encouraging them by his own fine spirits; and it is reported how once he laid hands on a distraught standard-bearer who was running to cover, turned him round, and suggested that he had mistaken the direction of the enemy.

All this was true enough, but there was also another side to Caesar's nature. He was a spendthrift, an extremely devious politician, a good (if partial) historian, and a rake. It was openly said, not only by his detractors but by his soldiers who adored

him, that in his youth he had gone through a homosexual phase. As Suetonius put it:
'His intimacy with Nicomedes [King of Bithynia] was a deep and lasting reproach,
which laid him open to insults from all quarters. I say nothing of the notorious lines
of Licinius Calvus: "Whate'er Bithynia had, and Caesar's paramour".'

The patrician Dolabella referred to Nicomedes as 'the Queen's rival, the inner
partner of the royal couch', while on one occasion when Caesar was addressing the
Senate on his obligations to the King, Cicero called out, 'No more of that, I beg you.
It's well known what he gave you, and what you gave him in return.' When he was
celebrating his Gallic Triumph the soldiers who followed behind his chariot are
reported to have sung the following verse:

> All the Gauls did Caesar vanquish, Nicomedes vanquished him;
> Lo, now Caesar rides in triumph, victor over all the Gauls,
> Nicomedes does not triumph, who subdued the conqueror.

At the same time he had acquired the reputation of being one of the most notorious
womanizers in Rome – and in the Rome of that period there was plenty of competition. Sir Charles Oman wrote: 'He was the inevitable co-respondent in every
fashionable divorce, and when we look at the list of the ladies whose names are
linked with his, we can only wonder at the state of society in Rome which permitted
him to survive unscathed to middle age. The marvel is that he did not end in some
dark corner, with a dagger between his ribs, long before he attained the age of
thirty.' He had seduced the wives of most of his friends, including Pompey, Crassus
and Gabinius – and this at a time when they were leaders of the political party to
which he belonged, whose goodwill he needed.

One of his greatest passions was for Servilia, the mother of Marcus Brutus (who
was to assassinate him), and it was widely rumoured that he was in fact the father of
Brutus. He gave Servilia pearls of immense value, and it was even said that one of
his reasons for invading Britain was that he had heard that the pearls from there
were of very good quality. Another verse shouted by his legionaries during his
Gallic Triumph shows that he did not confine his sexual activities to Rome. It went
as follows:

> Home we bring the bald adulterer,
> Romans, lock your wives away!
> Gold in Gaul he spent in dalliance,
> Which he'd borrowed here in Rome.

Suetonius describes his appearance as:

> Tall of stature, with a fair complexion, shapely limbs, a somewhat full face, and keen
> black eyes. He was of good health, except that towards his later years he was subject to

Julius Caesar in military costume

fainting fits and nightmares. He was twice attacked by the falling sickness [epilepsy] during the campaigns. He was very careful about his appearance, being always carefully trimmed and shaved, and even having superfluous hair plucked out. His baldness was something that greatly worried him . . . and because of it he used to comb his thin locks forward over the crown of his head. Out of all the honours voted him by the Senate there was none which he enjoyed more than the privilege of wearing a laurel crown at all times. . . . He was also fastidious about his dress, and wore a senator's tunic with fringed sleeves to the wrist.

This man, whom one of his enemies referred to as 'every woman's man and every man's woman', was at the same time unsparing of himself during his campaigns. It was for this that the hardened Roman legionaries loved him. He would be first to swim across a river, and insisted on a rate of advance that taxed even the youngest and strongest. A magnificent horseman, yet he could still keep up on foot with the steady pace of the legions. He ate sparingly and seems to have cared little about food, but he was a dandy when in Rome. He was a great connoisseur of gems, tessellated pavements and interior decoration generally. This descendant of Venus had a nature as passionate and contradictory as the goddess herself. Above all, he emerges as one of the most ambitious men in history. He had, to quote Plutarch, 'a restless passion after honour' – but 'honour' must be interpreted as a desire for fame. In money matters, as in sexual, he was completely unscrupulous. He had been married four times, his current wife being Calpurnia, the daughter of Calpurnius Piso who had been Consul in 58 B.C. It must certainly have made the Romans laugh when he divorced his third wife Pompeia, Pompey's sister, and made the famous remark 'Caesar's wife must be above suspicion'. It is certain that few of his friends' wives were – when he was in town.

A strange callousness, an *insouciance*, is the hallmark of his character. It was as if he felt – perhaps because of the supposedly divine origin of the Julian line – that the world was indeed his oyster. This immense self-confidence (which was ultimately to lead to his death) was shown early in his life when he was captured by pirates, and taken to the island of Pharmacusa off the coast of Miletus. They asked him to send for a ransom of twenty talents (several thousand pounds) to be paid for his release. Caesar laughed and said that he was worth at least fifty – a sum which he did ultimately pay them. He also assured the pirates that, when the ransom arrived and he was freed, the first thing he would do was to come back and have them all executed. Meanwhile, during the weeks of waiting, he joined in their carouses, but never for a moment let them forget that he was their superior. When he wanted to sleep he insisted that they all kept silence and, despite the fact that he was their prisoner, he ordered them about at his own convenience as if they were slaves, as well as chiding them for their coarse and uncivilized manners. No sooner was he freed than, true to his word, he collected a number of troops and came back to the island, captured the pirates and had them crucified. Even then the curious contradictions in his character were revealed, for – perhaps because he had developed some

Silver wineholders and a drinking horn from Pompeii, 1st century A.D.

rough feeling for them during his confinement – he ordered their throats to be cut rather than let them suffer the long and agonizing death on the cross.

In warfare, however, he was implacable. Perhaps this, too, was a part of his logical nature, for he reckoned that, if men dared to oppose the might of Rome they deserved no quarter. His thinking on this score might indeed be called Japanese – that if men went to war they intended to kill their enemy, and if they failed they must pay the penalty. In his Gallic campaigns he had thousands massacred and hacked off the right (sword) hand of many thousands of others who had fought against him. On one occasion, after making peace with two tribes, he attacked them when they were defenceless, and killed nearly half a million men, women and children. If it is true that all 'great men are bad men', then Caesar is a supreme example. However, he had charm. He was soon to meet another exponent of this quality, and one who in her own way was every whit as ruthless and ambitious as Caesar himself.

Settled in the comfortable palace at Alexandria Caesar decided that the best method of ending Egypt's civil war would be to summon Ptolemy to meet him. So he sent a message to Pelusium, telling the young King that he, Caesar, was now in the palace, and that he would like to see him in order to arbitrate between him and his sister. It is not difficult to imagine the haste this invitation was complied with – nor with what fury it was received by the triumvirate of Ptolemy's guardians, Achillas the general, Theodotus the tutor, and Pothinus the eunuch minister of finance. They saw at once the threat to their supremacy in Egypt with this Roman master sitting in the courts of the Ptolemies and giving orders to their protégé. But there was little that they could do for the moment except agree to Caesar's request. Ptolemy was accordingly despatched back to Alexandria.

Arriving with Pothinus early in October Ptolemy found his palace patrolled by Roman troops, and the city in Roman hands. This was bad enough, but as well this Roman was demanding an immense sum of money which, he claimed, he had lent Ptolemy's father in order to restore him to the throne. What was more, Caesar suggested that Ptolemy should stop the campaign and come to terms with his sister. The reaction of Pothinus (who seems to have been the real brains behind the administration) was immediate and instinctive. He decided to make life unpleasant for this Roman and his troops. After all, there were only about four thousand of them, and Caesar was only a man – just like Pompey. He arranged, accordingly, that the corn supplied to the Roman legionaries should be mouldy, or of third rate quality, and that the gold and silver plate of the palace should be exchanged for wooden platters.

Bronze table with three legs in the form of satyrs, 1st century A.D.

Caesar told Ptolemy (which in effect meant Pothinus) that his army must be disbanded and withdrawn from the frontier. Naturally enough the minister refused to agree, and sent a message to Achillas at Pelusium to bring his forces down to Alexandria. It seems he thought he would first eliminate the Romans, and then carry on the fight against Cleopatra. Caesar still held the trump card, for he had the young Ptolemy 'under his protection' in the palace – virtually a prisoner of his Roman troops – but his own position would become precarious once the Egyptian army arrived.

Caesar had already sent word to Cleopatra that he wanted her also to come to Alexandria, so that he could resolve the dispute between her and her brother. But the question was, how could this be achieved? Cleopatra knew that she could not make her way through the Egyptian lines facing her own forces, for Achillas would certainly have her killed. It was at this point that the courage, daring and quick wits, which were to characterize her life, showed themselves. She secretly embarked in a ship at Pelusium and set sail for Alexandria. Arriving off the city, she waited until nightfall and then had herself transported in a small boat by a faithful servant, a Sicilian called Apollodorus. He rowed the boat to a quay with which he was familar, just below the walls of the palace, where his appearance would occasion no comment. The Queen was now wrapped up in a roll of bedding or a carpet, which Apollodorus proceeded to tie together with cord. Shouldering the bundle, the Sicilian proceeded to walk into the palace, answering any questions from Caesar's soldiers to the effect that he was one of the palace servants. The sight of a man with a bundle over his shoulder would not have surprised them for in the East, to this day, it is not uncommon for a man to carry around all his worldly possessions rolled up in a rug, or in his bedding.

Having asked the way to Caesar's apartments, to which he would have been accompanied by armed guards, he entered and laid the bale on the floor – and untied it. To Caesar's utter astonishment the little Queen of Egypt rolled out, and sprang dishevelled to her feet. It was just the kind of gesture that would have appealed to him, revealing originality, independence of character and fiery courage. For Caesar knew as well as she did that if Pothinus or any of his faction had come across her first she would have been murdered and quietly disposed of in the harbour. 'This ruse of hers,' says Plutarch, 'is said to have opened the way to Caesar's heart,' while Dio Cassius writes that 'he was spellbound the moment he set eyes on her and she opened her mouth to speak'. He had known many women in many countries, but he had never met one like her. For the first time he had found a personality similar to his own.

It is probable (indeed, knowing Caesar's reputation, it is more than probable) that they became lovers that same night. But Cleopatra, if until now she had been physically innocent, was certainly no political virgin. Her whole life had been passed in the intricacies of that incredibly intricate court, and she was a typical Ptolemy in her desire for power. She knew that only from this Roman, this man

69

old enough to be her father, could she obtain it. What she loved in Caesar was the fact that he was the most powerful man in the world. She was determined to be Queen of Egypt. She had only one weapon that her brother, backed by his powerful advisers, did not have – her sex.

The next morning Caesar sent a message to her brother Ptolemy XIII saying that he required his presence in his apartments. When the latter arrived, probably accompanied by the eunuch Pothinus, he found Cleopatra comfortably at ease in the presence of the Roman dictator. After the shock of seeing her in the palace at all, his immediate thought must have been that she had presented her side of the case and and won Caesar over. Caesar said that he was determined to stop this civil war, and that brother and sister must declare themselves reconciled. Ptolemy rushed from the room, crying out that his cause had been betrayed. He ran to his friends – it must be remembered that he was only a boy – burst into tears, and dashed the crown from his head.

The news that Cleopatra, the Queen who had been exiled and prepared to invade Egypt, was in the palace with Caesar, was quickly communicated to the mob. Now the mob of Alexandria was notorious for being one of the most riotous and dangerous in the world, and in very little time the palace was almost invaded – indeed it would have been, but for the presence of the Roman legionaries on guard. To calm them down Caesar had finally to summon a meeting of all the people, read them the Flute-Player's will, and point out that as the representative of the Roman people he was only trying to do what was incumbent upon him – see that Cleopatra VII and Ptolemy XIII were joint rulers of Egypt. To placate the people, however, and possibly with a view to reconciling those hostile to Cleopatra, he said that he was restoring the island of Cyprus to Egypt, and that it was to be ruled jointly by the younger brother Ptolemy XIV and his sister Berenice. Thus, with typical nonchalance and a complete disregard for the feelings or wishes of the Roman people whom he represented, Caesar gave back to Ptolemaic control the island that Rome had acquired a brief ten years before.

A nominal reconciliation was now effected between brother and sister. But the former must have realized all the time that it was his grown-up sister who was going to rule, and not he. Dio Cassius states that he could see (and was no doubt told) that there was a personal relationship between Caesar and Cleopatra. The triumvirate of tutors, who had hoped to be the real rulers, could not be won over, even by the gift of Cyprus.

Cleopatra was delighted. She had the affection and protection of the ruler of the world, and her kingdom was restored to its former size. No doubt she dreamed that under her rule the Ptolemaic empire might once more return to its old power and glory. She was nothing if not ambitious. It was probably this quality which attracted Caesar to her, quite as much as her young body.

CAESAR AND CLEOPATRA

It soon became clear that Pothinus and Achillas were hatching a plot against Caesar, undoubtedly with the object of treating him to the same fate as Pompey and eliminating Cleopatra. The information reached Caesar from his barber, whom Plutarch describes as 'a man of unequalled timidity, but one who kept his ears open and was here, there, and everywhere'. Caesar did not hesitate to act. During a banquet that was being given to celebrate the supposed reconciliation of brother and sister his troops surrounded the banqueting hall and seized the eunuch minister. Pothinus was taken outside and executed. In the confusion, however, Achillas managed to escape and make his way back to the army. Soon afterwards he began the investment of the Roman garrison in the palace.

In the judgment of most early historians it was Caesar's infatuation with Cleopatra that led him to put his head into a noose, and caused him to endanger his life at the very moment when he was sovereign master of the Mediterranean world. There is some justification for this viewpoint, but when Caesar first reached Egypt he can have had little idea of the real political situation there, nor of the particular web of intrigue that flourished in the royal palace. In what was to become known as the Alexandrian War he now proceeded to show all his old brilliance, extricating himself from what at times seemed an impossible situation. As a first step he sent his friend Mithridates of Pergamum to raise reinforcements in Syria and Asia Minor that would march to his relief. If he could hold the palace for a sufficient length of time, he rightly calculated that these troops would be able to sweep down and take the Egyptian army in the rear. Meanwhile he held all the Ptolemies as security in the palace, and settled down to await events with his customary sangfroid.

The Egyptian army at that time consisted of about twenty thousand men with some two thousand cavalry. It was a heterogeneous collection: legionaries left behind by Gabinius, slaves and criminals who had escaped from Italy, together with Greek mercenaries. Although no match for disciplined Roman legionaries, they were nevertheless a formidable force, and outnumbered Caesar's troops by five to one. As soon as they reached the outskirts of Alexandria nearly all the inhabitants of that ever-disputatious city rose to greet them. Caesar was now faced not only by an army, but by the Alexandrian mob. The first of his worries came when the freshwater canals that fed the palace complex were either dammed up or tainted with seawater. Undaunted Caesar set his troops digging along the seaward side of the palace grounds, being well aware that adjacent to limestone headlands are often

Ptolemaic torso of a goddess-queen, c. 280 B.C.; 65½ inches high

to be found veins of fresh water. His practical advice was soon proved correct, and his men were once again comforted by the knowledge that their leader was as clever as he was brave.

Quite early in the course of the war Cleopatra's younger sister Berenice managed to escape from the palace along with her tutor Ganymedes, another court intriguer of the same stamp as Pothinus. There was little love lost between the Ptolemies, and Berenice appears to have hated Cleopatra quite as much as her brother Ptolemy XIII did. Making her way to the army, Berenice was now seen as the new centre of the popular revolt to evict the Romans and remove Cleopatra. This was not to the taste however of the general Achillas – whose protégé was Ptolemy – so Berenice and Ganymedes had him murdered. Ganymedes now became the leader of the Egyptian forces and the director of the revolt.

Caesar meanwhile had heard that the Thirty-Seventh legion from Asia Minor was already anchored off the Egyptian coast, but was unable to proceed on account of contrary winds. Knowing that reinforcements were near at hand, he was emboldened to make a stroke against the Egyptian fleet, which was a grave threat to his sea-communications as well as posing a danger to the safe arrival of the legion. He made one of those lightning surprise-attacks which were the hallmark of so many of his successes, and set fire to the Egyptian fleet. In the conflagration that followed a large part of the dockyard went up in flames, as well (it is said by some) as part, or all, of the great library of Alexandria. It is quite possible that some of the library may have been destroyed, but its total loss would have been such a disaster that it could hardly have escaped comment by ancient writers. On the other hand, the fact that Mark Antony later made a present to Cleopatra of the great library of Pergamum suggests that there may have been some truth in the story. Certainly Caesar, in his own account of the events, does not mention the destruction of the library, but then it would hardly have been something to boast about. The poet Lucan, however, who was pro-Pompey and anti-Caesar, might surely have been expected to hurl this charge of vandalism against the great dictator in his poem *Pharsalia* which describes the course of the civil war, yet he says nothing about it. As in the case of so many other events in the ancient world, the truth will probably never be known.

Other passages in the Alexandrian War which show Caesar in his best capacity as man of action are his taking charge of the Roman ships in harbour when they went out to escort the vessels bearing the Thirty-Seventh legion, and his attempt – unsuccessful though it was – to capture the island of Pharos. In the first case, when the ships carrying the legion were trying to enter the eastern harbour, Caesar himself embarked with his small galley force, with only the Rhodian sailors to man them (he left his troops behind to garrison the beleaguered palace). The Egyptians, who undoubtedly had spies within the palace, hearing that Caesar himself was aboard, brought round their fleet from the western harbour. Caesar, however, not only managed to bring in the troops but, on his way back, fought a brilliant sea-battle and soundly trounced the Egyptian fleet. His attempt to capture the Pharos, even though he failed and nearly lost his life, shows the calibre of the man, and why his troops, whether in Britain, Gaul, Greece, or here in Egypt, would follow him anywhere.

His plan was to make a double assault by sea and across the waters of the eastern harbour, capture the island and then swing back across the great dyke Heptastadion. He would thus have had the whole of the area to the north of the city in his hands. Perhaps the weakness in his concept was that, even with the new legion to reinforce him, he would then have occupied too large a territory for his men to hold. The landing on Pharos was made satisfactorily, and he managed to secure the northern end of the Great Dyke. Caesar himself led the contingent that stormed over to take the southern, or city, end of the Heptastadion. Unfortunately for his plans, the Egyptians made an uncharacteristically bold move and landed a force behind his men on the Pharos side of the dyke. The Romans now found themselves trapped on the dyke itself, with the enemy hemming them in on both sides. Their galleys and other boats, however, immediately came to their rescue. Caesar embarked in a small boat which, owing to the weight of the survivors, soon afterwards overturned and sank. He was forced to swim two hundred yards to another vessel holding, so a later story went, important despatches in one hand to keep them out of the water. Whether this is correct or not, it certainly seems true that – to his chagrin – he was forced to leave behind in the hands of the victorious Egyptians the purple general's cloak, upon which he set great store.

Up to now it would appear that he had been treating the Alexandrian War as if it were all something of an escapade. But the loss in this struggle over the Heptastadion of four hundred legionaries, as well as a great many sailors, convinced him that he must revert to his earlier policy and play for time. He knew that Mithridates's army was coming down from Syria to force Pelusium and effect his relief, so he decided to adopt to the other role in which he was a master: that of politician.

He most probably had information that Cleopatra's sister Berenice and her adviser Ganymedes had failed to win the affection of the Egyptian army – most of whom were still clamouring for Ptolemy to be restored to them. This youth, the technical husband of his mistress, was no more than a nuisance to Caesar. Ptolemy had conspired to drive Cleopatra from the throne, and Caesar knew that he would have killed her if he could. The answer was obvious – restore him to these Egyptians who professed to love him. Then, when the relief army came marching through Egypt, and the Egyptians had to stand and fight – let him flee the country or die in the battle. Thus Cleopatra, who Caesar already knew was going to bear a child by him (they had now been together four months), would become sole and un-disputed Queen of Egypt. He could marry her off, technically, to her youngest brother. The latter was only ten at the time; and honour, in theory at any rate, would thus be satisfied. His mistress would be Queen of Egypt; Egypt would be friendly to Rome and indeed would have to be, since Cleopatra would be maintained on her throne by Roman legions. Furthermore, if the Queen bore him a son, it would be easy for Rome in due course to bring the country under direct Roman rule. Cleopatra would be glad to see her odious brother leave the palace, and undoubtedly she now felt secure, since she was carrying Caesar's child, that he would not desert her interests.

LEFT: *Sculptor's trial head of Isis or of a queen, Ptolemaic period.* RIGHT: *silver coin of Cleopatra VII, c. 30 B.C.*

In the extraordinary affair between Caesar and Cleopatra it must always be borne in mind that both of them were devious and ruthless politicians. But it is more than likely that there was a very real affection between them, quite apart from sexual passion. Caesar, who was an aging fifty-two and who had had immense experience with women, was probably flattered and, as it were, rejuvenated by the body and attentions of this young woman – and a woman who was furthermore a queen. Cleopatra's feelings were probably very different. True, Caesar was still an extremely good-looking man, but one fancies that her love for him was largely attributable to the fact that he was amusing, witty and intelligent. He was also the most powerful man in the world. These are good enough reasons for any woman to love a man. There may have been yet another. If, as seems quite likely, Cleopatra was a virgin when she met Caesar, then Byron's lines come immediately to mind:

> In her first passion woman loves her lover,
> In all the others all she loves is love.

Caesar, having devised the means of getting rid of her rival and enemy, now sent for the young Ptolemy and told him that he proposed to restore him to the Egyptian people, since he was clearly unhappy in the palace. Ptolemy, protesting that he loved Caesar and that he did not want to go back to his people, burst into tears. Some historians have suggested that these were 'crocodile tears', but Ptolemy almost certainly saw that the Egyptians could not win, but he would nevertheless be forced to fight and die with them. Caesar maintained that Ptolemy's duty was with his people, and dismissed the weeping King to the arms of his enthusiastic subjects. No sooner was he back with the army than Ptolemy, true to the traditions of his family, removed Berenice and Ganymedes from power.

It was at about this time that Mithridates of Pergamum, whom Caesar had sent to raise the army of relief, arrived at the fortress of Pelusium, stormed it, and moved into Egypt. He advanced down the Pelusian branch of the Nile towards Memphis, where, after an easy victory over the Egyptian forces, he crossed to the western bank of the river and prepared to march up to Alexandria. Young Ptolemy, showing more spirit than his father would have done, now put himself at the head of his troops and moved off to give battle. As soon as he heard that the Egyptian army was leaving the city Caesar embarked his troops, leaving only a small guard in the palace, and sailed off eastwards as if he was going in the direction of Pelusium. Under the cover of darkness, however, he reversed his direction and sailed back west of Alexandria, where he disembarked his men. By this ruse he outmanoeuvred the Egyptians, who presumed him gone. He now proceeded to prepare an unpleasant shock for the Egyptian army. (The episode shows, incidentally, that the tale that he was trapped in the palace throughout these months is quite untrue. He could have left by sea at any time that he wished.) Proceeding by forced marches through the desert west of Alexandria, he joined up with Mithridates's forces a little north of Memphis. The allied army at once headed north to meet the Egyptians.

Ptolemy and his troops had taken up a position on a fortified mound, which had a marsh on one side and the Nile on the other. A two-day battle ensued but, despite the strength of the position they had occupied, the Egyptian army could not withstand the weight of the allied attack. Their camp was stormed, and the army to all intents and purposes was annihilated. In the ensuing mêlée many tried to escape by small boats across the Nile, Ptolemy among them. The boat into which he jumped was crowded with fugitives, and it overturned and sank. Ptolemy was drowned. He was only fifteen, but he had at least shown some of the ancient Macedonian spirit in his last days. His body was later found and identified by the golden corselet that he wore. Caesar had it sent to Alexandria so that the citizens could see that he was indeed dead, as well as to prevent any legends arising around his name, or any future troublemaker pretending to be Ptolemy XIII and raising the standard of revolt.

On the evening of 27 March (actually 14 January) 47 B.C. Caesar entered Alexandria in triumph. The citizens received him in mourning garments, and sent deputations to him begging for clemency and for forgiveness for their part in the recent war. Caesar was prepared to be lenient. He had won, and the whole of Egypt from the Nile delta to the capital had now seen for themselves the might of Roman arms. He could be confident that there would be no more trouble. Egypt was pacified, and he could have made it a Roman province without any difficulty. That he did not do so, but installed Cleopatra as Queen, can be taken as evidence of his real affection for her. At the same time he proclaimed her young brother Ptolemy XIV, by now eleven years old, co-regent with Cleopatra, no doubt calculating that he was too young to make any difficulties for his sister. But in order to make quite sure that her hold on the throne was secure Caesar arranged to leave

View from the Nile westwards towards the limestone cliff with the recess chosen by Queen Hatshepsut for the construction of her mortuary temple at Deir el-Bahri

three legions behind in Egypt under the command of an able officer who was entirely devoted to him.

After five months the Alexandrian War was over. Caesar, with comparative ease, had achieved a political as well as military triumph. He had overthrown the opposition to the Romans, and he had installed on the throne of Egypt a queen who was his mistress, and who was about to bear his child. There can be no doubt that, despite one or two moments of hazard, he had enjoyed his Alexandrian winter: the pleasures of the palace; amorous pleasures with a brilliant and amusing young woman; and (perhaps to Caesar the greatest) the pleasure of outwitting his enemies and bringing them to their knees. It might have been expected that in view of the unsettled conditions in Italy, and the presence in several parts of the Mediterranean of powerful pro-Pompey forces – as well as a fleet bigger than his own – that he would have hastened back to put his house in order. Everything was calling for his presence at home, yet he still lingered on in Egypt for several weeks. The fact was that he had fallen in love (if one may use the term of such a cynic) not so much with a woman as with Egypt itself.

It was during this period, when the fact could no longer be concealed that Cleopatra was pregnant, that the supposedly divine origins of the Julian line began to be made use of as a piece of political propaganda. This was designed to satisfy the Egyptian people that the child Cleopatra was carrying was not just the product of an illegitimate union: that she was not Caesar's mistress; but that he was, as it were, a god on earth. No one could maintain that he was a Ptolemy, or a Pharaoh, so another reason had to be invented for his presence at the Queen's side – and in the Queen's bed.

It is possible, although there is no evidence for it, that some form of marriage ceremony took place between the two of them. Certainly the story was circulated for the benefit of the superstitious Egyptians that Caesar was an incarnation of the god Amon (who was more or less equivalent in the Egyptian Pantheon to Zeus or Jupiter in the Greek and Roman). His incredible success at the head of these armoured Romans may well have helped to effect their belief in this legend, even if the sophisticated Alexandrians almost certainly made mock of it. Sculptured bas-reliefs have been found at Hermonthis, in the vicinity of Thebes, which show Cleopatra in conversation with Amon, as well as depicting the birth of the divine child. There is an epitaph dating from the last years of the Queen's reign, which is inscribed 'in the twentieth year after the union of Cleopatra and Amon'.

Cleopatra, in her capacity as Queen of Egypt, had always been held as synonymous with the goddess Isis; Caesar, too, now 'joined the royal family', and became a god. He had a good precedent, for Alexander the Great, after his visit to the famous temple of Amon at Siwah in the Libyan desert, had become known as the son of

---

From Deir el-Bahri towards the eastern bank of the Nile. The mud-brick construction in the centre is the remains of the tomb-chapel of Mentuemhat, the fourth prophet-priest of Amon, c. 660 B.C.

Amon. (Coin portraits show him with the ram's horns of the god projecting from his head.) That Alexander or Caesar ever believed the identification is doubtful, but there is no doubt that both made use of it, and that to one degree or another it influenced the course of their lives. Caesar had already been called at Ephesus the 'Descendant of Ares and Aphrodite, God Incarnate, and Saviour of Mankind', so the transition to being identified with the god Amon was not difficult. It has already been suggested that some of Caesar's nonchalance and indifference to danger might be ascribed to his belief in his divine ancestry. Now that this was even further confirmed this aspect of his nature, as well as his will to power, became increasingly dominant.

Marble head of Jupiter with the characteristic curling ram's horns of Amon

CLEOPATRA, CAESARION AND CAESAR

In the spring of 47 B.C. Caesar and Cleopatra embarked aboard the state barge for a pleasure voyage up the Nile. Caesar was eager to see something of this country which was a legend for its ancient history, long preceding that of the Greeks from whom the Romans had inherited almost everything worthwhile in their own civilization. Caesar was not only a general, a law-giver and a historian, but he was (like Napoleon after him) a man of insatiable curiosity. He wanted to see something of this fabulous kingdom, its monuments, temples and ruins. No doubt, as an immensely practical man, he also wished to make a personal assessment of the wealth of Egypt: of the value and the contribution that it could make to the steadily increasing Roman Empire, an empire which he, more than any other, had helped to found. Certainly he will also have been fascinated to learn more about Egypt's trade routes with the East – evidence of which he will have seen during his Alexandrian winter – another potential source of revenue for Rome.

The royal barge in which Cleopatra and Caesar now made their way up the Nile was something even more lavish and grand than the sea-going galley in which she was later to seduce his successor. Writing nearly three centuries afterwards, but basing his work on earlier historians, the Alexandrian Greek Athenaeus describes a Ptolemaic state barge of this time as having been about three hundred feet long, forty-five feet on the beam, and rising about sixty feet above water. It was not so much a ship as a floating palace. It was propelled by several banks of oars, and contained banqueting rooms, colonnades and courtyards, shrines, grottoes and garden areas. Behind it followed a whole fleet of galleys and supply vessels, and – on this occasion – several thousand of Caesar's troops; no doubt as a precaution against any attempt on the part of the Egyptians to challenge the power of their Roman-sponsored Queen.

This imposing fleet, which the historian Appian describes as having numbered four hundred vessels, moved slowly up the Nile, transporting the god Amon and the goddess Isis through the heart of Egypt before the eyes of thousands of her peasant subjects. It was a magnificent exercise in the art of propaganda, and Cleopatra's hold over her subjects was immensely reinforced by being seen at the side of this all conquering Roman. Caesar was now able to appreciate in peace and comfort the richness and the strangeness of a land which, by virtue of his conquest of the Egyptians as well as their Queen, he may well have felt was almost his personal possession. Italy was still in a troubled state, Pompeian factions were still active in

ABOVE: *limestone relief of cranes from the mastaba tomb of Manufer, Saqqara; Old Kingdom, c. 2300* B.C.
OPPOSITE: *the Sphinx at Giza; Old Kingdom, c. 2500* B.C.; *a gigantic 66 feet high*

Africa and Spain, Asia Minor was seething with revolt, but here in Egypt he looked in peace upon the fertile delta of the Nile and the giant buildings and temples that had existed centuries before Rome was founded. Like Alexander, he must have realized that 'there is no new thing under the sun', that everything had happened before. Perhaps in this knowledge he even found a tranquillity that he had rarely known in his tempestuous life.

The fleet went up the Nile as far as Heliopolis, where Caesar – and probably Cleopatra too – had his first sight of the immense pyramids and the Sphinx, lonely and disturbing in their desert landscape under the intense blue sky of Egypt. Even to a man as ambitious as Caesar these astounding monuments to rulers so long dead must have been daunting. What was Rome with its noise, bustle and squalid streets, what was Alexandria, even, with its marble palaces, compared with these?

The fleet then went on as far as Aswan and the First Cataract. At this point, according to Suetonius, the Roman troops showed signs of mutiny, and Caesar therefore turned back. Whether this is true or not, it is doubtful whether he went any further, for the task of hauling the vast State Barge up the cataract would have been almost impossible. Caesar had seen enough however to reassure himself as to the wealth and the organization of this ancient land. He had seen the canal cut by the Ptolemies, which connected the Nile with the Red Sea at the town of Arsinoë, and had doubtless observed the many cargo-carriers that passed down the Nile laden with the luxury goods of the East. Perhaps, again like Alexander, he dreamed of one day expanding the Empire all the way to India.

Upon his return to Alexandria he received alarming news from the East. Pharnaces, the King of Pontus, who had taken advantage of the Roman Civil War to extend his dominions, had defeated one of Caesar's generals. Roman prestige in this important area was being eclipsed, and it seems that Caesar immediately despatched three legions to Asia Minor, instructing them to wait there for his arrival. The one fact that is in dispute between historians is whether Caesar himself left Alexandria before or after the birth of his son by Cleopatra. Plutarch says he left for the East before the child was born. Appian, on the other hand, who is (it must be admitted) a less reliable historian, says that Caesar stayed in Egypt for nine months, and Caesarion (as he was to be generally called) appears to have been an eight-month child. It is difficult to believe that he would not have waited for Cleopatra's confinement, for the sex of the child was all important and, since the death of his daughter Julia, Caesar was childless. On the other hand he had never shown himself a man of any great sentiment in private affairs, and the necessity for his presence with the legions may well have speeded his departure before the child's birth. In attempting to get to the truth of the matter one is hampered by the fact that later historians, writing under the Roman emperors, were inclined to disguise the fact that the son whom Cleopatra bore was Caesar's. Since he was subsequently killed on the orders of Octavian/Augustus, Caesar's adoptive heir, it was embarrassing to discuss the subject when writing in the reigns of the successors of Augustus.

BELOW: *hunting hippopotamus and crocodile in the marshes of Egypt. From a limestone relief in the tomb of Mereruka, Saqqara; Old Kingdom, c. 2300 B.C.* OPPOSITE: *an inundated palm grove*

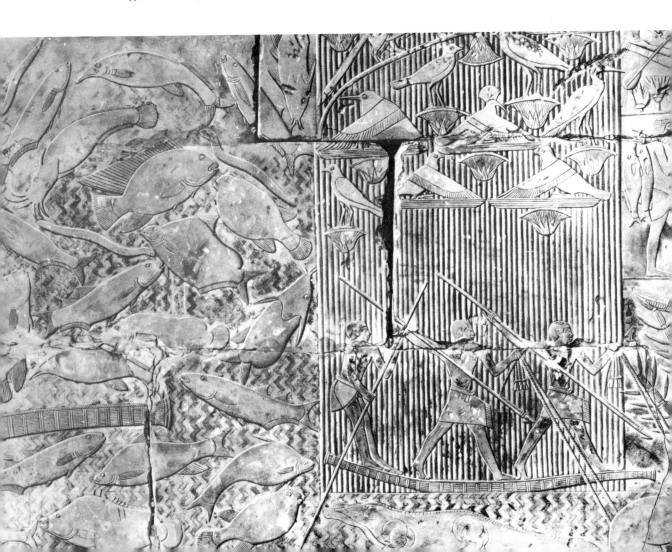

There can be little doubt, however, that the child that Cleopatra bore, sometime in late June or early July 47 B.C., was indeed Caesar's. The very fact that the Alexandrians, ever prone to snide comments about their rulers, called him 'Caesarion', 'Little Caesar', seems to prove that he was indeed regarded as Caesar's child, and, as has been seen, there is small likelihood of him having been fathered by any other man. The fact that Cornelius Oppius, a friend and protagonist of Caesar, later wrote a pamphlet designed to prove that Cleopatra's son was not Caesar's means nothing. Oppius was merely determined to defend Caesar's memory – as well as to preserve the claim of Augustus to be the real inheritor of the dictator's power and image. This son of Cleopatra and Caesar was formally named Ptolemy Caesar. He was the last of Caesar's line.

Caesar was to send for Cleopatra and his son after he had returned to Rome, but his immediate concern was to settle affairs in the East. First he appointed Antipater procurator of Judaea, and exempted the Jews from military service and the payment of tribute. Caesar had an affection for this clever nation, and it was one which the Jews returned. (For instance, during the recent disturbances in Alexandria the Jews had been conspicuous by their absence from the riots, and had refrained from harassing the Romans.) Caesar now moved on from Judaea to join his three legions. In a short but brilliant battle at Zela, about four hundred miles north of Ephesus,

he totally defeated Pharnaces. Having thus restored Roman rule throughout the East, as well as having far more than an ally in the Queen of Egypt, Caesar could well feel triumphant. Far distant were the days when he had wept because he felt that he could never rival Alexander. It was in this mood that he now wrote to his friend Amantius in Rome the famous words: 'Veni, Vidi, Vici' – 'I came, I saw, I conquered'. After the success of his Egyptian winter, and after this new and spectacular triumph, it is hardly surprising that Caesar's self-confidence was total. A vein of megalomania, always present in his character, came more and more to the surface.

When the news of his victory reached Rome there was no longer any doubt among his enemies that their position in Italy would be untenable upon the return of this all conquering general. Accordingly, Scipio, Cato and Faustus Sulla, among others, crossed to Africa where they had a friend in the local ruler King Juba. Many, however, who had previously been in the anti-Caesar camp now turned their coats and became (on the surface at any rate) his devoted supporters. As for his friends and the general populace, it seemed as if Caesar could do no wrong. His tide was now at the full, the Senate appointed him Consul for five years and dictator indefinitely. He was in effect the King of the Roman people and, by virtue of all his other conquests, ruler of the Mediterranean world. It only remained for him to deal with the last of the Pompeian faction. But first of all he set sail for Rome to settle local affairs, for there had been a mutiny among the legions stationed in Campania in the south. Mark Antony had tried to pacify them but had failed. It needed the presence of Caesar, of his reputation and dynamic aura, to restore order. Nothing at this moment in his life could go wrong for him. He was on the crest of the shining wave of success. By one speech, and by the distribution of money and land among the dissatisfied, the legions were once more loyal – and his to a man.

In the winter of 47 B.C. he crossed to Sicily with his troops, and in the following April, at Thapsus in North Africa, he defeated and utterly routed the Pompeian forces. Three of the leaders, Sulla among them, were put to death, while the others, including Scipio and Cato, committed suicide. 'Cato,' as Stewart Perowne has written, 'was, in a sense, the Last of the Romans. He was a patriot of the old school, prickly, prim and prudish; but inflexibly honest. . . . A Latin poet of the next century, Lucan, was to bestow upon him one of the noblest epitaphs of all time: *Victrix causa deis placuit sed victa Catoni*: The vanquishing cause pleased the gods: the vanquished Cato.' And Caesar was now one of the gods.

To all intents and purposes the Roman Republic was at an end. Caesar had killed it, and had laid the foundation for the future Empire under its quasi-divine, all-powerful monarchs. The Republic had begun to wither with every fresh accession

---

The temple of Luxor: Queen Nefertari clasping the leg of Rameses II; New Kingdom, c. 1300 B.C. OVERLEAF: the open court, constructed by Amenophis III, c. 1417–1379 B.C.; the columns are carved like tied bundles of papyrus.

of foreign territory. It was a noble dream of men like Cato to preserve it, or try to revive it – a dream impossible to fulfil. Caesar by his vast pattern of conquests had made its successor, the Empire, inevitable. The influence of Cleopatra and that Egyptian winter upon him had been profound. From now on the shadow of the Hellenistic god-kings was to determine the pattern of Rome and its civilization.

Except for Spain, where Pompey's sons were busy raising an army to continue their father's cause, all the Mediterranean basin was Caesar's, and he now presented Rome with immense territories in Africa. The problem of Spain would have to be dealt with but for the moment Caesar felt that he was entitled to his triumph and his laurels. He returned to Rome where the preparations were begun to celebrate his victory in Egypt, his defeat of Pharnaces, and his success in Africa. No man is capable of exercising so much power and receiving so much adulation without his head being turned, and there is little doubt that the events of this astonishing year – in which which he had been worshipped as a god – were to cloud Caesar's later judgments and attitudes. But for the time being the sun shone upon this extraordinary man as he applied his abilities to trying to settle the many problems in Italy that had arisen from the Civil War.

To prepare for the celebration of his Egyptian triumph the royal family, Cleopatra and her eleven-year-old brother Ptolemy XIV, were summoned to Rome. It was Cleopatra and his son Caesarion that the Dictator really wanted to see. But it was deemed impolitic to leave Cleopatra's brother behind, in case – in accordance with the family traditions – he and his advisers should make an independent bid for the throne. The unfortunate Arsinoë, Cleopatra's sister, was destined to walk among the prisoners in the triumph, together with Ganymedes and various others who had taken part in the rebellion against the Queen and Caesar. Apart from any private reasons of wanting to see his mistress and his son, Caesar had an excellent political reason for inviting Cleopatra to Rome. It must be seen by everyone that he was not celebrating a triumph over the established ruler of Egypt and the Egyptian people; but only over a section of the population who had disputed her, and his, authority.

The arrival of the Egyptian Queen with all her retinue of slaves, eunuchs, elaborately dressed bodyguard and courtiers, must in itself have caused something of a sensation in the city – as well as a scandal. Caesar promptly installed her in a house of his which stood on the right bank of the Tiber and was surrounded by gardens. Calpurnia, his legitimate wife (whom he had seen little of since his marriage to her in 59 B.C.), undoubtedly remained in his town house. It seems that Caesar made little or no attempt to disguise his relations with Cleopatra. The paternity of Caesarion was an open secret, and it must have become clear to all – and horrifying

Nomen of Rameses II carved on the back of a red granite statue of the King erected in the first court of the temple of Luxor; New Kingdom, c. 1300 B.C.

91

to the old republicans – that Caesar was contemplating a legitimate union with the Queen of Egypt, and the establishment of a royal line. He made no secret of his intentions from those who could read the signs for, during the celebrations not long afterwards, he dedicated in the centre of the Forum Julium (which he had built at his own expense) a temple to Venus Genetrix, Venus the Mother of All. This in itself was understandable, since the Julii claimed descent from the goddess. But Caesar went even further than this and had a gold statue of Cleopatra installed next to the statue of the goddess. The implication was clear enough: 'I am the descendant of Venus. Cleopatra is the incarnation of Isis who is the Egyptian equivalent of Venus. *Ergo*, we are both of divine origin.' Caesar anticipated Nietzsche by many centuries in claiming not only to be the Superman, but 'Beyond Good and Evil'.

Caesar's successive triumphs, which lasted four days, were the most splendid – and the longest – that Rome had ever seen. On the first day he was acclaimed as conqueror of Gaul. Followed by his legions declaiming their bawdy verses about 'the bald-headed adulterer' he ascended the Capitol with an escort of forty elephants. This well earned Gallic triumph was marred by the fact that Vercingetorix (the

BELOW: *bronze head of Juba II of Mauritania.* OPPOSITE: *Gaulish coin of Vercingetorix*

great leader of the Gauls who had surrendered in order to save his people from further suffering, and who had walked in his chains through the streets of Rome) was led back to his prison and put to death. This execution, although traditionally customary at the end of triumphs, was an unnecessary act. Caesar's reputation would have been enhanced if he had acted with clemency towards a man who had been a brave foe. The Egyptian triumph was celebrated with immense ceremony on the second day. A statue of the Nile god, a model of that wonder of the world, the Pharos, and innumerable reminders of the campaign such as portraits of the defeated Achillas and Pothinus; all these were paraded through the city. They were followed by a number of exotic animals, such as the giraffe, which few Romans had ever seen before. Arsinoë was later granted her liberty. It would have been singularly bad politics to have executed the sister of Cleopatra – even though the latter might not have hesitated to do so. Ganymedes disappears from history, so he may well have shared the fate of Vercingetorix.

On the following day Caesar's victory over Pharnaces, and the conquest of Pontus, was marked among other things by the procession of a great tablet bearing the words 'Veni, Vidi, Vici'. His defeat of King Juba (which had in reality been the defeat of Romans and of his political enemies) concluded the spectacle. 'After the triumphs,' Plutarch writes, 'Caesar gave his soldiers large gifts and entertained the people with banquets and spectacles, feasting them all at one time on twenty thousand dining-couches, and furnishing spectacles of gladiatorial and naval combats in honour of his daughter Julia, long since dead.'

Nowhere do we find any mention of Cleopatra, and it is most unlikely that she would have watched the Egyptian triumph. This would have been impolitic though she might not have minded the degradation of her sister. Undoubtedly though, she must have revelled in the general spectacles, all of which made the stature of her dictator-lover greater even than she could have imagined it during their Alexandrian days. Then he had been greatest of the Romans; but now, with all his subsequent victories, he appeared almost to transcend human limitations. If, as seems likely from his recorded actions, Caesar was planning a formal Roman marriage with Cleopatra, she must at this moment have felt secure that a magnificent future was assured for her and her son. East and West would be united, and she would be Caesar's Queen-Empress.

One further military action remained to Caesar – the destruction of the Pompeian factor in Spain. Early in November he left Rome and, moving with his customary speed, reached southern Spain with his legions less than a month later. Despite a series of inconclusive minor engagements it was not until March 45 B.C. that he managed to bring the Pompeian forces to a major confrontation. It was one in which he very nearly lost his own life. Pompey's sons had assembled a large and well disciplined army of Roman legionaries, similar to those who opposed them. Battle was joined near Munda, a town not far from Cordòba, and it took all of Caesar's generalship and even a personal rallying of his troops to bring it to a successful conclusion. He is later reported to have said: 'I have often fought for victory, but this was the first time I had to fight for my very life'. The elder son of Pompey the Great was killed, but the younger escaped. It made no difference: the Pompeian forces were crushed. Caesar was the sole and unchallenged master of an empire which stretched from Britain in the north to Asia Minor in the East. At this moment of absolute triumph he was certain that he was not only the descendant of a goddess, but a very god himself.

Allegorical representation of the Nile, found in Rome about 1513, perhaps originally from the Iseum; 5 feet 6 inches high

EMPEROR OF ROME

Caesar was now fifty-six, a queen and his son by her awaited him in Rome, and he was master of a world that had been united under Roman rule almost solely by him. But, god though he might be, he was aging like any mortal. A coin which was struck two years later – the year of his death – shows a balding man with wrinkled forehead, hollowed cheeks, a scrawny dewlap and a withered neck. It is still a face of unmistakable power, however, and the large eyes are confidently confronting the future. In every respect except for drink and gluttony he had driven himself hard since he was a young man, pressed forward by the relentless urge of his ambition. He had fought battle after battle, swum rivers, tamed so-called unbreakable horses, and campaigned in the cold north as well as in the burning desert. Intellectually, too, he had pushed himself, from writing books to duties of administration and law-giving, as well as the conduct of vast campaigns ranging over nearly all the known world. Few human beings could have withstood such physical and intellectual punishment as he had inflicted in himself.

There seems to have been another reason for his premature aging. All his life he had been subject to epileptic fits. The 'falling sickness', or the 'divine malady', has often been associated with great brilliance of intellect, as if its victims had such active brains that sometimes they literally exploded under the pressure of the thought-processes streaming through them. Lombroso, the Italian criminologist and one of the founders of psychiatric studies, pointed out that many of the great religious leaders and men who believed themselves to be either the Voice, or the Messenger, of God, were epileptics. Caesar had several times been stricken with the malady in the course of his business, and even, apparently, during the battle of Thapsus. The attacks seem to have come upon him more often in his later years. One medical definition of epilepsy states that it is 'a recurring, abrupt loss or alteration of consciousness, [and] includes many types of seizures, e.g., convulsions, emotional explosions, irritable periods, vertigoes and psychic clouding. . . . Epilepsy appears to exert no necessarily injurious effect upon the general health, and is quite consistent with great bodily vigour. It is very different, however, with regard to its influence upon the mind.' Another medical authority, J. A. C. Brown, remarks that: 'Numerous great men have been epileptics and in many respects the novelist Dostoievsky who was a sufferer is typical of the epileptic character with its violence, its love of mysticism, its persecutory beliefs and impulsiveness'. Caesar certainly had 'great bodily vigour', and a 'love of mysticism' – at least in regard to himself –

ABOVE: *denarius of Julius Caesar, 42 B.C.* OPPOSITE: *the Forum Julii, the square and market built by Julius Caesar, with the temple of Venus Genetrix, Rome; from a reconstruction by Olindo Grossi*

had increased. Cleopatra may have had her belief that he was superhuman strengthened because he suffered from the 'divine malady', for it was generally believed that during a seizure the body was inhabited by a god.

Upon his return to Rome Caesar celebrated another triumph for his victory in Spain. This time, however, it was felt by many that he was behaving in a tasteless and unnecessarily boastful fashion. The victory which he had just gained had been over fellow Romans, and over the sons of the great Pompey, whose memory was still held in considerable and deserved reverence. But Caesar was by now consumed with *hubris* and, in accordance with the classic law, *nemesis* was waiting in the wings.

He had been nominated consul for ten years and Dictator for life, and he was from now on to be known as Imperator, or Emperor. This title had usually been conferred on successful generals in the field of battle (rather like a medal in later times), but Caesar took it as a permanent prefix to his name. It was furthermore arranged that, though he had as yet no legitimate children, it should be handed on to his children's children. Once again, one sees the shared intentions of Caesar and Cleopatra. At the moment Cleopatra was no more than his mistress in Roman eyes, but divorce was easy enough to obtain in Rome. All Caesar had to do was put aside the unfortunate Calpurnia, marry Cleopatra, and legitimize Caesarion. Even if this son were scorned for having been born outside wedlock, there was every likelihood of Cleopatra bearing him other children. Caesar's ambition extended beyond the grave. He intended to establish a dynasty.

In this last year of his life it must not be thought that he neglected home affairs. Indeed, now that he could for the moment dismiss warfare from his mind, he threw

himself into the reconstruction of the Roman polity with all his customary brilliance and vigour. The Civil Wars had left the whole fabric of life in Italy in tatters, and Caesar set about the necessary task of surgery and reconstruction. First of all, his veteran soldiers had to be rewarded for their services, so he settled them on land in Italy and in the provinces. To deal with the problem of unemployment he sent eighty thousand settlers to two new colonies, Carthage and Corinth (both of which had been destroyed by the Romans a century earlier), and to Hispalis (modern Seville) in Spain. He also tackled one of the greatest problems in Rome itself, the bread-dole. This free distribution of bread to the needy had got out of hand and contributed to a demoralizing laziness. Caesar, accordingly, after a house-to-house census to determine the real needs of the people, cut the dole by a little over fifty per cent – from three hundred and twenty thousand recipients to one hundred and fifty thousand – and fresh recipients were only to be placed on the list where vacancies occurred through death. This drastic reduction played an added part in Caesar's designs, for it encouraged the emigration of the indigent, or out-of-work citizens to the new colonies. Rather than starve in Rome, they would emigrate. To lessen the danger of slave revolts, and to ensure that native-born Italians were not pressurized to leave the soil by cheap slave-labour, he passed a law requiring large land-owners to employ one-third freemen among the labourers on their estates. To regulate the flow of Roman citizens to the new territories a further law stated that no man between twenty and forty, unless on military duties, should be absent from Rome for more than three years. This gave a young citizen the chance to complete his education in Greece, or a merchant to trade in Africa, Spain, or the

East; but it ensured that they, and the fruits of their learning or earning, would come back to their native land.

Work started on a complete revision of the Criminal Code while, to eliminate the many anomalies in the Civil Law, a new codification of all the laws was begun. To encourage the arts and medicine in the new Rome that he hoped soon to see rising above the ungainly pattern of the old city, citizenship was automatically to be granted to doctors and artists (most of whom were Greeks). Further to all these projects, he initiated the very necessary reform of the Roman calendar – an idea which had probably come to him in Egypt when talking with the *savants* of the Mouseion. It is almost certain that Sosigenes, the great Alexandrian astronomer, was the author of the new Julian calendar. Prior to this, the Roman calendar had been based on the lunar year of three hundred and fifty-five days which meant that there was an annual discrepancy of ten and a quarter days between it and the solar calendar. This meant that, unless an adjustment was regularly made, it was necessary every so often to insert an additional month into a year in order to bring the months and the seasons into line. This primitive system was abandoned. Caesar decreed that the year 46 B.C. should be extended by some ninety days, so as to begin the new year of 45 on the right date of 1 January. Every fourth year a 'leap year' was instituted, by the introduction of an extra day in February. One month, our modern July, was to be named Julius in honour of Caesar.

Quite apart from all his law-giving and intellectual tasks, Caesar determined that to create a tranquil spirit in the new Italy he would show clemency to his former enemies. Cato, who had died by his own hand, had earlier said: 'As though he were their lord, he pardons those whom he has no right to rule'. But even Cicero, who can hardly be counted among his admirers, was ready to concede that Caesar in victory behaved with humanity. As he remarks in one letter: 'He is naturally humane and ready to forgive . . . . What kindness he showed to us! He appointed Cassius as one of his legates, and made Brutus Proconsul of Gaul, Sulpicius Proconsul of Greece, and Marcellus, against whom he had the greatest grievances, he allowed to return.' These were all men who had fought for the Pompeian faction against Caesar. At the time it must have seemed to him that his actions were those of an intelligent man, and politically sensible, for he could not possibly harry down all those who had been on the other side in the Civil Wars.

He had grandiose, but feasible, projects for the city of Rome, its port Ostia, and for other places in the Empire. Almost certainly he had been influenced in Alexandria by the sight of this great city which had been planned from its inception; where there were splendid public buildings, efficient water-supplies, drainage systems, and where a road-plan operated throughout the capital. Rome was a city that had just grown;

Just below the First Cataract, Aswan. Rock-hewn tombs of nobles of the Old and Middle Kingdoms overlook the Nile immediately below the Muslim shrine of Kubbet el-Hawa.

unplanned, embellished here and there with marble palaces and temples, but overall a higgledy-piggledy mess of winding streets and small squalid squares; and with a totally insufficient housing capacity for its ever-increasing citizenry. He planned, in effect, a complete rebuilding of the city. He had already endowed it with the new temple of Venus Genetrix, but now he proposed the erection on the Campus Martius of a vast temple to the God of War. Culture and entertainment were not to be forgotten, and he intended to build a large theatre similar to that of Athens at the foot of the Tarpeian Rock. Work was started on the Curia Julia in the Forum Julium for meetings of the Senate within the city walls. The Pontine Marshes were to be reclaimed (not in fact achieved until the dictatorship of Mussolini in the twentieth century). The Tiber was to be joined to the river Anio by a canal, which would then run down to Tarracina over fifty miles away, to facilitate the passage of commerce to and from the city. A road was contemplated that would run from Rome across the Apennines to the Adriatic. Finally, envisaging that Corinth would soon become a thriving commercial city (as it had been formerly), he proposed to drive a canal through the Isthmus, thus linking the Aegean with the Gulfs of Corinth, Patras and the Ionian Sea. (An attempt at this was later begun by the Emperor Nero, but the rocky terrain proved too hard for the tools of the time, and it was not in fact dug until the late nineteenth century.)

What was this Rome like, this city from which Caesar ruled the Empire? It is difficult to visualize it now, since the many buildings of the later emperors overlaid the capital that Caesar knew. But its atmosphere was probably not dissimilar from that which Juvenal, writing over a century later, described:

> The waggons thundering past
> Through those narrow twisting streets, the oaths of draymen
> Caught in a traffic-jam. . . .
> If a business appointment
> Summons the tycoon, he gets there fast, by litter,
> Tacking above the crowd. There's plenty of room inside:
> He can read, or take notes, or snooze as he jogs along –
> Those drawn blinds are most soporific. Even so
> He outstrips us: however fast we pedestrians hurry
> We're blocked by the crowds ahead, while those behind us
> Tread on our heels. Sharp elbows buffet my ribs,
> Poles poke into me; one lout swings a crossbeam
> Down on my skull, another scores with a barrel.
> My legs are mud-encrusted, big feet kick me, a hobnailed
> Soldier's boot lands squarely on my toe. Do you see
> All that steam and bustle? The great man's hangers-on
> Are getting their free dinner, each with his own
> Kitchen-boy in attendance. Those outsize dixies,

Marble bust of Julius Caesar, provenance unknown. Augustan copy of an original of about 40 B.C.; 10¾ inches high

Three reliefs of the 2nd century A.D. ABOVE: *Roman travelling wagon.* OPPOSITE, ABOVE: *butcher's shop, Rome,* BELOW: *metal-worker's shop*

And all the rest of the gear one poor little slave
Must balance on his head, while he trots along
To keep the charcoal glowing, would tax the strength
Of a musclebound general. Recently-patched tunics
Are ripped to shreds. Here's the great trunk of a fir-tree
Swaying along on its waggon, and look, another dray
Behind it, stacked high with pine-logs, a nodding threat
Over the heads of the crowd.

(trans. Peter Green)

In Caesar's time Rome, at least compared with Alexandria, was still a provincial city, but very conscious of itself as the acknowledged capital of the world. One cannot help wondering whether Caesar was toying with the idea of making it the second capital, and dividing the administration of the Empire as Constantine was to do centuries later. It was in the East that the greatest wealth was found, and it was in the East also that there still existed the greatest unconquered enemies of the Roman Empire. No Roman could ever forget the disaster of Carrhae in Mesopotamia, in 53 B.C., when the Roman general Crassus had been killed and nearly all his army wiped out by the Parthian horsemen who, with their mobility and showers of arrows, had proved that in certain circumstances at least the armed legionary was no match for light cavalry. One of Caesar's last dreams was to tame the Parthians, and then (perhaps) to drive his way south to India. If he could succeed in doing this he would have eclipsed Alexander in every respect; for Caesar already had an empire in Spain, Gaul and the north, an area which Alexander had never even known.

Cleopatra, lodged in her comfortable house, surrounded by her courtiers, busy with plans for her and her son's future, cannot have seen very much of Caesar at this time. From the absence of references to her it would seem that she tactfully kept to herself and did not enter into the life of the city which lay just across the water. She will not have known much, if anything, of that Rome so brilliantly described by J. W. Mackail:

> The drip of water from the aqueduct that passed over the gate from which the dusty, squalid Appian Way stretched through its long suburb; the garret under the tiles where, just as now, the pigeons sleeked themselves in the sun and the rain drummed on the roof; the narrow, crowded streets, half choked with the builders' carts, and the pavements ringing under the heavy military boots of guardsmen; the tavern waiters trotting along with a pyramid of hot dishes on their heads; the flower-pots falling from high window ledges; night, with the shuttered shops, the silence broken by some sudden street brawl, the darkness shaken by a flare of torches as some great man, wrapped in his scarlet cloak, passes along from a dinner-party with his long train of clients and slaves. . . .

This was Rome: violence, squalor, beauty and brutality – and power.

THE IDES OF MARCH

Cicero wrote of Caesar in his Second Philippic that, 'after planning for many years his way to royal power, with immense labour and accompanied by great dangers, he had achieved his purpose. By means of public spectacles, by monumental buildings, by bribes and by feasts, he had conciliated the unreflecting masses. He had bound his own friends to himself by favours, and his opponents by a show of clemency.' What was so soon, and so tragically, to be proved was that there were some of his opponents who did not feel themselves so bound, and who remained devoted to the idea of the Republic. Caesarism in fact had triumphed, and he himself had laid the foundation of the monarchical system that would henceforth rule Rome and its Empire. But it was in the hands of another and far younger man that the Emperor principle was to be perfected. Caesar himself, had he only moderated his behaviour, might indeed have died peacefully as Dictator and Imperator, and founder of a Julian–Ptolemaic dynasty. He was driven, however, by that same ambition which had all along prompted his astonishing meteoric career, to excesses that could only outrage men of conservative, or even moderate, persuasions.

An example of this occurred on 15 February, when the annual festival known as the Lupercalia took place in Rome. This was a day when the whole city was *en fête* in celebration of an ancient fertility rite whose origins were obscure, but which almost certainly dated from Etruscan times. Lupercus, who was identified in Roman eyes with the nature god Faunus or Pan, represented the return of the spring and, by natural identification, the growth of plants, the mating of animals, and fecundity in human beings. After the sacrifice of a goat and a dog, two young nobles who belonged to the Order of Lupercus cut the skins of these animals into strips known as *februa* (hence February) and using them as whips ran through the streets striking out at every woman they passed. The belief was that any woman touched would become pregnant during the year, so that there was great competition between women who wanted to bear a child to be struck by the *februa*.

On this particular occasion in 44 B.C. Caesar, who was president of the ceremonies, was seated on a golden throne in the Forum, and Mark Antony by chance (or possibly by arrangement?) was one of the *Luperci*. As he bounded into the Forum,

The Appian Way, south of Rome

followed by the usual dense crowd who always ran behind the 'Faun-men', Antony hailed Caesar as Lupercus himself. He then ran forward and, mounting the rostrum, attempted to place a crown upon Caesar's head. At this dramatic moment a claque of Caesar's supporters, stationed at various points in the Forum, shouted out and begged him to accept it. Had he done so, this would have made him not only Dictator and Emperor, but King of Rome as well.

It is difficult to understand why Caesar, who already had all the power of the state in his hands, should have wished to be ordained King – difficult, that is, unless one accepts the fact that he had it in mind to marry Cleopatra, and to found a royal line. There can be little doubt that the whole of this episode was planned by Caesar and Cleopatra in association with Antony as a test of the feelings of the Roman crowd. But the very name Rex, or King, connected with the Etruscan Tarquins – the last of whom had been expelled about 509 B.C. – had very deep emotional over-tones. It reminded the Romans of the long fight of their ancestors to rid themselves of Etruscan rule. The crowd stayed silent or made hostile protests, and Caesar, sensing their mood, handed the crown back to Antony. His action was loudly applauded – something which must have been profoundly depressing to the Dictator, who was suffering one of the first major checks to his ambitions. Antony, however, (as his life was later to prove) was less sensitive and much less intelligent than Caesar. He persisted, perhaps thinking that Caesar was only making a gesture of refusal, and once more offered him the crown. Again the crowd showed their disapproval, and Caesar, bowing to their mood, this time emphatically rejected it. At his action, the booing and the clamour ceased, and the people broke into tumul-tuous cheers.

Caesar, concealing his disappointment (which must have been deep indeed), now gave orders that the diadem should be taken and placed upon the head of Jupiter's statue in the Capitol, and that the whole incident should be recorded in the public records, to the effect that: 'On this day, acting on the wishes of the people, Mark Antony offered Caesar the royal crown, but the Dictator refused to accept it'.

The citizens of Rome may have thought that the incident was closed, and that Caesar by his rejection had showed that he understood their feelings. Perhaps some may even have thought he had contrived the whole situation in order to prove to them that he had no desire for the kingship. But there were others – and they were more knowledgeable about the true state of affairs – who felt differently. Even before this scene at the Lupercalia the band of conspirators had begun to meet to discuss ways and means of doing away with the Dictator. A nexus of senators, some intelligent pro-Republicans, and others intent on their own ends, had already set in train the plot that was to end with Caesar's death.

Model of Flavian Amphitheatre in Rome, completed in A.D. *80, known as the Colosseum, one of the most famous surviving ancient buildings. The poles supported an awning.*

Marble relief depicting two men with spears attacking a bull. From Naxos, Greco-Roman period; 1 foot 6½ inches high

---

These senators had many grievances, several of them legitimate – for Caesar at various times had showed with fatal arrogance that he regarded the Senate with contempt, and most of its members as men of straw. On one occasion, for instance, the whole Senate led by Antony (who was Consul) had presented themselves to him in the Forum Julium. Caesar received them outside the Temple of Venus Genetrix seated on his gold throne, but did not even bother to rise in courtesy to the Senate. He received their homage and conferment upon him of the title of Dictator for life in a way which was clearly intended to show his contempt for the Senate as a body. He had already packed the Senate with his own supporters, even, so it was said, with Gauls and other foreigners who hardly knew how to wear the Roman toga. (A joke subsequently went the rounds of the city that if any new Senator was to ask the way to the Senate House no one was to tell him where it was.) Now the Senate as a body had promised always to protect Caesar, so in his certainty that no one would ever harm him, he dismissed his bodyguard. His friends warned him that his life was in danger, but his life, he said, was of more value to Rome than to him and in any case. it was better to die than to live in the fear of death. In

108

this he echoed another remark of his, that when the time came he wanted to die swiftly.

His last weeks were occupied with his forthcoming campaign in the East, where he intended first of all to establish the Empire's frontiers in Dacia (modern Hungary and Rumania), and then to strike south through Armenia against the Parthians. Preoccupied with so many things, as well as with his private monarchical dreams, it is little wonder that, even though he received these warnings from his friends, he chose to disregard them. He would soon be away from Rome. He must have felt completely confident that there could be no denying him the coveted crown, the repudiation of Calpurnia and a royal marriage with Cleopatra.

It was later rumoured that, after his departure with the army, he had arranged for a bill to be introduced enabling him to marry again, since Calpurnia was childless and he wished for offspring. Possibly what really determined his fate – and its date – was a saying found in the Sibylline Books. In view of the imminent departure of the army and the extreme importance of the Parthian campaign, it was natural enough that Caesar should order them to be consulted. What was less natural was that, for a second time, the saying which emerged exactly suited his ambitions. While his friends may have smiled, his enemies must have been furious at what was almost certainly a blatant tampering with these ancient oracles. Consulted about the prospects in Parthia, the books (as interpreted) stated unequivocally that no war could be successful against the Parthians unless the Roman armies were led by a king. The implication was clear to all: 'Before he leaves, Caesar must be made King'. This ruse, which may have seemed clever to him at the time, was to be his ruin. He had only to wait, to win, and return to Rome, and it would have been almost impossible to deny him the kingship. But Caesar, like many an aging man, was in a hurry: he could not wait. On 15 March, the Ides of March, the advice of the Books was to be debated in the Senate, and a proposal in connection with it was to be laid before the members. There can be no doubt what that proposal would have been.

Since the explosion of the Sibylline pronouncement occurred so shortly before Caesar's departure, it meant that any act to prevent the Dictator's clear intention must be made with the greatest speed. It was this fact which prevented the plot from leaking out through that great whispering-gallery that was the Senate of Rome. One of the leaders of the conspiracy was Gaius Cassius, an able general, who had also been one of Pompey's admirals, and who had been among the many pardoned by Caesar in the amnesty. Cassius had long been an ardent Republican, and had all his life detested autocracy. His motives were easily comprehensible, although he may have had other personal reasons for hating Caesar. The latter had, indeed, suspected for some time that Cassius was up to no good, and had once remarked that he mistrusted him: 'Cassius looks so pale. What can he be up to?'

Brutus was quite a different type of man. Young, scholarly, an intellectual, he provided for the conspirators the moral justification, as it were, for their proposed

ABOVE: *the embodiment of Roman republican virtues, once thought to be Junius Brutus; Etruscan-Italian bronze bust, 3rd–2nd centuries* B.C. OPPOSITE: *coin commemorating Caesar's death, issued 43–42* B.C.

action. Caesar had had a notorious affair with Brutus's mother Servilia before and after his birth, and it was widely rumoured that he was Caesar's son. Brutus, however, naturally claimed descent from Servilia's legal husband, and he was thus descended from the great Junius Brutus who had expelled the Tarquins. Whatever the truth of his ancestry, there is no doubt that Caesar treated Brutus like a son. He had even given special orders at Pharsalia that Brutus was not to be harmed in the battle; orders that were repeated during the flight of the Pompeians after Caesar's victory. If Brutus was clever, he was also something of a prig, and his moralistic stand on various matters when speaking in the Senate had once caused Caesar to say: 'I don't understand what the young man means, but whatever it is, he means it vehemently'. Other leading conspirators were the two Casca brothers, Trebonius (whom Caesar had just appointed Proconsul of Asia), and a number of men such as Tillius Cimber and Servus Galba, both of whom had been supporters and confidants of Caesar. To judge from the offices that many of the conspirators had held through Caesar's good favour, his policy of clemency towards the Pompeians had not succeeded. Perhaps it would have if he had never raised that deadly question of kingship. Among the principal leaders of the plot there was a mixture of idealism, personal hatred of the Dictator, self-seeking and a confused desire to return to the days of the Republic. But it is, as Oskar von Wertheimer put it, 'horrible to think that these murderers saw him daily, pretended to share his views, his plans and his

interests, and feigned friendship, the noble Brutus no less than the fanatical Cassius and Decimus Brutus Longinus – horrible even for the Rome of that day, in which horrors abounded.'

Various schemes were propounded as to what date and place would be best for the assassination. In the end it was decided that, since Caesar's last visit to the Senate before joining the army was to be 15 March, and since this was the occasion when it was suspected he would ask for the Kingship 'to ensure victory', the Ides of March would be the date, and the Hall of Pompey – where the Senate would be meeting – the place. There could not, of course, have been a more effective (or ignoble) plan; for they knew that he would be unarmed, without the bodyguard that he had dismissed, and placing his trust in the fact that all the Senators had solemnly declared that they would never see him harmed. How the idealistic Brutus could have squared all this with his conscience is difficult to see. Indeed, it is said that he was in such a state of mental torment, trying to resolve the issue in his mind, that he could not sleep at night, and tossed and turned, finally causing his wife Portia to ask him what was troubling him. Thereupon he revealed the details of the plot, thus risking the lives of all the conspirators as well as involving his own wife in their corporate guilt. To such a depth can the heights of idealism reduce a man.

The murder of Caesar made such an impression upon ancient historians that it was natural they should describe innumerable portents foretelling his end. There is little reason to doubt that in the weeks before his death the atmosphere of Rome was sombre in the extreme. The legions were about to march against the dreaded Parthians – and without a king at their head as the Books prescribed; small groups of men were known to be meeting behind barred doors in private houses, and everywhere there was a feeling of unease. Only a few days before the Ides it was said that the horses Caesar had consecrated to the gods on crossing the Rubicon had declined to eat, and had wept vast tears. Spurinna, an old soothsayer, of whom there were many in Rome (who naturally had to keep their ears to the ground for their supposedly 'magic' information), had come to him and warned him to beware of the Ides. On 14 March it was said that a small bird, bearing a sprig of laurel in its beak, had been seen flying into Pompey's Hall, pursued by a flock of other birds which had attacked and killed it. An ancient tablet was said to have been dug up by some of Caesar's veterans who had been settled at Capua, which purported to be from the grave of Capys, the founder of the city. On it was written Greek words to the effect that if ever the founder's bones were disturbed, the crime would have to be expiated by the death of a descendant of Julius, at the hands of his own fellows, and at a heavy cost to Italy. All these 'prophecies' were of course written with the benefit of hindsight. They show, however, how deep an impact the murder of Caesar made on the Roman world – and in none of them is there the faintest suggestion that a noble act of tyrannicide was committed on the fatal Ides.

On the night of 14 March, so Plutarch tells us, as Caesar was lying next to Calpurnia in his town house, all the doors and windows of the room suddenly burst open as if struck by a massive gale of wind. At the same time the ceremonial armour of Mars, which Caesar, as Pontifex Maximus, kept in his house, fell with a crash from the wall. Calpurnia is said to have had terrible visions and nightmares; to have lain moaning in her sleep and, on Caesar awaking her, to have said that she had dreamed he was murdered. She begged him not to leave the house that day.

In the morning Caesar, who may have been genuinely indisposed or, quite probably, troubled by the soothsayer, the strange events of the night and his wife's entreaties, sent for Antony with the intention of postponing his visit to the Senate. He now received a report from the augurs, stating that the sacrifices for the day had proved inauspicious. All these things, combined with the advice of his doctors that he should stay at home, ought to have been sufficient to convince Caesar that he would be unwise to attend the meeting. The conspirators, meanwhile, were on tenterhooks as the time dragged by and still the Dictator failed to make his appearance. There can be little doubt that they were in an agony of fear. Suppose their plot had leaked out, and Caesar was even now on his way with the legionaries who loved him, to surround Pompey's Hall and take his vengeance? In their terrified quandary they sent as an emissary the man who is the Judas of the story. This was Decimus Brutus Albinus. He had been a close friend of Caesar's, and the latter had made him Governor of Cisalpine Gaul, as well as destining him for the Consulship in the following year. He arrived at Caesar's house to find him on the point of postponing his visit.

Decimus chided Caesar on his delay, pointing out, no doubt, that there was a lot of business to transact before Caesar left Rome with the legions. He may even have stressed the fact that it was all-important that Caesar came, since he must be made Rex before the Parthian Campaign. There is no evidence of this but, in view of the omens and his own feelings, it is difficult to understand what other bait could have drawn Caesar to the meeting. It was the only important piece of business as far as he was concerned.

Caesar was now persuaded – and he trusted Decimus as much as he did Brutus – and agreed to come. Decimus, elated, hurried back to tell the conspirators that he had done his job well, and that the Dictator was on his way. The assassins had hidden their daggers either under their cloaks or in their stylus cases. (These were the holders in

Bas-relief of an emperor performing a sacrifice, 2nd century A.D.

which Romans kept their writing equipment together with the sharp-pointed stylus, with which writing was scratched on a hard-wax tablet.) Caesar meanwhile, borne through the streets, was to receive one further warning. The same soothsayer approached him again, and when Caesar said jokingly: 'Well, the Ides of March have arrived!' Spurinna replied 'Yes, but they are not yet past.' At a later point on his journey a man darted from the crowd and thrust into his hand a small scroll containing details of the plot. Caesar was used to receiving many such petitions. He did not bother to open it at the time, but put it aside with the other documents he was carrying. (It is said to have been recovered beside his body a few hours later.)

In the Hall of Pompey the priests offered up sacrifices and, once again, the omens proved unfavourable. Antony, among others who were present, said he was not going to attend. This, as it turned out, was a further blow. Everything pointed to disaster. But Caesar adamantly maintained that, having come this far, and because the Senate awaited him, he would go within. After the deliberate disrespect with which he had treated the Senators in recent months one can only conclude that he was convinced he was at last to be acclaimed Rex.

At this late hour there was to be a further moment of apprehension, even terror, for the conspirators. The news ran round that Brutus's wife Portia was either dead or dying. (She had fainted from the strain.) Could she at the moment of death have betrayed the whole plot? Worse was to come, when a senator, Popilius Laenas, whispered to Brutus and Casca, 'I wish you luck with your scheme, but I

113

Head of Julius Caesar, 18th century

advise you to be quick, for people are talking'. They had another fright when another man came up to Casca and said, 'You kept it well secret, but Brutus has told me everything'. It turned out later that he was referring to the fact that Casca was applying to be an aedile or magistrate. The same may well have been the case with Popilius Laenas. But it did not help the conspirators' nerves when they saw the latter approach Caesar as he stepped from his litter and start talking to him. For a moment it seemed as if all was lost; then it became clear from the senator's manner that he was not passing on information, but asking a favour. Their hands relaxed on their daggers. It will never be known whether Popilius Laenas, as he bent to kiss Caesar's hand, was just a harmless Senator hoping to have obtained a favour for himself.

Caesar now entered the building and the whole Senate rose to their feet. It seemed like many another meeting, although Caesar must secretly have hoped that he was nearing the moment of his greatest triumph. He walked over to his throne and took his place. While the Senate as a body was paying the usual formal tribute of respects to the Dictator, the conspirators – as though to ask him questions or favours – gradually gathered round him in a half circle, so as to cut him off and screen him from the main body of the Senate. Tillius Cimber was one of the foremost. He asked Caesar a favour: that he would recall Cimber's brother from exile. Caesar refused his request, but Cimber continued to implore him and then, in that characteristically Italianate gesture of supplication, stretched out his hand to Caesar's robe. The latter drew back, but Cimber, as if turning from pleading to outright indignation, laid his hand upon the Dictator's purple robe and pulled it down off his shoulders. It was the signal. The other conspirators crowded round Caesar, who now stood there clad only in the simple Roman toga. They had stripped him of his Emperorship. Caesar, as if divining the symbolism of the act as well as the hostility surrounding him, cried out: 'But this is violence!' Casca, who was standing behind him, struck the first blow at the victim's neck but, missing, pierced only his shoulder. Caesar, wheeling round, caught Casca's arm and ran it through with his stylus, crying out, 'You villain Casca! What are you about?' But, in that brief moment, he must have known.

A second later Casca's brother stabbed him in the side, and Cassius struck his dagger into his face. They were all onto him like a pack of wolves, one striking him in the thigh, another in the back. Caesar, says Appian, fought for his life like a wild animal.

He had fought all his life; it was not in his nature to give up; but this was to be the last fight of the old 'leader of the pack'. The conspirators were madmen. Inflamed with blood-lust and hate, they struck about them so wildly that several of their own number were wounded. Caesar, striking out left and right with his stylus, managed to break through the circle of his enemies. Once more he grasped Casca by the arm, fighting to the last, slowly sinking to the ground at the foot of the statue of his old enemy, Pompey. It was at this moment, so tradition says, that he saw Brutus among the others, coming towards him with a dagger in his hand. His last words, spoken in Greek, were to Brutus: 'And you too, my child!' So, covering his head with his toga, he slid to the floor and died. Twenty-three dagger wounds were later counted upon his body; but it was so mangled that there may well have been many more. They were wounds that would be paid for over and over again in the body of Italy.

AFTERMATH

Cleopatra must have been one of the first to hear the news of Caesar's death. What her feelings were when a messenger burst into the villa that Caesar himself had lent her it is hard to imagine. A human and natural grief there must certainly have been – the man whom she had loved was dead. Close on the heels of this initial anguish must have come practical considerations. Those twenty-three wounds that had destroyed Caesar had also destroyed all Cleopatra's hopes. She was not to sit on another golden throne at the side of Caesar; nor was three-year-old Caesarion to be legitimized and proclaimed the lawful descendant of his father and the future Emperor. The dream of a Julian-Ptolemaic dynasty was at an end. For the moment there was nothing she could do but guard the doors and prepare for violence; for the thought must surely have occurred to her that if the conspirators had been prepared to go so far as murdering Caesar, she herself might well be included in their future plans.

But the conspirators had no future plans. This was the final and complete absurdity of their whole action. They had murdered Caesar – largely for a political motive, it is true – but beyond this point they had no political motives whatsoever. Childishly they seem to have believed that with the Dictator out of the way the Republic would somehow or other rise like a phoenix from its ashes. The rules of the tyrannicides of earlier days – like Harmodius and Aristogiton, for instance, in sixth-century Athens – no longer applied. In simple communities it had been enough to kill the 'tyrant' and all was well. But Rome and its vast Empire was no simple community, and the murder of Caesar, far from cutting any Gordian knot and producing a solution to the state's problems, only aggravated them. Caesar had very largely created the Empire; he himself had been the State; but now everything from distant Gaul and Spain to equally distant Asia Minor was put in question. Who, for instance, would lead the legions against the Dacians, let alone the Parthians? Who would pick up the reins of administration? Not the enfeebled Senate, that was sure. The murder of Caesar was the last gasp of the old Roman upper class, its last vain struggle to assert an independence of action that no longer existed. Brutus, who may be regarded as the keystone of the conspiracy, was a deluded romantic who saw himself cast in the role of his forefather but failed to see that killing Caesar was not the same thing as expelling the Tarquins nearly five centuries earlier.

Roman aqueduct, Segovia, Spain

116

From the very beginning it was clear that the murderers had failed in their aims, if their aims were anything other than the death of the Dictator. While the blood-stained body still lay warm at the foot of Pompey's statue the conspirators turned to the body of the Senate, expecting to find a wave of excitement, a cheering crowd shouting 'Liberty!' and 'Long live the Republic!' Instead they found a terrified mass of men all jostling to get away. The deed had failed: the Senators could not comprehend it. They fled from Pompey's Hall, each felt that he might be next on the list for assassination. The magnitude of the crime – the murder of the greatest Roman of all time, and moreover a man whom every Senator had promised to keep inviolate – deeply shocked them. Within a few minutes, the streets outside the hall were full of the billowing togas of frightened men as they ran for their homes and safety, crying out that Caesar was dead. Brutus, who turned with, no doubt, a neatly prepared speech on his lips, found that there was no one to address – except his fellow conspirators. This was not what he, or they, had expected. Well, then, they must make known to the citizens of Rome that the great deed was done, and that the tyrant was no more.

Holding the folds of their togas over their left arms like shields and brandishing their bloodstained daggers, they made their way across the Campus Martius calling out to all and sundry: 'The tyrant is dead! Long live the Republic!' There were some among the Senators who joined them, but these were bitterly to expiate their mistake when Antony and Octavian later took their vengeance on the conspirators, not bothering to differentiate between the actual murderers and their associates. The people, however, did not respond to these ancient cries about liberty and the Republic. Neither of the words meant anything to them. They cared about peace and prosperity, food and amusements, their private lives and pleasures – and Caesar was the man who, in their opinion, had not only increased the power of Rome, but had cut short the Civil War and begun to restore law and order to a ravaged Italy. Senators and the Senate meant nothing to the people. Who were these terrifying-looking men, waving daggers and with their robes stained with blood, crying out that they had killed Caesar? The crowd could no more understand the situation than the body of the Senate had been able to. They ran to their homes, they closed their shops and, as they ran, they shouted to one another the incomprehensible news 'Caesar is dead!'

Antony, too, on hearing of the murder, tore off his consular insignia and, disguising himself as a commoner, hurried back to his house and barricaded himself inside. He felt that as the next most powerful man in Rome he was probably next on the murder list.

The conspirators now made for the Forum, where once again they proclaimed that liberty was restored, the tyrant dead, and that Brutus like his great ancestor had

Section of the Roman road built by the Emperor Trajan from Aleppo to Antioch. The carriageway is 20 feet wide, constructed of well cut blocks of hard limestone.

freed the Roman people from oppression. The people did not respond: they were struck dumb, and numbed by the terrible news. The conspirators, together with a band of gladiators whom Decimus Brutus had hired in case of need, made their way to the Capitol and occupied it. It must have already been clear to the more astute among them that something had gone very wrong with their plans – their noble deeds and aspirations. They had lived for weeks in a dream of the nobility of tyranni-cide, and now the cold light of day was beginning to penetrate their obscured minds. They were not going to be regarded as liberators, but as cold-blooded, treacherous assassins. For the moment, however, they continued to be sustained by their delusions, which were reinforced when Cicero, among others, came to visit them on the Capitol. Cicero immediately pressed for an emergency meeting of the Senate, but his sound advice was disregarded. A Senate meeting at that moment, while the Senators were still in a state of shock, would undoubtedly have produced a great majority who, if only out of fear, would have proclaimed themselves ardent Republicans. By failing to arrange it the conspirators lost the initiative – which was very soon to pass to Antony.

Meanwhile people crept up to the Hall of Pompey and peered inside, but dared not venture to inspect more closely that fallen figure – 'imperious Caesar, dead and turned to clay'. A little later three of Caesar's slaves entered the chamber, placed his body on a litter, and bore it back to his home on the Forum, 'with one arm hanging down'. He had been unfaithful and unkind to Calpurnia, but it was to his wife, and not to his mistress, that he ultimately returned.

Some time that night it would seem that Antony left his home and secretly made his way to Calpurnia. There, for the first time, he saw the dead and mangled body of his arrogant, brilliant and awe-inspiring master. Even the extrovert Antony must have found it a sobering sight. But Antony was now the most powerful man in Rome for, with the aid of his Master of the Horse, Lepidus, he had command of a whole legion quartered in the city. His position was even further reinforced when Calpurnia turned to him as Caesar's friend and confidant, entrusting him with the dead man's will and documents, together with his private fortune and the state treasure. Against Antony's secure position as Consul, master of a legion, and holder of Caesar's money and secrets, the conspirators could muster no more than a handful of gladiators – and their mistaken belief that all Rome was republican at heart.

The conspirators could possibly have won Rome and Italy the following day, for Antony kept cautiously out of the fray. However they did no more than hold a public meeting in the Forum, where their speeches – and particularly one by .the intellectual Brutus – fell on deaf ears. Antony, with his handsome appearance and his bluff soldier's manner, was far more likely to appeal to the crowd and, whether by accident or design, the fact that he held back undoubtedly contributed to his

MVNIFICENTIA.PII.SEXTI.P.M

ultimate success. As Consul he convened the Senate for a meeting next morning – two days after Caesar's death – which was to be held in the temple of Tellus, a place deliberately chosen because it was as far away as possible from the fateful Hall of Pompey. Antony held the trump card, Caesar's will, and he opened and read it to the Senate. Perhaps he knew its contents beforehand, but it must certainly have astonished everyone else present. There was no mention of Caesarion at all; three-quarters of his estate was bequeathed to his great-nephew, Octavian, who was also named as his heir, while the other quarter was to be divided between his two nephews Lucius Pinarius and Quintus Pedius. A further clause named a number of guardians if a son should be born to Caesar after his death. It cannot have escaped note that the principal of these was Decimus Brutus Albinus – whose powers of persuasion had lured Caesar to his death – nor that the will went on to make him the main inheritor should Octavian predecease Caesar. Thus, even in death, Caesar's magnanimity served to embarrass and discomfort his assassins. The Roman crowd now heard that Caesar had bequeathed three hundred sesterces to every citizen, as well as leaving them all his large gardens on the right bank of the Tiber (in whose grounds stood the villa where Cleopatra was residing). Just as that line from the Sibylline Books had helped determine Caesar's fate, so his will largely determined that of his murderers. No ordinary Roman who heard it could fail to recall Caesar's warm and brilliant personality, his love of his soldiers and the people, and his open-handed munificence. Against this was set the meanness of his end, and the treachery of his enemies.

Antony must have known that this would be the people's mood, and that it would work for him and his ambitions. Meanwhile, he had the Senate to deal with, and he prudently let them have their head. Some of the out-and-out republicans were all for declaring the conspirators heroes of the State, and throwing Caesar's body into the Tiber. This was too much for the majority, and Cicero's suggestion that a general amnesty should be granted was adopted. The most that the republican wing could secure was the concession that the conspirators should be immune from punishment – small enough reward for men who had expected to be hailed as liberators of the Roman people! At the same time all Caesar's acts were declared valid (if they had not been, many of those present would have been deprived of their positions). It was further agreed that not only his published acts but even any others that might be found among his private papers should be accepted. Far from being thrown into the Tiber like a criminal, he was to have a public funeral. Except for the death of one man, the conspirators had accomplished nothing. By removing Caesar, however, they had left a vacuum at the head of the state. In their desire to restore the Republic, they had inadvertently precipitated that struggle for power, a Civil War, from which Caesar had only recently rescued Italy.

On 20 March, five days after his death, the body of Caesar was borne from his house on its way to the Campus Martius, where a great funeral pyre had been

Marble head of Cicero, set in a modern bust; 29½ inches high

erected. The cortège, however, had to pass through the Forum, where a rostrum had been erected for speakers to make funeral orations in praise of the dead. This was the moment for which Antony had been waiting. He knew the mood of his Roman crowd, and knew too that his simple but forceful style would appeal to the people far more than any clever oratory by Cicero or others. Antony's famous speech, so beautifully embellished by Shakespeare, rings down the ages. There is no doubt that, even if the words were not strictly accurate, the poet's genius enabled him to catch the very mood of that day. While the women wailed, and the soldiers clashed their shields together, Antony proceeded to destroy the conspirators by extolling the greatness, the talents, and the virtues of the dead. Italians, then as now, are not given to emotional reticence, and Antony had the whole crowd in the grip of hysterical grief within a few minutes. The crowning touch came when he held aloft on a spear the blood-stained robe, punctured with dagger thrusts, in which Caesar had died. There could be no holding back the crowd. Caesar's body was not to go to the Campus Martius, but was to be cremated there and then in the Forum which he had loved, and where they had loved and honoured him.

Soldiers and citizens began running to adjacent houses and public buildings, seizing tables, benches, chairs and any available woodwork to build the pyre. Some legionaries thrust brands into the assembled mound, while actors threw onto it their rich robes, weeping women cast in their jewelry, and the smoke shuddered and twisted into the March sky. An innocent bystander, Helvius Cinna, being addressed by a companion, was thought by the mob to be the Cinna who had been in the conspiracy, and was torn to pieces. Other raging bands made their way to the houses of the chief conspirators, including those of Brutus and Cassius, intending to burn them down. Order was only restored by Lepidus's legionaries.

It was clear enough what the people of Rome felt about the death of Caesar. They mourned the Father of their Country, and – although quite unconsciously – they were already looking for another father to take his place. It seemed the whole of Rome – with the exception of a small group of dissatisfied Senators – had loved the dead man, and found his loss almost unbearable. The Republican cause received its death-blow on that night, as endless crowds of people surged forward, hurling more and more goods and chattels into the pyre. As Cicero was to write to his friend Atticus a few weeks later: 'Do you remember how you said we were finished if Caesar ever had a public funeral?' He knew the answer.

Cleopatra's dilemma was a terrible one. She was no more than a visiting foreign queen, and the occupant of an insecure throne that was propped up only by the force of Roman arms. The contents of Caesar's will, futhermore, must have been a great shock. There can be little doubt that Caesar had contemplated another one had he been made King; and it is just possible that such a will had been drawn up, but was destroyed by Calpurnia, or even Antony. Calpurnia, certainly, had nothing to gain by the declaration that Caesarion was the Dictator's child, while as far as Antony was concerned Octavian may have seemed a remote and unknown figure who would probably be happy enough to inherit Caesar's treasure, and forgo politics and the harsh battle for power.

Neither of them could have been more mistaken. The little known Octavian was to prove himself the worthy inheritor not only of Caesar's fortune but also of his political ability. This was coupled with an astute knowledge of human nature and situations such as has rarely been found in any human being. Caesar, when he made Octavian his heir and adopted son, had picked the right man. In her predicament, it seems most likely that Cleopatra consulted Antony as to her best course of conduct. The latter no doubt suggested that she would be best advised to wait in Rome until they could see the trend of events. Was it now, one wonders, that

Antony first saw himself taking Caesar's place, and that Cleopatra saw in Antony Caesar's potential successor as ruler of the Roman world?

Caesar's nominated heir was at this time studying at Apollonia, a town in Illyria on the western coast of Greece, well known both as a place of commerce and a centre of learning. His father, born of obscure parents, had been diligent in pursuit of the Roman course of power at establishment levels. He had raised up the family to a point where his marriage into the Julian house – to a daughter of Julius Caesar's sister – had secured his hold upon such necessary offices as quaestor, aedile and finally, Governor of Macedonia. He seems to have been an honest and upright man, while his wife was something of a blue-stocking, taking no part in the fashionable world of Rome. Octavian, who was mostly brought up in the country, was a quiet and studious youth – the type of young Roman whom even Cato would have admired. There was no hint as yet that he was every whit as ambitious as his great-uncle. Delicate, and always constrained to be careful about his diet and his health, he had joined Caesar in the Spanish campaign that had seen the rout of the Pompeian forces, although he was ill at the time and had been shipwrecked on passage. There must have been something in this young man (he was only nineteen when Caesar was assassinated) which had alerted the Dictator's interest; some quality that others nearer to Caesar in blood did not possess. He was certainly good-looking in a fragile way, with a long neck, long nose, high forehead and large, brilliant, luminous eyes. If one compares coin-portraits of him and Caesar it is easy to see a distinct resemblance, particularly in brow, nose, eyes and chin. Until the publication of the will he had not known that Caesar had made him his heir, and it was not until ten days after the event that the news reached Apollonia that Caesar was dead and that his great-nephew had inherited three-quarters of the Dictator's fortune. For some young men this would have been enough, but Caesar had chosen rightly in picking one who had as great political aims and ambitions as he had himself. In spite of the entreaties of his mother and his friends Octavian decided to leave the quiet and safety of Apollonia for the unknown – and possibly extremely dangerous – shores of Italy. As heir to Caesar he acted exactly as if the late Dictator had already established the principle of hereditary monarchy.

In Rome in the meantime it had become perfectly clear to those who had conspired against Caesar that their position was no longer tenable. Cassius and Brutus had virtually been prisoners in their own houses since the night of Caesar's funeral, and all the conspirators felt themselves constantly threatened by assassination. The Caesarians, at whose head stood Mark Antony, were in emotional, political and military control of the city. The 'liberators' found it best to leave this troublesome and dangerous climate, taking themselves either to their estates or the provinces to which – ironically enough – Caesar had earlier appointed them. Thus, Decimus Brutus was in his province of Cisalpine Gaul by April, while Brutus and Cassius were on their country estates. Antony, so it seemed at the time, had inherited the mantle of Caesar. But the real heir, unknown to the swashbuckling soldier, had

already landed at a small port to the south of Brundisium (Brindisi), and was preparing to march on the city and claim his inheritance.

Octavian proceeded cautiously. He knew that Antony had, in the general judgment, succeeded, and that, while Antony was a well known figure and a famous soldier, he himself was only a youth known to almost nobody. But a codicil in Caesar's will, adopting him into the Julian family, gave him the right to call himself Caius Julius Caesar Octavianus. He was inspired not only by the memory of his great relative, but also it seemed as if the very name which he now bore conferred upon him a tenacity of purpose that was to rival Caesar's. Historians have subsequently, for convenience, called him Octavian; but he was never known as such in his own lifetime. To his contemporaries he was always C. Julius Caesar or, more simply, Caesar. From the moment of his adoption by the dead man, Octavian determined to live up to his new name and rank. He soon discovered, as he travelled through the south of Italy, that the soldiers and the veterans settled on their plots of land had no doubt as to his being Caesar's rightful heir. Soldiers, freedmen, slaves and friends of the murdered man flocked to Octavian to declare their loyalty. With the acquisition of Caesar's name he had acquired also, by that intricate web of Roman patron–client relationship, thousands of those who had been Caesar's men. He did not hasten. 'Festina lente', 'Hasten slowly', might have been Octavian's motto (and it is significant that Suetonius attributes the remark to him). He made his way from southern Italy to Puteoli (Pozzuoli) where, apart from seeing his relatives, he wished to discuss matters with Cicero. If Rome seemed safe, he must go there next, have his adoption officially ratified, claim his inheritance and carry out the bequests laid upon him in the will.

It was at some time during this period that Cleopatra, probably acting on Antony's advice, decided to leave Italy and return to her kingdom. She could read the signs on the wind, and there was clearly a danger of civil war between the pro-Caesar faction and his murderers. Now she learned that Caesar's adopted heir was coming to Rome to claim his inheritance. What his attitude would be towards Caesarion, who was really Caesar's flesh and blood, she could not know, but in all respects it seemed politic to absent herself from the centre of the Roman stage. The first phase of her life had ended with Caesar's death. It seemed, perhaps, that the best she could ever hope for now was to retain her throne, and ensure that Caesarion followed her in due course. Besides, once safely back on the sidelines of Egypt she could watch and await developments in the cockpit of the Mediterranean. She had backed the winner once – to be foiled only by a senseless murder. If it came to civil war again, she must be quite sure that the power, the wealth and the legions of Egypt were not misused but diverted to the side of the ultimate victor.

Sandstone relief of the goddess Hathor suckling the infant god from the mammisi *at Denderah, built in the time of Augustus and decorated subsequently*

ANTONY

The man who held the commanding position in Italy was a strange mixture of virtues and vices. He was tall and well built, with a thick neck, a handsome strong face and abundant curly hair. He was muscled like a gladiator, and, indeed, his whole appearance gave some credit to his own claim to be descended from the god Hercules. (He was later during his association with Cleopatra to identify himself with Dionysus, which was appropriate enough, since Antony was a very heavy drinker.) In his youth, like Caesar, it seems that he went through a marked homosexual phase. His relationship with the younger Curio, the son of the wealthy Caius Scribonius Curio, was notorious. It resulted in the father forbidding Antony to enter his house, saying that he was debauching his son. Antony's interest in Curio was not only sexual but monetary, for the youth had offered to stand surety for Antony's debts to the tune of six million sesterces. When the date for repayment arrived, Curio found that he could not raise the sum, so he went to Cicero and begged him to prevail on his father to give him the money. If Antony, he said, was forced to flee from Italy he would certainly go too, since he could not live without him. The money was produced on Cicero's advice, but conditional on this was that the relationship between the two young men should stop. Curio later married Fulvia, the former wife of Publius Clodius (who has been described as 'one of the most profligate characters of a profligate age'), and Fulvia was subsequently to become the second wife of Antony.

Antony's good looks and magnificent physique made him irresistible to women – an advantage of which he made abundant use. Cicero, who hated him, described him as a 'kind of butcher or prize-fighter', and certainly two men can hardly ever have had less in common. Antony's rise to power was almost entirely due to his association with Caesar, for he had been with him in Gaul, and had played an important part in Caesar's struggle against Pompey in Greece. He later distinguished himself at Pharsalia, and he was generally regarded as the finest Roman general after Caesar himself. At the same time, he had none of his master's intellectual distinction and though Caesar was a rake, Antony was notorious as a drinker and womanizer. At one time in his career he had travelled throughout Italy in company

Marble statue, over 10 feet high, of Hercules, a Roman copy of an original attributed to the Greek sculptor Lysippus, a contemporary of Alexander the Great

with his mistress, the actress Cytheris, accompanied by a train of musicians, whores, actors, actresses and brothel-keepers. Renan wrote of him that he was 'a colossal child, capable of conquering the world, but incapable of resisting a pleasure'. It was inevitable that, with the extravagance of his life, Antony should have been constantly in debt. A classic instance of this occurred when Pompey's splendid town house had been put up for sale after the latter's death. Antony had acquired it, feeling sure that Caesar would never ask his most faithful supporter for the money. He had little reckoned on Caesar, who at once demanded payment. During the period of Antony's tenancy many of the works of art, silver plate and paintings had already been wrecked (or given away) in innumerable orgies. Antony's slaves even slept in the purple coverlets that had belonged to Pompey, and the whole value of the property had vastly depreciated. To Antony's fury he was very nearly forced to sell at a loss. It was only Caesar's departure for his Spanish campaign that caused him to be reconciled with his first-lieutenant, and to allow him to continue living in the house.

But, now that he was first man in Rome, Antony, together with Fulvia, who was as unprincipled and unscrupulous as any woman of her day, proceeded to recoup their private fortunes by pillaging the state. Along with Caesar's private fortune, as well as the state treasury (which Calpurnia had trustingly but foolishly placed under his control), Antony had inherited, as it were, Caesar's amanuensis, a certain Faberius. With the aid of Faberius he now proceeded to falsify documents that had come into his hands, as well as to forge others that were purported to have been found among the Dictator's papers. It soon became common knowledge that anything in the Empire was for sale at Antony's house – estates, offices, towns, titles, dues and privileges. Cicero wrote that, through the invocation of the dead Dictator, 'everything was now possible'. The new senators whom Antony appointed on 'instructions from Caesar', were dubbed Charonides – men put in power on the instance of Charon, the ferryman of the underworld. Provinces, even, were for sale, the governors who purchased them knowing full well that by increasing taxes they could soon pay back their investment and make themselves fortunes. In the scale and enormity of Antony's corrupt mishandling of the Roman world there is, as always in his actions, a certain vast prodigality – like a boy let loose in a sweet shop – that can hardly fail to raise a smile. Many other Romans in positions of power had been grossly corrupt, but they had at least made hypocritical gestures, or tried to hide their misconduct. Antony, with that extraordinary openness of temperament which was one of the reasons so many of the common people and soldiers loved him, did not even bother to disguise what was going on. Caesar, whatever he may have been putting aside for himself, had been trying to get the affairs of Italy and the Empire back on a sound and even keel. Cicero and his friends,

Augustus as Pontifex Maximus

the conspirators, and others of the Republican persuasion, must have realized with horror that they had, as it were, only exchanged King Log for King Stork. There can be little wonder that, when Octavian at last appeared in Rome, Antony's attitude towards him was patronizing and arrogant in the extreme. There was also no doubt a certain anxiety on Antony's part. He had been misspending both Caesar's and the State's, resources. Now that the heir was come to claim his inheritance there would have to be a certain reckoning with accountancy problems.

It was in April 44 B.C. that Octavian arrived in the capital. He had already gleaned from Cicero, as well as other sources, the way in which things were being conducted, or misconducted, but he had no intention of provoking any immediate or open breach with the powerful and popular consul. He acted studiously and quietly on the Asquithian basis of 'Wait and See', a form of tactic ideally designed to irritate Antony, and to provoke him to unthought immediacy of action. 'Wait and See' was the kind of counsel that Mark Antony could never have understood. Octavian was also favoured by the fact that, on the very day he entered Rome, there was a halo round the sun – not so unusual in that latitude when a depression is on the way, but esteemed in those superstitious days as a mark of some signal or divine favour. It was natural enough that the crowds, eager to receive their promised presents from Caesar, should hail the young man; but many former Caesarians also made a point of calling upon him to pay their respects and tender their loyalty. Not only had Antony's conduct affronted some of them, but they desired to acknowledge that this was the undoubted heir – and that Antony had been no more than a temporary guardian of Caesarism.

From the beginning relations between the two men seem to have been strained. Antony treated Octavian as if he was only a presumptuous young puppy, suggesting that it was absurd for him to claim Caesar's inheritance, let alone the mantle of the great dead. Octavian was polite, but insisted on making his public claim to be Caesar's heir, and his acceptance of adoption into the Julian clan. He promised also to pay the citizens the money that Caesar had bequeathed them – even if it was at his own expense. There is no surer way to the public's heart than the promise of money, and when Octavian capped this with an assurance that he would pay for the public games to be held in Caesar's honour that summer he had already cut a great deal of ground from under Antony's feet. It is noteworthy also that he omitted to mention in his speech that the amnesty for Caesar's murderers – which Cicero had proposed and Antony had tacitly accepted – still held. Octavian was determined to give himself latitude for manoeuvre. Whether it was desire for vengeance, or merely a determination that the murderers of one dictator should not be left free to plot against his successor, he seemed to ignore the conspirators, as if they had never existed. Cicero began to sense uneasily that not only had the Republicans lost when Antony had taken charge of the scene, but that this newcomer might be an even greater danger.

Antony continued to show the foolish and impetuous side of his nature. Instead

LEFT: *gold coin of Mark Antony, from Asia Minor, 41 B.C.;* RIGHT: *Octavian;* BELOW: *Lepidus.*

of coming to terms with Caesar's heir – standing at his right hand as soldier, guide and mentor – he seems to have gone out of his way to provoke Octavian. He slandered him, saying he had been made Caesar's heir only because he had been the latter's partner in sodomy. Before long relations between them were so strained that there was open talk in Rome of another civil war breaking out. A patched-up reconciliation, however, was arranged and for a few months, on the surface at least, it appeared that some working arrangement might be reached between the nominated heir and the *de facto* ruler of Rome.

Octavian does not always seem to have behaved with the studied tact which determined most of his actions (one must remember that he was not yet twenty), and on two occasions tried to occupy Caesar's golden chair as if he were indeed the hereditary, reigning Emperor. The first time, forbidden to do so by a tribune of the people, he was applauded by the spectators for stepping down. But on the second occasion, during the funeral games for Caesar, although forbidden by Antony from occupying the Dictator's throne, he was applauded in his attempt by the bulk of the crowd. Give them games, give them bread, spare them war and improve their lives, that was all they asked – like most people. It was on the last day of the celebration of the Games that a portent appeared which, like the halo round the sun that had ushered him into Rome, seemed to show that the gods were on the side of Octavian. A comet, immediately designated the Julian Star, appeared in the sky. It was taken to be not only a sign that Julius Caesar had joined his ancestress, Venus, among the immortal gods but also an indication of his blessing conferred upon his adopted son. Antony could only gaze bleakly into his wine cup, realizing that the tide was swinging against him, and that the wind of popular favour was setting firmly in Octavian's sails.

Antony had formerly been appointed to the province of Macedonia, and to the command of the legions stationed there. But this was too far away from the main theatre of Italy, so he assigned it to Decimus Brutus, acquiring for himself the nearby province of Cisalpine Gaul. But he retained command of the Macedonian legions. This was good strategy, for if Octavian tried to acquire power in Italy Antony would be able to menace him from the north and the east. After much manoeuvring and near civil war the two rivals officially effected a reconciliation in the autumn of 43 B.C. But their mutual mistrust is said to have been such that they searched one another for hidden weapons before sitting down to talk. It was finally agreed that a Triumvirate should be formed, consisting of Antony, Octavian and Lepidus, the Master of the Horse. It was felt that Lepidus, an old friend of Caesar's, would act as buffer between the conflicting ambitions of the other two and prevent them coming into open collision. The three men were to govern Italy jointly, but the important provinces were divided between them in such a ratio that Antony and Lepidus received the greater portion, Octavian being assigned only Africa, Numidia and the Mediterranean islands. By assigning Sicily and Sardinia to Octavian the other two Triumvirs had saddled him with a very difficult task, since the younger son of Pompey the Great, Sextus Pompeius (who had escaped during Caesar's campaign in Spain) still had an immense fleet, and was virtually master of the Mediterranean Sea.

One of the first actions of the Triumvirate was to take vengeance on Caesar's murderers. It now became clear why Octavian had omitted any reference to the amnesty in his earlier speech. As the dead man's adopted son, and the bearer of his name, he could hardly have been expected – especially in the climate of those times – to exercise mercy and forgiveness. Similarly Antony and Lepidus had both been Caesar's men, and were eager to avenge his death. The only person who must have been troubled by the reconciliation of Antony and Octavian was Cleopatra. True, she could not but rejoice that the Triumvirate had decided to act against Caesar's murderers but Octavian had dispossessed her son Caesarion and inherited the mantle which she had felt was really his. All Cleopatra's actions were now designed to see that she held the throne secure in trust for Caesarion. He might, she may well have felt, still inherit the world – if only Octavian were to lose his life in the war that was about to break out against the conspirators.

In order to finance their campaigns against Cassius and Brutus, who were raising

Round temple, commonly called the temple of Vesta, Rome, restored and embellished by Augustus

a large army in Greece, the Triumvirs now set about an orgy of murder and proscription that was among the most sordid and bloodstained in the history of that bloody century. One hundred senators and some two thousand other rich and prominent men were named as conspirators and supporters of the crime. Fathers betrayed sons, sons fathers, and everywhere throughout Italy slaves and spies were at their infamous tasks of seeking out the condemned men and handing them over – for suitable rewards. Cicero was among the many who were condemned and killed, principally because he had infuriated Antony by his series of speeches, the 'Philippics', in which he had condemned the consul for his behaviour and his scandalous mishandling of Roman affairs.

He was also betrayed to the Triumvirs by Popilius Laenas. It is difficult to understand why Octavian, who had been helped and befriended by Cicero, allowed him to be put on the list. Probably it was done as a sop to Antony, but possibly also because Cicero's republican ideals had no appeal for one who already had his eye on the Dictatorship. Cicero was a spent force, and of no further political use. Octavian was a cool and calculating young man, who had no purpose for sentiment. The old philosopher, orator and perhaps the greatest writer of Latin in history met his death with the courage that he had shown earlier in his life during the Catiline conspiracy. Stretching his head out of the litter in which he was being borne to safety and escape by ship from Italy, he bared his neck. The centurion who had been sent to capture him struck, and cut off his head – and then the hand with which he had written the Philippics against Antony. All the heads of those who had been proscribed had to be taken to the Triumvirs for identification, and it is said that Antony's wife, the odious Fulvia, even stuck a pin through Cicero's tongue because it had spoken against her husband. Rome in those days was great only because of its power: in other respects it was vile.

With loot that they had gathered during this period of massacre the Triumvirs proceeded to raise legions to destroy the rest of the major conspirators. Only Dolabella, one of the most villainous among the men who had plotted Caesar's murder, managed to become reconciled with Antony, thus escaping the general pogrom. He did not escape death, however, for he was defeated by Cassius near Laodicea in Syria, and committed suicide. Cleopatra, although he was one of Caesar's murderers, had decided to support him against Cassius whom she detested but, fortunately for her, the four Egyptian legions did not reach him in time. She was able to call them back, to protect her frontiers should Cassius strike down through Syria.

The threat to her throne, her country and herself (for any of the Republicans would willingly have killed the woman who had aspired to become Empress of Rome), was not eliminated until 1 October 42 B.C. Then, in two battles near the

Heroines of Greek mythology playing 'five-stones'. Monochrome painting on marble from Herculaneum, 1st century A.D., based on late 5th-century B.C. Greek original

town of Philippi in eastern Macedonia, the last of the Republican forces, headed by the two principal conspirators, Brutus and Cassius, were cut to pieces. Cassius was killed in the first battle, while the remaining troops under Brutus were completely routed in the second. Brutus, who had survived, was advised by one of his companions to make his escape. But in that bitter moment he knew that all was over: that the Republican cause was dead, and that the Caesarians had triumphed. 'Fly?' he replied, 'Yes, we must fly, but not with our feet – with our hands.' He then fell upon his sword and killed himself. This was the end of the man whom Shakespeare was later to describe as 'the noblest Roman of them all'. It is difficult to agree with the poet. Brutus was by any standards a traitor, even if he did not think so himself because of his belief that Caesar was betraying Rome. He murdered a man he had sworn to protect, a man who had always loved him, who had spared his life at Pharsalia, and who was very probably his father. One cannot help wondering whether Brutus's dagger-stroke was inspired, not by idealism at all, but by the knowledge that he was Caesar's bastard, and a desire to wipe out the stain on his mother.

The news of the victory at Philippi undoubtedly delighted Cleopatra. The hero of the hour was Antony (Octavian had been too ill to take much part in the battle), and Cleopatra had the advantage of knowing Antony well. Octavian she did not know, and disliked and mistrusted for obvious reasons. It was probably during this time that she came to the conclusion that Antony was destined to take Caesar's place as sole master of the Roman world.

Silver drinking cup from Pompeii

138

NEW DIONYSUS

The immediate task of the Triumvirate, after their victory at Philippi, was the reorganization of the Empire. In plain fact, it was now really a Duumvirate, for Lepidus was completely eclipsed by Antony and Octavian. He was also suspected of being in collusion with Sextus Pompeius, whose fleets still ranged the Mediterranean and threatened Rome's supply routes. Lepidus, accordingly, was assigned the province of Africa where he could do little or no harm. Italy itself was nominally to be ruled between the three, although the homeland remained in effect in the hands of Octavian. The latter also received the province of Spain, as well as Cisalpine Gaul, which was now regarded as part and parcel of Italy.

It was to Antony that the richest plums fell, as was natural since it was he who was the real victor of Philippi. In the redistribution Antony received six provinces – Macedonia, Greece, Bythinia, Asia, Syria and Cyrene. Egypt was to be regarded as still an independent kingdom. He was also to be master of all Gaul, which would provide him with some twenty-four legions. These were commanded by generals who were faithful to him, so he could more or less disregard this part of his legacy and concentrate on the East. From his previous campaigns Antony already knew this theatre well, and it was rightly considered the richest part of the Roman Empire. The wealth of the whole area was held to be almost inexhaustible, which it certainly was when compared with war-scarred and impoverished Italy. Besides all this Antony was bent on completing Julius Caesar's grand design of moulding the East into one giant unit (possibly assimilating Egypt in the process), and then taking his legions against the Parthians. Once they were crushed there could be no limit to his ambitions. India beckoned, as it had beckoned both Caesar and Alexander.

Accompanied by a large army he proceeded on a triumphal tour through Greece, which magnified a vanity that was never of modest proportions. Everywhere he was hailed as the new Caesar, the Conqueror, Hercules, the God of War, and of course Dionysus Redivivus, the New God of Wine. To his simple and boisterous temperament these flattering epithets seemed no more than his due, and he enjoyed the whole atmosphere of wine, women and adulation which swam in his triumphal wake like phosphorescence in the blue Aegean. He was now forty-two, just twice as old as Octavian. But during these years in which the latter was quietly putting his house in order, suppressing various minor revolts in Italy (including one in which Antony's wife Fulvia played a leading role), Antony was to embark on his grandiose concepts in the East. The latter, like a *fata morgana*,

was to lure him over the next decade deeper and deeper into those desert sands where all ambition finally perishes.

After leaving Greece he embarked for Asia Minor, where once again he was everywhere hailed as the all-conquering god – and feared equally, for it could be no secret that he had come to look at his estates and see how much could be wrung from them. For a time he stayed at the rich and famous city of Ephesus, which he entered as the New Dionysus preceded by women dressed as Bacchantes, and men and boys in the roles of satyrs and fauns. Living in ostentatious grandeur like an oriental despot, he set about the oppressive taxation that caused one of his tax-gatherers to say that, if he intended to raise two taxes a year, he must also see to it that each year contained two summers and two autumns. Antony did not care. Unlike Caesar he could not look ahead and, while enriching himself, make sure that he left stable foundations. He lived for the moment, surrounded by his extra-ordinary court of fiddlers and dancers, actors and actresses, mountebanks, whores and tumblers – anybody and anything that could satisfy his senses, or make him laugh.

From Ephesus, in the late summer of 41 B.C., he proceeded to the ancient city of Tarsus, the capital of Cilicia, which stood on the river Cydnus about twelve miles above its mouth. Pompey the Great had made it the capital of the new province. It was therefore the administrative centre – which, from Antony's point of view, meant tax-gathering. Since Egypt was protected by Roman legions which came under his command, and since its Queen was personally known to him, it was natural enough that he should want to see Cleopatra as soon as possible. He had almost certainly learnt when talking with her in Rome that this was no ordinary woman, no spoiled and stupid eastern potentate, but a politician of a calibre that even Caesar had valued. Among the rulers of Asia Minor and the East there was no one who could compare with her, and Antony may well have felt

---

BELOW: *relief from a marble sacrophagus depicting the procession of Dionysus, 2nd half of 2nd century* A.D.
OPPOSITE: *bas-relief of a Maenad, in the time of Augustus*

Actors playing a tragedy. Wall-painting from Herculaneum, 1st century A.D.; 15¾ inches high

that she could give him a better picture of the whole area than anyone else. Quite apart from this there were other material considerations: her country was immensely rich and her capital was second only to Rome in importance. Indeed, as Antony must have remembered from his brief visit all those years ago, it was superior to Rome in its palaces, public buildings and administrative capabilities. Even as early as this he may have envisaged a close alliance – if no more – with its Queen, so that he could use Alexandria as the centre of his eastern empire. Accordingly he despatched a message to Alexandria, asking Cleopatra to meet him at Tarsus.

Cleopatra was conscious enough of the use that she and her country could be to Antony, and she was conscious, too, that she was a queen, and 'the descendant of many kings'. In the eyes of her subjects she was Isis incarnate, whereas this Roman, however powerful, was only a commoner, even if it was true that he claimed descent from Hercules. She knew all about Antony, both from report and from her own personal observation. She knew his tastes, his love of voluptuousness and excess, and his vigorous sexual appetite. She was not going to hasten to meet him like a vassal: she would come in her own good time. Meanwhile all the sophistication of her court and the Mouseion should be dedicated to seeing that, when she arrived, her vessels, her entourage and her appearance should be such that this unsophisticated Roman would at once realize the immense superiority of the Hellenistic world.

The Queen's arrival at Tarsus created such an impression that over two thousand years later it still lingers in human memory. This is largely because Shakespeare, transcribing North's translation of Plutarch's Life of Antony almost word for word, immortalized the occasion:

> The barge she sat in, like a burnish'd throne,
> Burn'd on the water: the poop was beaten gold;
> Purple the sails, and so perfumed that
> The winds were love-sick with them; the oars were silver,
> Which to the tune of flutes kept stroke, and made
> The water which they beat to follow faster,
> As amorous of their strokes. For her own person,
> It beggar'd all description: she did lie
> In her pavilion – cloth-of-gold of tissue –
> O'er-picturing that Venus where we see
> The fancy outwork nature: on each side her
> Stood pretty dimpled boys, like smiling Cupids,
> With divers-colour'd fans, whose wind did seem
> To glow the delicate cheeks which they did cool,
> And what they undid did.

The royal barge, followed by its attendant escorts and supply ships, sailed up the river Cydnus until it reached the lake on which the city stood. Antony, who must have been kept constantly posted as to the Queen's progress, had seated himself at the public tribunal in the market place, thinking no doubt that she and her courtiers would come ashore and present themselves to him. He was mistaken. Cleopatra had no intention of behaving as if she were any ordinary mortal. She had heard of Antony's adoption of the title the New Dionysus (one which she was well aware had been borne by her father), and she was now presenting herself to the people of Asia Minor not in her role of Isis, but as Venus Anadyomene, Venus risen from the waves. The streets, the market place, indeed the whole city itself, became

143

deserted as the people flocked down to the water's edge to gaze at this fantastic vessel, from which the scent of incense drifted across the water; and where the Queen of Egypt reclined under a golden canopy in the guise of Venus, surrounded by her Cupids, while her serving women, dressed as Graces and Nereids, struck picturesque attitudes about the ship. It was a masterpiece of theatre and the crowd were enchanted. Soon the saying was going round (possibly arising from a claque implanted by Cleopatra) that 'Aphrodite had come to revel with Dionysus for the good of Asia'. Certainly to the common people, the sight of this extraordinary ship and the display of this prodigious wealth must have suggested that this was no mortal woman, but a goddess incarnate. Antony, his guards, and a few other Romans, were left in the market place alone.

Cleopatra had, as it were, won the first round. She now proceeded to win the second. When Antony sent a message to invite her to dinner, she declined it, but politely invited him back. His natural curiosity, inflamed no doubt by reports of the almost miraculous luxury of the state barge, prompted him to accept. The golden spider's web which Cleopatra's artists and artisans had woven out of the sciences and skills of Alexandria would have entrapped any man – except a Stoic philosopher like Diogenes. Antony had a taste for luxury; but his concept of sensual pleasures was similar to that of a simple soldier or sailor – lots of food, quantities of wine, and an ample supply of available young women. He was now to discover the 'infinite variety' of civilized and sophisticated entertainment that had been evolved in the Hellenistic-Egyptian world during three centuries of Greek rule.

The royal barge moved across and moored to the quay on the city side of the lake, and Antony, followed by his staff officers and the chief dignitaries of Tarsus, stepped aboard. From the very first it would seem that he was fascinated by Cleopatra. She was now twenty-nine years old, and at the height of her physical and intellectual powers. The voice and manners, the sparkling conversation, the erudition and wit that had fascinated Caesar, overwhelmed his simpler lieutenant. Antony had known innumerable women over the years, but he had never known one like this. He had admired her qualities during his visits to Caesar's villa while she was in Rome, but now, as he must have realized, all these powers of seduction, all this graceful luxury and sophisticated entertainment were designed solely for him. He was being offered the place at her side that had formerly been occupied by his master. For it was he, Antony, who was the master of the world, the new Caesar – not that sickly youth, Octavian.

After the first formal meeting and reception, the presentation of his officers and the town officials, the company moved below to the banqueting hall. Antony was

---

An intimate party, in a wall-painting from Herculaneum, 1st century A.D.
OVERLEAF: *mosaic of an idealized landscape of the Upper Nile, found at Praeneste, Italy, 1st century* A.D.

familiar enough with ships, but he had never seen what the Alexandrians could do when they built a state barge for their Queen. This was no ship, but another floating palace. The walls were hung with purple tapestries, embroidered with spun gold, while the whole room was brilliant with light, reflected from innumerable mirrors. The air was delicately scented with incense, the composition of which was an art for which the Egyptians were world-famous. Twelve embroidered dining couches were ready to receive the guests, and in front of each was set a table with goblets of gold and golden dishes inlayed with precious stones. On Antony's expressing amazement at such a banquet, Cleopatra expressed her regret that there had not been time to do more, but that if he would return the following night she would see that things were better ordered. On the conclusion of the meal the Queen made him a present of everything used in the banquet – couches, vessels of gold, goblets and embroideries. The company now moved out onto the upper deck, where during their withdrawal below servants had been hanging illuminated lanterns from branches which had been suspended above their heads. It was as if they stood in an enchanted forest. The thousands of watchers on the shore felt as if they had a vision of how the gods lived on Olympus. Again the murmur went round that Venus was feasting Dionysus for the good of Asia.

On the following night Cleopatra was true to her word, and the entertainment was such that the first banquet seemed almost contemptible. As each guest departed, he was made a present of the banqueting couch and the plates and goblets that he had used, while the principal guests, as well as receiving the same, were given litters to transport them back to their homes, together with Ethiopian boys to run before them carrying flambeaux. Other guests received fine Arab horses with golden accoutrements. Antony had known the rich and prodigal life of Rome and many other cities, but he had never before known the refinements of luxury as practised by the Ptolemies. The man who had once come drunk to the Senate and vomited while making a speech began to see that the senses could be more delicately titillated than he had hitherto realized. Cleopatra was a master in the art of hospitality, and in a style of theatrical presentation unknown in Rome. She was bent on turning him from gourmand to gourmet.

Antony did his best to repay the Queen's hospitality, and on the following day invited her to a banquet ashore for which he had exhausted the resources of Tarsus. It could not help but be a provincial affair compared with the Egyptian Queen's entertainments, and Plutarch describes it as marked by a certain 'rustic awkwardness'. Antony, however, was not the man to pretend to graces that he did not possess, nor to hide his shortcomings under a pompous exterior. He had a sense of humour, and turned his failure as a host into a joke. Already, so early in their relationship – quite

Bronze head of Augustus, 18½ inches high, with inlaid eyes; from a statue probably erected at the southern frontier of Roman Egypt. Found at Meroe, Republic of Sudan

149

apart from what she had known about him before – Cleopatra perceived that this Roman, if she was to become his mistress or wife, would have to be treated in a very different style from Caesar. The latter, while a sensual man, had the studied quiet of an intellectual, and the *savoir faire* and conversation of a man of the world. Antony, by comparison, was a gigantic adolescent. So, to quote Plutarch's Life of Antony: 'Noticing that his conversation and style was rough and course, savouring more of the soldier than the courtier, she dealt with him in the same way, and quickly fell into his manner without any reservation or difficulty.' The consummate politician early realized that 'when in Rome [she must] do as Rome does'.

Antony, who had summoned her to Tarsus partly on the complaint that she had not sufficiently helped the Caesarian cause, now found that the tables were turned. Cleopatra explained, no doubt, how at one moment she had put out with her fleet from Alexandria to join the fleet of the Triumvirs in the action against Brutus and Cassius, but had been compelled to put back again by a sudden storm. (She was the first woman in history since the famous Queen Artemisia of Halicarnassus – who had accompanied Xerxes in his invasion of Greece – to take a fleet to sea.) She told him, too, how she had tried to get her legions to Dolabella before he had failed in his action against Crassus in Syria. Antony was convinced – not only by her record, her life with Caesar, her being the mother of Caesar's son, but by her whole manner and bearing. He saw then that only with this woman at his side and with the wealth of Egypt at his command could he be certain of eliminating Octavian in the struggle for the world.

BELOW: *silver-gilt drinking cup decorated with scenes from the vineyard; Greco-Roman period.*
OPPOSITE: *Roman copy of Hellenistic bronze figure of Aphrodite at her bath; 31 inches high*

AN ALEXANDRIAN WINTER

Cleopatra proceeded yet further to bedazzle Antony with the style of her life and entertainment. At another banquet she had the whole floor of the saloon covered with roses to the depth of several feet, the roses being held in place by nets attached to the side walls, so that the guests found themselves walking upon a solid, scented carpet of flowers. Then there was the famous episode of the pearl. Antony was a gambler – something it will have taken the Queen very little time to find out – so she wagered him that she would spend a sum of about a hundred thousand pounds upon one meal. Disbelieving that, even with her amazing extravagance, she could spend so much money, Antony accepted the bet. The banquet was indeed luxurious, but no more so than on other occasions and after it was over Antony's intermediary, a certain Plancus, costed it up and said that she was still short of the agreed sum. Cleopatra smiled and maintained that she would now spend more than the deficit upon herself alone. A table was brought in, upon which was set a solitary cup. Antony did not know there was a little vinegar in the cup. The Queen, who was wearing two huge pearls in her ears, removed one of them, and held it up for inspection. It was appraised as being worth far more than the missing sum. She threw the pearl into the cup, where it disintegrated, and drank it. She was even prepared to add the other, when Plancus protested and declared she had more than won the wager. This gesture has usually been described as if it was no more than an extravagant folly, but few of Cleopatra's actions were thoughtless, and this one too had a political point behind it. She was illustrating, in the simplest manner, the immeasurable wealth of her country, where choice pearls from the Red Sea (which would be priceless in Rome) were no more than expendable baubles.

If Cleopatra had amused and entertained Caesar, she completely overwhelmed Antony. When at some time during this Tarsus period they became lovers it seemed as if the whole world smiled upon him. He was master of the East, master of Egypt through its Queen, and would soon be master of the Roman Empire.

How much Antony really loved Cleopatra, or she him, is something that it will always be impossible to tell. Both had so much to gain politically by an alliance – and an alliance that was cemented by a sexual union was likely to be that much more durable. It was the common practice for powerful families, as well as countries, to bind themselves together by marital ties. Antony must have been aware – like Caesar before him – that by making Cleopatra his mistress he was in effect saying to her, 'In due course, I will make you my wife'. As has been suggested, it is likely that the young Cleopatra was seduced by Caesar rather than the reverse, although even then it is very doubtful if her head did not rule her heart. In the case of Antony, it is clear from their first meeting that she set out to seduce this impressionable Roman. What her real feelings towards him were cannot be known, any more than his towards her, but nearly all women love men of power – and Antony was not only that, he was also very good-looking in a florid way. He, for his part, must have known many more physically attractive women, but his vanity was tickled by being the Queen's lover, and while his sexual experience was infinitely greater than hers, it is doubtful whether any Ptolemy was unversed in the sophisticated erotic techniques of the East. While Antony was healthy, virile and (one suspects) a bit boorish in his approach to women, Cleopatra will have known how to arouse and maintain his physical passion for her. Love, as envisaged in later societies, most probably entered their relationship very little. A few years afterwards, when she had born him children, and when their destinies had become indissolubly linked, it is almost certain that – on Antony's part at least – love did indeed bind him to Cleopatra. The ancients often used to pray to be spared from love, although revelling in sexuality as such. It was a combination of love and a constitution weakened from his excessive cultivation of the wine-god that were ultimately to destroy Antony.

Cleopatra exploited her superiority from the very beginning of their relationship. Within only a few weeks she achieved a victory such as she had never won over Caesar. When Caesar had held his Alexandrian Triumph in Rome Cleopatra's sister Arsinoë, who had conspired against her, had been forced to walk in chains through the streets of Rome along with the other captives. Caesar had then spared her from either execution or any further humiliation, and she had been permitted to retire to Asia Minor where she had subsequently been living in the sanctuary of the great temple at Ephesus. Here, much to Cleopatra's fury, she was treated with honour and respect, the High Priest going so far as to address her as 'Queen'. Whether Arsinoë was conspiring against Cleopatra or not, the latter was taking no chances. Arsinoë was the sole other survivor from the Flute-Player's five children, and Cleopatra was determined to have her out of the way. She prevailed upon Antony – as she had not been able to with Caesar – and Arsinoë was executed. Cleopatra even went so far as to try and have the High Priest killed for having hailed her sister as Queen, but was persuaded by cooler counsellors to abandon the idea.

There was now the matter of Cyprus to be attended to. This had originally been given by Caesar to Arsinoë and her brother Ptolemy XIV, but the gift had probably never been ratified. The island was at the moment governed by an Egyptian viceroy, Serapion, who had favoured the cause of the conspirators and had loaned his fleet to Cassius. He had backed the losing side and he too was executed. Antony made Cleopatra a present of Cyprus, so that she was now the sole ruler of the old Ptolemaic empire of both Cyprus and Egypt. Only one minor threat to her position remained. After Ptolemy XIII had been drowned, Caesar had carefully had the body identified to prove to the citizens that he was dead and to prevent any pretender arising and causing trouble. Nevertheless this was exactly what had happened, and a young man was now claiming to be the dead King. It is indeed quite possible that he and Arsinoë, and even the High Priest, had been in correspondence in a plot to obtain the throne of Egypt during Cleopatra's absence. This pretender, who at the time was living in Phoenicia, was also despatched on Antony's orders (but at Cleopatra's instigation). Antony was certainly proving more pliant in the Queen's hands than his predecessor had been, and Cleopatra must have felt confidently secure in her kingdom and her future when she finally left Tarsus for Alexandria. Ever since Caesar's death both she and her son had been menaced and threatened. But by her wit, charm, extravagance and sex she had now reversed the tide of fortune. Once again it must have seemed possible that she would reign at the side of a Roman husband as mistress of the Mediterranean, and Queen of the whole Roman Empire.

The affairs of the East, which he had been sent to administer, urgently called for Antony's attention. The Parthian threat to the Roman provinces loomed ever larger. Roman renegades, former companions of Cassius and Brutus, had thrown in their lot with the Parthian King and were assisting him in a massive reorganization of his army. In Syria, Antony had to install a new governor, one of Caesar's best generals, while there was trouble in Judaea where Antony had made Herod and his brother co-rulers, contrary to the wishes of the Jews, who preferred the claim of Antigonus who came from the family of the Maccabees. There was plenty for him to attend to, but statesmanship was a quality that always eluded him. He seems to have done little more than some hasty reorganization, coupled as always with some heavy tax-gathering, before sailing in the autumn of 41 B.C. to join Cleopatra in Alexandria. There was, indeed, one good reason why a visit to Egypt might be considered fruitful: it might serve as a useful base from which to organize the legions for the campaign against Parthia. The Egyptian fleet would also be an asset. These were matters that could be attended to in weeks, or at the most a month or so, but Antony was to spend the whole winter in Alexandria, engaged not in state-craft or military preparations, but in a riot of banquets and entertainments, drunken orgies, gambling and every kind of excess. It would not be too much to say that it was this Alexandrian winter which destroyed Antony, not only sapping his health, but weakening his moral fibre – never, except on the battlefield, his strongest point.

Plutarch got most of his information for his Life of Antony from his grand-father, who had known a Greek doctor who had been in the city during that winter. No doubt the stories, though improved with time, had their basis in reality. From the very first, it would seem that Antony fell in love with that strange city. What-ever his real feelings about Cleopatra (and there seems no doubt that these were immeasurably strengthened during this period), his love affair with 'The City' was real enough. He remembered it from his youth but now, in his forties, he was experiencing a second youth, coupled with the heady knowledge that he was no longer just a young cavalry officer but the most powerful man in the world. Cleo-patra, by her intelligent assessment of his character and his weaknesses, bound him

Ivory plaques of the Ptolemaic period showing a young woman offering a bowl of wine to a naked youth with a goat's tail, and the god Pan as half goat, half man

to her with ropes of silk, that were yet as strong as steel. She needed him for her own designs, but he was to end needing her for almost everything except his sword-arm. Antony had been well trained in acquiescence to an intelligent female by his second wife, Fulvia, who had the strong character and a political bent that he never possessed. Like many extrovert men who are great wenchers and drinkers, Antony was putty in the hands of a clever woman.

'It would be tedious', writes Plutarch, 'to chronicle Antony's many follies in Alexandria' – and proceeds to do so. Antony was to become more Alexandrian than the Alexandrians. Such expatriates often seem indistinguishable from the locals, but do not possess the locals' necessary industriousness and application to work. (The Mediterranean is still littered with such figures.) Antony is the classic example of a man who fell in love with a foreign country.

Very quickly he adopted the Greek dress – something that his master Caesar would never have done – and he began to appear in public in the Greek tunic and white Attic shoes. He spoke Greek well, for he had been trained in rhetoric in Athens, and he no doubt enjoyed the company of the Greek courtiers who frequented the Lochias palace. To them he was – apart from his power – probably little more than a gigantic Roman bull let loose in their exquisite china shop. He proceeded to found an exclusive club, known as 'The Society of the Inimitable Livers', whose members had to contrive ever more extravagant banquets and entertainments for each other. 'Let me astonish you!' might have been their motto. It is said that in the palace itself the kitchens were always ready at any hour of the day or night to produce a feast, should Antony or Cleopatra require it. On one occasion a visitor inquired what great banquet was being prepared since there were eight wild boars turning slowly on spits. The head cook laughed and said that they had only a small party that night but, since they never knew quite when a meal would be

ABOVE: *Roman kitchen, from a sarcophagus, 3rd century* A.D. OPPOSITE: *fowling, in a Theban tomb wall-painting – the owner of the tomb stands in a papyrus skiff; New Kingdom, c. 1400* B.C.

required, they always had several going at different times so that everything could be ready in a few minutes.

It was Cleopatra who dominated those winter months. It was she who instructed the Roman in the elegances of court life, while at the same time she pandered to the simple soldier in his nature. She was royal, infinitely sophisticated, an administrator, a linguist, something of an intellectual, and if she was indeed a hedonist at least one of a rarefied sort. She knew her man, and knew that only by enslaving him to his pleasures could she keep him by her side. Aware, for instance, of Antony's gambling propensities, she would play dice with him; aware of his drinking capacity, she would drink with him; and aware of his love of practical jokes and crazy high-spirits she would join with him on escapades through Alexandria. Did Antony want to go on a drunken carousal through the city, disguised as a private citizen, in order to rap on people's doors and play jokes on them? Well, she would go too, disguised as a female slave. All this would seem to have been very far from her real nature for, although she was still young and had a sense of fun, she was very conscious of her dignity, her nobility, and her divine equation with the gods. But it was Antony that she had to captivate and, whatever her deepest feelings, she must have recognized the undoubted charm of this strange rough soldier who had taken over from the quiet and civilized Caesar. It was during this period, if not before, that she became pregnant by Antony. In due course she would bear him twins.

Meanwhile in Italy Antony's wife Fulvia together with his brother Lucius had taken up the battle against Octavian, and were bent on driving Caesar's adopted heir out of the homeland. Fulvia probably hoped that her husband would see that the centre of power still lay in Rome, and she no doubt hoped that her actions would bring Antony to her side. With the legions at his disposal he could have come to her aid, left his Egyptian mistress behind, eliminated Octavian, and ruled the world from its real centre, Rome. In all of this she was conspicuously more far-sighted and intelligent than her husband, but the fact was that Antony was enslaved by Cleopatra, her city and kingdom, and a whole way of life that appealed completely to his simple temperament. He ignored the true issues, and continued to trifle away his life in the happy hedonism of the Alexandrian world.

Cleopatra would provide hunting and fishing expeditions in the wild land beyond the Greek city's walls, boating on Lake Mareotis, as well as coming down with her court to watch him exercise in the gymnasium and practise his swordsmanship or indulge in feats of strength. If he was Heracles/Dionysus she was entirely Isis/Aphrodite. She must have felt, with the new life stirring in her womb, that (like the ancient Mother-Goddess who had once dominated all the Mediterranean) although the man was necessary, it was the female principle that finally ruled the world.

Quite apart from the elaborate banquets and entertainments with which she diverted her lover throughout the pleasant winter of Alexandria, she was quite capable of the kind of simple practical jokes which appealed to his sense of humour. (In many respects Antony reminds one of King Edward VII of Britain, with his fondness for women and high living, horses, and sport in general, and a schoolboy taste in humour and horseplay.) On one occasion Antony, who had been fishing in the harbour and had failed to make any catches, paid a local diver to swim down and affix large fishes to his hooks. Cleopatra, who was not deceived, arranged next day for another diver to make quite sure that her lord and master was successful. When

Antony felt the sudden weight of a large fish upon his line he immediately struck and drew it up to the surface – only to be astounded, and chagrined, to find that the trophy he was so proudly displaying in the sunlight was a salted fish from the Black Sea, one of the staple diets of the poor during the winter months. Cleopatra and her courtiers burst into shouts of laughter. There can be no doubt that Antony laughed too, for, whatever his faults, he was never pompous. Cleopatra now called out to him (and there was a seriousness at the back of her laughter): 'Leave the fishing rod to others, General – to rulers like us who bear sway over places like Pharos and Canopus. *Your* game lies in cities, provinces, and kingdoms.'

Bronze statue of Isis holding a sistrum, a kind of rattle ; from Puzzoli, southern Italy, Greco-Roman period

THE YEARS BETWEEN

While Antony was spending in Alexandria what the orator Antiphon called 'that most precious of gifts, Time', elsewhere in the Mediterranean events were taking place which would soon force him to take some positive kind of action. In Italy his brother Lucius and his wife Fulvia were failing in their campaign against Octavian. In the East the Parthians had advanced into Syria and Antony's recently installed Governor had been killed. The Parthians next pushed on into Judaea, capturing Jerusalem in the process, and Herod was forced to take refuge in the mountain fortress of Masada. Antony's failure to make proper provision for the eastern provinces was already making itself felt, while his neglect of his Italian homeland had allowed Octavian to obtain a secure foothold from which to base any future operations. In the struggle for power between Octavian and Antony one is inevitably reminded of Aesop's fable of the Tortoise and the Hare.

'At last,' in Plutarch's words, 'like a man aroused from sleep after a deep debauch,' Antony realized that he must leave his mistress and the city. In February 40 B.C. his brother Lucius was compelled to surrender to Octavian. The latter's success was largely owing to the remarkable Marcus Vipsanius Agrippa, who had been a student with Octavian at Apollonia. He devoted his whole life to being Octavian's right hand man, yet never attempted to compete with him for the leadership of the Roman world. Antony's wife Fulvia was now compelled to flee to the East, while the province of Gaul also fell under Octavian's control. Indeed everywhere that Antony looked he could see only chaos and disaster. After a brief visit to Tyre during which he made ineffectual efforts to reorganize and stabilize his eastern frontiers Antony made his way via Cyprus and Rhodes to Athens where his wife Fulvia was awaiting him. Their meeting cannot have been a pleasant one, for while she could reproach him for his desertion of her for Cleopatra, he in his turn could reproach her for the failure of his cause in Italy.

There was nothing for him to do but go to Italy and either fight or make terms with Octavian. The latter now held the trump cards – Italy, Gaul and Spain, while Antony's Eastern Empire was tottering. Antony landed near Brundisium, and for a while it again looked as if the two rivals were destined to plunge Italy into the turmoil of yet another civil war. Then fate took a hand. The unfortunate Fulvia, exhausted by her ordeal, fell ill and died. This left Antony technically a widower for whether he had gone through any formal ceremony with Cleopatra or not it was certainly not recognized in Rome. With the death of his wife it became comparatively easy for

Antony to put the blame for the war in Italy on her shoulders, and for Octavian to accept his version of events. It also happened that the latter had a recently widowed sister Octavia. In a licentious and immoral age she was that rare thing – a Roman woman of virtue coupled with intelligence. What more natural than for Octavian to propose that Antony should marry Octavia, thus sealing the agreement between them to run the two halves of the Empire without further discord?

The politics of it seemed sensible enough to Antony. With the Parthian problem on his hands he could not afford to quarrel with this young man whose power increased from month to month. In the late autumn of that year Antony was formally married to Octavia amid great public acclamation, for the Italian people were heartily tired of the civil wars that for so long had ravaged their country. Even the professional soldiers had no wish to find themselves yet again matched against one another because of the ambitions of their leaders. They wanted to settle down on the farms and small-holdings that had been allotted to them, and live the tranquil and industrious life. Let their arms hang on the wall, and let their hands turn to the plough: those were their sentiments.

While this marriage with Octavia might seem to the Italian people to contain the promise of peace and prosperity, it must have been regarded by Cleopatra as the ultimate disaster. It was a betrayal of a particularly squalid kind, for it occurred only a few weeks after she had borne Antony twins, a boy and a girl, whom she had named Alexander Helios and Cleopatra Selene. Politically it looked a calamity for Egypt, for a close alliance between Antony and Octavian might well mean the incorporation of Egypt as a province of the Roman Empire. That Octavia was younger than she and known to be as wise as she was beautiful must have further increased

Coin portrait of Lucius Antony, Mark Antony's brother, 41 B.C.

Cleopatra's misery. Everything that she had played for and schemed for since her first arrival in Tarsus and throughout that Alexandrian winter seemed to be lost.

There was nothing that she could do but bide her time, and hope that Antony's promiscuity would estrange Octavia from him and lead to a breach between the two Romans. It is possible that Octavian had this in mind. He may well have foreseen that Antony would provide him with the opportunity to say that his sister's honour had been slighted, an ideal excuse for making war. Octavian was quite capable of such foresight and, as his whole life was to show, he was a consummate politician who had absolutely no scruples when it came to the battle for power. Octavian regarded marriages as political moves, as he now proceeded to show by marrying Scribonia, a woman much older than himself, who had already had two husbands but who could be helpful to his schemes since she was a relation of Sextus Pompeius. This last of Pompey the Great's sons was still master of much of the Mediterranean and it was quite as important to Octavian to neutralize this threat to his interests as to make peace with Antony.

In the following year, 39 B.C., the three men met at Misenum near Naples, the fleet of Sextus Pompeius lying off at anchor, while the forces of Antony and Octavian were drawn up on the shore. An agreement was finally signed between them that in return for control of Sicily and Sardinia Pompey's son would use his ships, not to harass the supply routes, but to keep down the pirates with which the Mediterranean had become infested during the long period of the civil wars. In the course of the mutual banquets and entertainments that accompanied the reconciliation it fell to the lot of Pompey to invite Antony and Octavian to a feast. On Antony inquiring where it would be held, Pompey, in Plutarch's words,

> pointed to his admiral's barge with its six banks of oars and said 'There, for this is the only ancestral home that is left to Pompey.' He said this by way of reproach to Antony who was occupying the Rome house that had once belonged to his father. He then brought his ship in to anchor close to the shore and made a kind of bridge between it and the headland of Misenum so that the visitors could pass on board. Pompey gave his guests a hearty welcome. When the festivities were at their height, accompanied by many coarse jokes about Antony and Cleopatra, Menas the pirate came up to Pompey and whispered so that the others could not hear, 'Shall I cut the cables and make you master, not only of Sicily and Sardinia, but of the whole Roman empire?'. Pompey brooded over his words in silence for a time and then replied: 'Menas, you should have done this without saying anything about it to me beforehand: but now we must leave things as they are. I cannot break my word.'

In this he showed a decency of conduct rare at that period, but befitting the son of so distinguished a father.

With the conclusion of this agreement it seemed for a time as if the golden age of peace and harmony forecast by Virgil in his famous *Fourth Eclogue* was indeed about to occur. But the Roman world was now in effect ruled by four men rather than three and it was unlikely that such a division would be any more effective than the Triumvirate had been. At the apex of the power pyramid there was room for only one man.

In the autumn of this year Octavia bore Antony a daughter, Antonia, something which might have been expected to bind him and his brother-in-law even closer together. However Antony was soon off to Greece, where he made his home in Athens, resuming the same style of life that he had enjoyed in Alexandria. Neither Cleopatra, it seemed, nor Octavia, both women of considerable distinction and character, could control for any length of time the irrepressible buffoon that was latent in Antony. In his role of Hercules he liked to boast of the innumerable children he had fathered, while in his role as the New Dionysus he indulged in orgies and drinking parties that astonished even the pleasure-loving Athenians. Yet there was something immensely good-natured, even childlike, about him, and it was this that endeared him to the people as in the past it had done to his troops. His general popularity received a further and immense boost when news reached him from Parthia that a very able general Ventidius Bassus, whom he had despatched to stabilize the frontier, had completely routed this formidable enemy. In a further engagement he drove them back with even heavier losses. Among the dead were the King's son, a number of the Roman defectors and the Parthians' best general.

It soon became clear that the alliance made at Misenum was not going to work in the central basin of the Mediterranean. Pompey's forces – many of whom were probably not really under his control – soon began harassing Rome's supply routes and cutting off the grain ships that were so essential to the economy. Octavian realized that he would have to act against Pompey and began a massive ship-building programme, designed to give him a superiority at sea over any other fleets in the Mediterranean. In the meantime he had met the woman who was to dominate his life. This was Livia Drusilla, of the ancient house of the Claudii. She was nineteen years old and already married, but this in no way deterred Octavian. When he wanted something no scruple whatsoever deterred him from the pursuit of his objective. Despite the fact that Livia was pregnant with her second child by her husband Tiberius Claudius Nero, Octavian declared that her marriage with him was dissolved. At the same time he ordered the dissolution of his own marriage with Scribonia.

There is no doubt about Octavian's passion for Livia, but the dissolution of his marriage with Scribonia was also a political act. Since he soon intended to make war upon Sextus Pompeius he no longer wanted to have any marriage ties with the Pompey family. Unlike Antony, Octavian was not openly indiscreet about his love affairs, although it was said that in private he was as dissolute and vicious as any

Marble statue of Livia, from Pompeii; 6 feet 4 inches high

Roman of his time. His marriage with Livia, however, was to endure all his life, and she was to prove herself exactly the right woman to be the wife of the first Emperor of Rome. He acted now in his usual cool and indeed in this case callous way – annulling his marriage with Scribonia on the very day that she bore him a daughter. In January 38 B.C. he married Livia and three months later she bore her second son, who was called Drusus. Octavian sent the child to her former husband and had his action in doing so placed on public record. Naturally enough the cynical Romans were not going to ignore this strange situation, and verses were soon circulating congratulating the newly-weds on their miraculous feat of having a three-months child.

Octavian at this period of his life was not popular with the Romans. It was Antony whom they admired, Antony with his dash and charm and exuberance. Octavian with his sickly frame and unhealthy appearance – except for his fine luminous eyes – coupled with his lack of military ability, did not seem 'the man most likely to succeed'. If Antony had at this moment decided to challenge Octavian seriously it is conceivable that he could have won the Empire for himself. But like many people who are born with a weak constitution Octavian looked after himself very carefully, while Antony squandered the gifts of his splendid physique and constitution in a senseless round of over-indulgence. Octavian always wore heavy, warm clothing during the winter, and a sun hat in the summer. . . .

At about the same time as the great success of Roman arms over the Parthians – the first in history – the situation became more favourable for Antony. Octavian failed miserably in his first clash with Pompey at sea, and lost a large part of his new fleet. This was in the spring of 38 B.C. Some part of the blame may well be laid at Antony's door, for when asked to assist Octavian he had done little more than counsel him that the Treaty of Misenum should be maintained. He may perhaps have been acting politically, determined not to aid his rival, or this may have been symptomatic of the lethargy which was steadily overtaking him; but at this point one might clearly discern Octavian's discontent with his fellow Triumvir. Lepidus was harmless, tucked away in Africa; Pompey still remained to be dealt with; Antony, last on the list, would one day have to be eliminated. Octavian, as nearly always in his life, had his priorities right.

Something else that Octavian always had to his advantage was the unswerving allegiance of the brilliant Agrippa, and he knew how to bind to him other men of considerable stature. Rich and influential men like Maecenas together with poets like Virgil and Horace were to enrich his life and ensure that what would one day to be called the 'Augustan Age' would be a landmark in history. Antony with his whores and acrobats was hardly of a calibre to compete.

The Cilician Gates, the narrow entrance to the Kulak Bughaz (Taurus Mountains), one of the longest and most difficult passes in the world. OVERLEAF: *fresco from the villa of Livia, near Rome*

AN UNEASY ALLIANCE

In January 37 B.C. the Triumvirate, which had expired, was renewed for a further period of five years in what became known as the Pact of Tarentum. Some of the credit for this must certainly go to Antony's wife Octavia who, whatever she may have felt about her husband's manner of living, was certainly eager to prevent any conflict between him and her brother. Both men had ambitious projects in view: Octavian the naval war against Sextus Pompeius; Antony a further large scale Parthian campaign in which he intended not only to destroy their army, but also to bring the whole area within the Empire. Octavian therefore needed ships, and Antony needed men. The pact was sealed by Antony agreeing to give Octavian one hundred and thirty ships for the conduct of his war, while the latter was to give Antony twenty thousand legionaries.

Meanwhile Octavian's faithful friend Agrippa had been summoned back from Gaul where he was Governor to take charge of the impending operations against Pompey. Agrippa was not only a fine general – he had just advanced Roman arms beyond the Rhine – but a brilliant planner and administrator. He was determined that the next operation against the 'Son of Neptune', as Pompey now called himself, should not fail through lack of preparation. This time there was to be no mistake. Throughout the whole of the year he concentrated his abilities on training up a fleet and crews designed to eliminate once and for all this threat to Rome's lifelines. As Stewart Perowne writes:

> The first requirement was a really good harbour, protected from storm and foe alike. We may still admire Agrippa's creation. Near the shore east of Misenum, at the northern end of the Bay of Naples, there are two lakes, Lucrinus and Avernus. Agrippa joined them by canals to each other and to the sea. Here the new fleet could be assembled in absolute security. Freed slaves were instructed in oarsmanship for a whole year, and in the manipulation of a new device of Agrippa's whereby grapnels were shot from catapults to facilitate the holding and boarding of an enemy ship.

While Octavian was preparing to eliminate the first of his rivals Antony was on his way back to the East. He took his wife Octavia with him as far as Corfu, at which

---

Ploughing, a detail from a mosaic of agricultural scenes. From Caesarea (Cherchell) in North Africa, 3rd century A.D.

point he sent her back to Rome on the pretext that since she was once again pregnant any further sea travel would be dangerous to her health. There can be no doubt that this was no more than an excuse to have Octavia out of the way. She could easily have been confined in Corfu, or indeed in Athens, for the sea voyage to Greece was no further than it was back to Italy. His other excuse, that he needed to concentrate on the impending war, had equally little validity. It seems almost certain that Antony had decided to ally himself once more with Cleopatra (he would need the large Egyptian fleet against the one that Octavian was building) and, after conquering Parthia, return out of the East and make himself master of the West as well.

Probably there were also personal reasons. Octavia is portrayed as good, domestic, gentle and a paragon of virtue – a Roman matron of whom even Cato would have approved. All these concepts were anathema to Antony, who only felt happy amid excess and extravagance. Very probably when she had been with him before in Athens as well as recently back in Rome, Octavia had given him the standard wifely lectures on not drinking too much, keeping away from other women, and looking after his health. His previous wife Fulvia had been a strong minded woman of similar stamp, and had doubtless read him many a 'curtain lecture'. Antony had had quite enough of these women who thought men should conform and behave themselves. He remembered how Cleopatra suited herself to his moods. This was the kind of woman he could understand, and this was the kind of woman with whom he could rule the world. He needed not only her money and her fleet, but also her intelligence, her political insight – and her vivacity.

Antony's act of sending Octavia back to Rome must also be interpreted as a political one. In much the same way as Octavian's studied divorce of Scribonia had been a statement to Pompey that relations between them were at an end Antony's despatch of his pregnant wife to Rome said to Octavian: 'Have your sister back. I don't want her or her children.' He had thrown down the gage and the battle for the world would soon be joined.

That this interpretation of the event is true seems proved by the fact that soon after reaching Antioch he sent a trusted friend to bring Cleopatra to meet him. Plutarch tells the romantic version of the story: 'Antony's dire passion for Cleopatra, which people thought had been lulled or charmed away by more sensible considerations, now broke out afresh. . . . And finally, like the stubborn and rebellious beast of the soul, of which Plato speaks, he flung away all sensible counsel, and sent Fonteius Capito to bring her to Syria.'

It is extremely doubtful, however, that it was passion alone which inspired him. After all he had not seen her for three and a half years, which was a very long time in Antony's simple memory of women. Furthermore he had married Octavia (even if it was only for political reasons) only a few months after he had left the Queen, and just after she had borne him twins. Antony, to judge by the record of his life, was no great romantic – something rare enough in the ancient world – but a healthy bull of a man with little consideration for the feelings of women. As has been said, Cleopatra's personality undoubtedly matched his, for she knew how to go along with him, but also he needed Egypt as a base for his Parthian campaign, and Alexandria as a capital city. His dream was the same as Caesar's: a Roman-Ptolemaic dynasty ruling the world, and basing its strength on the rich provinces of the East.

Cleopatra can have had few illusions about the nature of the alliance now projected. She would join with him in the conquest of the East, to be followed by a war against Octavian. In the autumn of 37 B.C. for the second time in her extraordinary life she left her capital and went to meet Antony. But the years that had passed had left many a discrepancy between them. They had been lovers before apart from any political necessity; they became lovers again more out of politics than love. Cleopatra, however, was in a stronger bargaining position than she had been, for Antony needed her help. She seems to have insisted on a legal marriage which, although it would not be recognized in Rome, would be perfectly binding in the East. Antony would annul his marriage with Octavia officially in Rome, and Cleopatra would become his Empress. He also seems to have agreed to recognize Caesar's son Caesarion as the legal heir to the Empire, while his own children by Cleopatra would inherit minor kingdoms within its framework. For himself Antony devised a new title Autocrator, 'Ruler Absolute'. This was more than Imperator, which merely meant Commander-in-Chief, and at the same time it would not offend the Romans as would the title 'King', which had proved Caesar's undoing. As absolute ruler of the whole East he was the regent of Egypt in concert with his Queen Cleopatra. He now intended to restore to Egypt an empire such as had not existed since the great days of the Pharaohs over a thousand years earlier. His and Cleopatra's dominions were to include Cyprus, the coasts of Palestine and Phoenicia (with the (exception of the free cities of Tyre and Sidon), Sinai, Central Syria, and a large part of Cilicia and Arabia Nabataea, possibly Petra, or at any rate a share in its trade, and the famous balsam-producing groves of Judaea. Judaea itself, against Cleopatra's wishes (for she hated Herod), he left in the hands of his old friend, who was not only faithful to Antony but who also provided a useful buffer-state against the Parthians. To commemorate the event a new system of coin-dating was instituted in which, apart from the previous dating as from Cleopatra's accession, there was added a further date as from 37 B.C., when there can be little doubt that their marriage was celebrated. Henceforth the heads of both Antony and Cleopatra appear together on coinage, he as Autocrator and she as Queen.

Cleopatra must have felt overjoyed at this sudden reversal of her fortunes. She was to be co-ruler of an empire larger than any of the Ptolemies' before her, and her children were confirmed in the succession. Twice before – with the death of Caesar and then with the desertion of Antony – she had known the bitterness of complete despair. But now a new order was to arise in the East and she would be at the heart of it. Antony, by his marriage to her as well as by returning Octavia to Rome, had made it clear that he intended to move against Octavian.

Coin of Antony and Cleopatra, minted in Asia Minor, 32–31 B.C.

The winter of 37 B.C. was spent by Antony and Cleopatra at Antioch. Antioch was a good base for making Antony's preparations. It was also a noble city, third to Rome and Alexandria in the Mediterranean. The capital of Syria, it was adorned with many fine buildings and works of art, as well as being agreeably situated in a well wooded countryside with many streams. There is no record of how the Autocrator and his Queen passed the winter, but knowing Antony there can be little doubt that in many respects it will have resembled that famous winter in Alexandria. But he was also a very busy man, for he intended to march against Parthia in the early spring of the following year.

In March 36 B.C. Antony set out with his legions and Cleopatra accompanied him. She intended to stay at his side throughout the campaign, but she got no further than Zeugma, a town on the Armenian frontier, when she realized that she was pregnant. Even then it was probably only at Antony's insistence that she made her way back to Alexandria. Her route took her down through Damascus, across the Sea of Galilee and along the river Jordan to Jericho. It was here that she met Herod, a man who distrusted her as much as she him, and who was naturally indignant that Antony had so high-handedly disposed of one of the richest portions of his territory, the balsam-producing groves of Jericho, to this Egyptian Queen. He knew well enough too that if Antony succeeded in becoming master of the whole Empire Cleopatra would almost certainly insist on adding his kingdom to her personal acquisitions. Our authority for this part of Cleopatra's life is the Jewish historian Josephus, who was writing nearly a century after the events concerned, and who, as the client of the Emperor Vespasian, naturally wrote with the traditional anti-Cleopatra bias. According to him Cleopatra now attempted to seduce Herod – unlikely enough since she disliked him, and even less likely since she was at that moment carrying Antony's child. What does seem to have happened is that Cleopatra agreed to lease the area of Judaea which Antony had given her to Herod for the sum of two hundred talents a year. Equally unlikely is Josephus's story that Herod planned to murder the Queen and was only dissuaded from this course by the advice of his councillors. 'They begged him,' the historian writes, 'to do nothing rash, for Antony would never countenance it . . . this woman was the most important of her sex in the whole world.' It is hardly conceivable that Herod, always famed for his skill at diplomacy, could have suggested such a course of action. No doubt he would have liked to have got rid of this enemy, but since he knew that she had concluded a marriage with Antony, the most powerful man in the East, and that she was pregnant by him it is impossible to believe that he ever seriously contemplated her murder. If one can dismiss this story of Josephus it would be reasonable to assume that one can also dismiss his other story that Cleopatra tried to seduce Herod. What had Cleopatra to gain by an affair with Herod – which would certainly get reported back to Antony? She was intent on becoming Empress of the World at Antony's side, and this petty King of Judaea can have meant nothing, politically at least, to her. This is one of the accretions to the Cleopatra legend put out by Roman propagandists to show her as 'a slave to her lusts' – a symbol of that 'decadent East' against which the 'pure Romans' must be cautioned.

What certainly did happen was the conclusion of the agreement between Herod and Cleopatra, after which he escorted her and her retinue as far as the frontier town of Pelusium. From here she made her way to Alexandria, where she settled down in her palace to await the birth of her fourth child. Some time later in the year she bore another son, who was given the name Ptolemy Philadelphus. During the months she was awaiting her confinement she must have felt more than happy at the prospect ahead. Antony would have a conclusive victory over the Parthians and would then bring the whole area under Roman control. After this there could be no denying him a massive Triumph in Rome, where the victor of Philippi and the conqueror of the Parthians – the avenger of Roman honour for the disgrace of Carrhae – would become all Italy's hero. Discredited, the unpopular Octavian would then be forced to slink from the scene, leaving Antony sole ruler of the Roman world. Antony's marriage with Octavia would be annulled; Cleopatra, already his wife in Eastern eyes, would become his wife under Roman law; and Caesar's child and Antony's children would be the heirs to the throne. She, Cleopatra, would reign as Empress over an area greater than even Alexander had ever imagined. Such no doubt were the dreams with which the Queen fed herself while she waited in her palace on Lochias promontory, feeling the sea wind as it rustled through the colonnades and listening to the fountains.

Antony meanwhile, having assembled his troops at Zeugma, prepared for his great onslaught into Parthian territory. His plan of action was a considerable improvement on that of his predecessors, who had always invaded Parthia from the west across the desert. Antony intended to take the enemy by surprise and, by a long circuitous march, come down on them from the north where they would not be expecting him. It was a good plan on paper, but it entailed a massive degree of organization – and organization was never Antony's strong point. The other drawback to it was that the movements of so large a body of troops as Antony had now assembled could never be kept secret. He had a grand total of about one hundred thousand men, composed of sixty thousand legionaries, ten thousand horsemen, and some thirty thousand troops from the eastern provinces. Among these were a large number of slingers who it was hoped would be more than a match for the famous Parthian archers. There was also a secondary train which was centred around a great number of engines of war, including one battering ram eighty feet long. This 'tail' was to prove Antony's undoing logistically. Although he would need these devices for the siege of cities, the speed at which they could progress compared with that of the legions meant, almost inevitably, that the two halves of the army would have to move separately.

Plutarch writes that 'all his preparations – which terrified even the Indians and made all Asia afraid – were rendered useless because of his desire to return to Cleopatra. So eager was he to spend the winter with her that he began his campaign too early, and before everything was properly arranged. No master of his own faculties, he was like a man drugged or under a magic influence, and he was ever thinking of her, and of his speedy return, rather than of engaging and conquering the enemy.' This can hardly be the truth for Antony knew as well as anybody else that his fortune depended upon a victory to ensure the Triumph which would ultimately make him master of the Roman world. Plutarch, who is usually objective, is again betrayed into a false reconstruction by the prejudice of the world in which

BELOW: *the Caspian Gates*
OPPOSITE: *fragment of bas-relief with an allegorical representation of Rome and Warriors, 2nd century* A.D.

he lived. Antony, drunkard and lecher though he may have been, was never the man to ruin a campaign for the love of any woman.

He and his legionaries now marched by a more or less direct route through northern Armenia and into Media. The other part of his forces, together with the siege train, took the easier route along the valley of the Araxes river. In company with them went two legions, as well as troops provided by the client kingdoms of Armenia and Pontus. For Antony to be successful he should have regulated the advance of his own legions to that of the much slower supply forces and siege train; but here as throughout his life he showed an impatience that was to be his ruin. Caesar had known how to use Antony's abilities – and how to control them. In modern terms one might say he was a good first-lieutenant but unsuitable to be a captain.

Antony's first major target was a city called Phraaspa, where he had learned that the family (and the treasure) of the Median King was to be found. Had he waited for his siege engines he would undoubtedly have taken this comparatively small town, but he relied on the belief that his name and his legions would be sufficient to cause Phraaspa to surrender. In this he was sadly mistaken. While he was preparing for the siege and had set his troops to build a great mound opposite the city walls he received the news that his second force had been attacked by the Parthians and massacred. All the siege engines had been captured or destroyed, and his ally

Model of a Roman battering ram; the head was reinforced with iron and the frame could be pushed forward.

the King of Armenia had fled with what remained of his men back into his own country. The King of Pontus, another of Antony's clients, had been captured by the Parthians. It was a disastrous blow but Antony was determined to carry on with the siege. The return of the victorious Parthians however, who continually harassed his troops without ever letting them get to grips in a pitched battle, was to prove the end of his hopes. The autumn was drawing on and soon the mountain passes would be heavy with snow.

With the loss of his supply train and his failure to take the city, provisions were running low, and starvation threatened the legions. Finally in October Antony was forced to seek terms from the enemy. His own troops had lost their morale and he had had to make an example of those who had been occupying the mound – but had fled before a Median counter-attack – by decimation: that is, putting to death one in ten of their number. At first Antony tried to arrange with the Parthian King that he should restore whatever Roman prisoners remained from the disaster of Carrhae together with the Eagles lost by Crassus. If only he could return to Rome with the missing Eagles, those symbols of Roman arms and prowess, his whole campaign would be justified – in the eyes of the people at any rate. But the Parthian King, naturally enough, was adamant against any such exchange. Antony realized that he was beaten. He must raise the siege and withdraw his forces as soon as possible, before 'King Winter' caught them all.

There is something about Antony's withdrawal from Phraaspa, as several writers have commented, which brings to mind Napoleon's retreat from Moscow. The circumstances were almost identical – the grand, disciplined and organized army, which had seemed destined to success, making its way back home through the snow

176

while bands of horsemen and guerilla fighters harassed it all the way. The Parthians, who seem to have promised to let Antony retire without further provocation, certainly did not keep their word, but maintained a continuous, mosquito-like attack on the flanks and rearguard of the marching legions. Antony's great campaign, the one that was to have made him master of the world, had failed. Throughout the retreat Antony himself behaved with conspicuous valour and despite his nature permitted himself no luxuries but ate as simply as his troops.

Whatever the shortcomings of Antony's character they were not cowardice or lack of sympathy. As Plutarch puts it:

> The respect which his soldiers felt for him as their leader, their obedience and goodwill, and the degree to which every man of them – whether good or bad, officers or private soldiers – chose honour and favour from Antony rather than life and safety, was something that even their forefathers could not have surpassed. There were many reasons for this: Antony's nobility of birth, his eloquence, his simple manners, his largesse, and the very way in which he loved to give to people, and his generosity whether it was in matters of pleasure or straightforward social relations. By the way in which he shared in the distress and difficulties of the ill and the unfortunate, giving them as far as he could whatever they wanted, he made even the wounded and the sick as eager to serve him as those who were well and strong.

Plutarch goes on to describe how on one occasion during their march through to Armenia the Romans formed the famous *testudo*, tortoise, as a defensive measure against the Parthians who were attacking them as they descended some steep hills:

> The shield-bearers wheeled about, enclosing the lighter armed troops within their ranks while they themselves dropped on one knee and held their shields out in front of them. The second rank held their shields over the head of the first, and the next rank likewise. This tactic produces a most striking appearance, rather like the roof of a house, and it is very effective against arrows, which merely skim off it. The Parthians, however, seeing the Romans dropping on one knee, thought that they were exhausted, so they laid aside their bows and came in at close quarters with their spears. Then the Romans suddenly sprang up, giving a battle cry, and killed the foremost of the enemy with their javelins, and put the rest to rout.

But despite several such successful actions cold and famine took a terrible toll of the once proud army.

Finally after a month's march the legions reached the river Araxes and crossed into the friendly territory of Armenia. A review of the troops was held and it was seen that in the campaign – but mainly in the retreat – some twenty-four thousand legionaries and horsemen had been lost. Even now their troubles were not at an end, for Armenia was under snow and in their march back to Syria it was estimated that another eight thousand men perished. Finally the army went into winter quarters at a small town north of Sidon called the White Village. Here Antony, who throughout the whole retreat had kept up the morale of his troops, and held them together by the strength of his personality, finally abandoned himself to despair. Despatches had already been sent to Cleopatra telling of the failure of the campaign and the state of the army – without money, with very little food, ill-clad and with most of their equipment lost. Antony as always when inactive or despondent turned to wine for consolation. But even here, 'in the midst of his drinking he would spring up from the table and gaze seaward, looking for the fleet of Cleopatra that would bring them succour'. She had needed his help in the past; the situation was quite reversed. From now on one sees the ascendancy of Cleopatra and the gradual decline of Antony.

Roman legionaries forming a testudo. *Detail from the column of Marcus Aurelius erected in Rome at the end of the 2nd century* A.D.

EAST AND WEST

It was not until late in the year that the Egyptian fleet was finally sighted coasting up to the White Village. Cleopatra herself came ashore to find Antony distraught amid the ruin of his hopes and his army. She had brought with her food and clothing for the troops, but comparatively little money, so Antony was forced to extort a considerable sum from his petty kingdoms and clients in order to pay the soldiers. He was gentleman enough however – and eager not to damage the Queen's prestige – to tell his officers and men that the money came from Cleopatra. In this way he bound them to her interests and to those of Egypt.

Cleopatra must once again have had a feeling of foreboding. Were all the golden hopes she had entertained during her recent pregnancy again to be reduced to ashes? Antony's failure against the Parthians was already being reported throughout the Mediterranean world. Octavian receiving his carefully veiled despatch would surely be able to read between the lines. The real truth would soon be out.

Cleopatra must also have been shocked at the decline in Antony's morale and at the fact that he was no longer drinking – as in the past – out of healthy good spirits but out of black despondency. There was only one thing for her to do: take him back with her to Alexandria, where in the comfort of the palace he could recuperate and revive a little. There were his children for him to see, including his new-born son Ptolemy Philadelphus. The Queen knew well enough that the material losses of the campaign could easily be made good over the winter, but more important was the damage to Antony's reputation. She herself had never been in favour of the Parthian expedition, and no doubt could not understand this Roman obsession with the area. But she knew that Caesar, just before his death, had been intending to march against Parthia and however much she may have distrusted Antony as a statesman she had had ample time to appreciate Caesar's brilliance in this sphere. By underwriting Antony's ambitions in the East she was only attempting to carry out the policy which Caesar himself must often have explained to her.

What made matters worse was that while Antony had failed Octavian had just achieved a remarkable triumph. His campaign against Pompey's son Sextus Pompeius had begun badly enough. Owing to bad weather he had lost a number of transports that were bringing troops up from North Africa to assist in driving Pompey out of Sicily. The plan of campaign (whether Octavian's or Agrippa's) was good enough in itself. Lepidus was to strike up from North Africa in the south of the island, while other troops were to be landed in the east and west. It was a

summer of unseasonable gales however, and Octavian suffered other naval losses particularly in the Messina Straits. The ships which Agrippa had constructed in his secret training-ground were all built much more heavily than those of Pompey, whose fleet was principally composed of the light and easily manoeuvrable type of galleys known as Liburnians. What largely turned the scales in the end was that Agrippa, who was in command of the main fleet, managed to seize the Lipari Islands, thus cutting off Pompey from Sardinia. Octavian got his troops ashore on the east coast and pitched camp near Tauromenium (modern Taormina) while Lepidus camped at Messana. Agrippa coming down from the north landed twenty-one legions near the promontory of Mylae. Pompey was in danger of being hemmed in on all sides and cut off from his supplies. Thereupon he decided to stake everything on one great sea-battle, for he felt confident that the superior seamanship of his well trained crews would easily afford him a victory.

The final engagement took place near Mylae – significantly enough the very place where many years before the Romans had won their first sea-victory over the Carthaginians by methods very similar to those now employed by Agrippa. In the Carthaginian war the Romans, aware of their inexperience as seamen, had devised a beaked bridge known as a *corvus*, which swept down on the opposing vessel and bound the ships together so that the legionaries could fight what almost amounted to a land battle. Agrippa's invention of catapults which hurled grapnels at the enemy, which were then winched in so that the opposing ships were held next to one another, was merely a refinement on the *corvus*. The effect of this was to neutralize the greater manoeuvrability of Pompey's ships and give Agrippa's 'heavyweights' a distinct advantage, since they held more soldiers.

On 3 September, when Antony was fatally engaged in the East with the Parthians, Octavian, largely through the brilliance of his lieutenant Agrippa, gained the victory he so badly needed to win favour in Rome and efface his reputation as the man who had been too ill even to take part in the battle of Philippi. The two fleets were, it would seem, almost equal in numbers. (Appian says that they mustered three hundred on each side, although this may well be an exaggeration.) Pompey, who was camped with his army on the shore, watched and waited for the victory that would lift him from master of the sea and Sicily to master of Rome and the western empire. He witnessed, upon those wind-freckled waters to the north, an engagement in which the last of all the Pompeian hopes went down. Agrippa's heavy ships seized one after another of Pompey's, and their greater manpower told in the ship-to-ship encounters that took place. A large part of Pompey's fleet attempted to flee but were driven ashore, captured, or run aground on that treacherous limestone coast. In the end only seventeen ships out of the Sea King's navy (which had so long dominated the Mediterranean) managed to escape, bear off to the east and round into the Messina Strait. Here Pompey, having abandoned his army, went aboard and set sail for the East. He had decided that in the battle for power in the Roman world his only hope now was to throw in his lot with Antony.

Taormina, Sicily

The troops that he left behind were rapidly disposed of, a large part surrendering to Octavian, while the others who were at Messana surrendered to Lepidus. The latter, who was always the weak link in the Triumvirate, now made a fatal mistake. Having promised the Pompeian forces equal rights and pay with his own he attempted to challenge Octavian, and claim Sicily as well as North Africa for his share in the empire. Nothing could have suited Octavian better. He had destroyed the power of Sextus Pompeius and removed him from the central Mediterranean, thus freeing the supply lines to Rome and ensuring for himself an instant popularity in Italy. He now had the chance of getting rid of yet another rival.

Lepidus's brief bid for power was soon over. Most of the troops were heartily tired of this seemingly eternal civil war and were not inclined to renew it. They had just got rid of one threat to peace and prosperity in their homeland and they were definitely not prepared to begin all over again in a conflict between Lepidus and Octavian. Besides, through Agrippa and his fleet Octavian was now master of the sea. And who could hold Sicily without naval superiority? Lepidus was forced to submit and was deprived of his triumviral office. Octavian, knowing that the man was a spent force and no challenge to his authority, was wisely clement and allowed him to retire to his home at Circeii where he lived for a further twenty-five years

182

on that beautiful promontory north of Naples called after the goddess Circe. Lepidus was probably luckiest of all those who at this time struggled for command of the Roman world.

Octavian was now in possession not only of Italy and the West but also of Sicily and Sardinia and the rich province of Africa. But he still had plenty of problems on his hands, among them the resettlement of the veterans, for he now had many more troops than he needed. There was little public land remaining in Italy, but what there was he turned over to the legionaries, and at the same time he resettled many of them in Provence as well as in Adriatic Illyria. Married to his adored Livia, having secured the affection of the Romans by removing Pompey's threat to their well-being, ruler of vast new territories, he could now look forward to a period of readjustment and administrative improvement. Before he tackled the problem of the last of his rivals Octavian needed to reorganize home affairs. Then, like a master chess-player, he could move from a position of strength to capture the queen and checkmate his rival.

Fortune does not always favour the brave. Antony's conduct during the retreat from Parthia though brave, could not exculpate him from his failure. No doubt during these winter months Cleopatra did all that she could to restore his morale and revive in him the feeling that he was destined to be master of the Roman world. He had her; he had his children; he had Alexandria; and he had potentially all the wealth of the East. The legions were reassembled and re-equipped; the Egyptian fleet was second to none; and he himself was a veteran general, matched against a young man who, in warfare at least, had never shown that he had any great personal capability.

Antony might still convince himself that he had some substantial achievements to his credit. Syria and Armenia, despite the overall failure of his campaign, were secure within the Roman aegis. There would yet be time to return to the Parthian problem. Even if they had managed to hold their kingdom against his massive onslaught they had been taught the lesson that the Romans could raise – and transport – great armies to the scene of almost any theatre in the world.

Technically at least Octavian and Antony were still co-partners ruling the Empire. Antony's failure had been disguised, while Octavian's triumph had certainly not been concealed. The advantages that had been Antony's had been nullified but Octavian's subsequent success had still not turned the scales. At this moment the two contestants were more or less equal: the one still with the wealthy eastern provinces behind him, and the other, although immensely enriched by the additions of Sicily and Africa, still hampered by the problems he had inherited in the Italian homeland.

Pompey's son, however, was still upon the scene. It was not long before he opened negotiations with the court at Alexandria, but Antony was disinclined to antagonize Octavian any further and Pompey's envoys received no encouragement. To Antony he was discredited and though he might have been helpful against

183

Octavian, with almost no fleet he was more of a liability than an asset. Antony (or Cleopatra) accordingly temporized. Young Pompey was now stationed in the island of Lesbos where he had laid up what remained of his fleet for the short but stormy Aegean winter. During this period, realizing that he could expect little or no help from Alexandria, he entered into negotiations with the rulers of Asia Minor. Like his father before him he saw the prospect of recouping his fortunes in the East. His father's name was still held in great respect in that quarter and many of the rulers and princes had been either installed on their thrones by or clients of Pompey the Great.

The only reason that Antony had loaned Octavian ships to proceed against Pompey was that he needed the legionaries whom he had been promised in return. All the evidence seems to show that Antony would have left Pompey in peace provided that he retired from the arena and did not stir up trouble in the East. But this was just what Pompey proceeded to do. He seized the city of Lampsacus in Asia Minor to serve as his base and began recruiting numbers of veteran legionaries, many of whom no doubt had once served his father. There was a likelihood that he might well acquire a considerable amount of local support in that area where Antony's tax-gathering habits had made him extremely unpopular. There was a danger also that Pompey would begin the construction of another fleet with which to make a further bid for power. Antony acted swiftly. He sent Marcus Titius the nephew of the Governor of Syria with a powerful force of legionaries to oppose Pompey before he should succeed in raising a large army. The Sea King was captured as he was trying to make his way to Armenia, possibly with the idea of going on to Parthia and selling his services to the Parthian King as other Romans had done.

Sextus Pompeius was taken to Miletus and executed. Whether this was on Antony's orders or not is open to conjecture. The act was not popular with the Roman people who, despite the hardship he had sometimes caused them, retained something of a sentimental regard for this 'outlaw and pirate'. Officially however the action was received with great enthusiasm: Antony had completed Octavian's work. The latter now honoured his fellow triumvir by having statues to Antony erected in the Forum. He also granted the latter the right, equal to his own, to hold banquets with his wife and family in the Temple of Concord. On the face of it this seems a relatively trivial matter, but it was a very clever piece of politics. Octavian was saying: 'This is where your place is, in Rome with your wife and family – not in Egypt'. He was reminding Antony of the family tie that technically united them. He was pointing out to him that he only had one real wife, Octavia, his fellow-triumvir's sister. It is interesting to speculate on the course of events if Antony had accepted this olive branch and returned to Octavia. But he had no intention of leaving Cleopatra and the East, or of losing his quasi-divine position of Autocrator.

Whatever Cleopatra may have felt about his Parthian policy Antony was as

Gold coin of Sextus Pompeius, issued in Sicily, 42–36 B.C.

determined as ever to prosecute the war. He now had an additional reason for doing so, the need to wipe out the memory of his recent failure. What finally determined him to prepare for a further campaign was the unexpected arrival in Alexandria of the King of Pontus, who had been captured by the Parthians when they had attacked the siege train, and had been held prisoner over the winter by the King of Media. The King now sent him to Antony with the more than welcome news that the alliance between Media and Parthia was at an end. He proposed therefore that Antony and he should form a new alliance and make a common cause against the Parthians. This was the most encouraging thing that had happened to any Roman general. It was the strength of Media and Parthia combined that had always proved too much in the past, and indeed the Roman disasters had all taken place in Median territory. Antony must have been overjoyed. Here was his chance to crush the Parthians and acquire that Triumph in Rome which was so necessary to his ambitions.

It seemed too good an opportunity to loose but there were still many preparations to be made. Probably on Cleopatra's advice he sent for the King of Armenia, asking him to come to Alexandria to discuss the future plan of campaign. But as he had deserted Antony when the siege train had been overwhelmed, he showed a marked reluctance to leave his native country. He may well have thought that at the very least he would be upbraided for his conduct, or else imprisoned, or even publicly humiliated and executed. Cleopatra, if it was her suggestion, can never really have believed that any suspicious oriental king would, in view of what had happened, put his head into the tiger-trap of Alexandria. This was either a deliberate delaying act on her part or she was perfectly well aware that Antony could never get things ready in time for a campaign that year. In any case she very soon had good reasons for keeping Antony by her side. His Roman wife Octavia arrived in Athens. Once again Antony had been politically out-generalled by his brother-in-law.

185

QUEEN TAKES QUEEN

The news of Octavia's arrival in Athens must have been immensely upsetting for Cleopatra. Octavian's motive in sending his sister to Greece was plain to the meanest observer. As Plutarch put it: 'He gave her permission to leave Rome for Athens, not as a favour to her, but in order that, were she neglected and treated with scorn, he might have plausible ground for war'.

If Antony went to see his wife in Athens, Cleopatra feared she would lose him. She knew his weaknesses. Octavia was an attractive woman and Athens was one of his favourite cities. Besides all this Octavian had added to the bait by sending money and gifts for Antony, his officers and friends; a large quantity of clothing for his soldiers; beasts of burden, and two thousand picked soldiers of the praetorian guard equipped in magnificent armour. All this, in theory, was for use in Antony's Parthian campaign, and in return for the ships that he had lent Octavian for his war against Pompey, seventy of which were returned by Octavian for Antony's use in the East. It was later represented in Octavian's propaganda as a lavish gift which Antony had spurned – at the same time as he spurned his wife. But the two thousand legionaries were little enough, and no replacement for the thousands that had been lost in Parthia as Octavian well knew. Furthermore, since he had promised Antony twenty thousand men in return for the ships that Antony had lent him they were almost an insult. They were in fact no more than a bodyguard for Octavia. (When Antony's previous wife Fulvia had travelled through Greece, she had had an escort of three thousand cavalry.)

Prior to Octavia's arrival in Athens Antony had sent a letter to await her in which he stated that he was busy in Syria preparing for his campaign, and told her to stay in Athens until she heard further from him. Cleopatra had one great advantage over her rival – she was with him in Syria, and able to influence him day and night. The only real danger was that, if absence does indeed make the heart grow fonder, Antony might remember an idyllic Octavia and hasten to her side. She had borne him three children (as had Cleopatra), and she was a younger woman than the Queen. To add to Cleopatra's worries a friend of Antony's now arrived from Athens direct from Octavia. Cleopatra saw how closely her position was threatened. The two women were almost face to face, and it was a battle between them. Thus they faced each other across the chess-board, one Antony's wife in Roman eyes and the sister of the ruler of Italy and the West, and the other his wife in eastern eyes and Queen of Egypt.

Basalt head of Octavia, sister of Octavian and wife of Antony, 2nd half 1st century B.C.; 10½ inches high

Cleopatra was fortunate that Antony was no Caesar. The latter had always kept his eye on the main objective and could never have been turned from his path by an appeal to the emotions. Antony, as he had shown in his relations with Fulvia and indeed for a time with Octavia, was a simple man when it came to women, and could be easily swayed or dominated. As he had always demonstrated with his soldiers – something of which Cleopatra must have been well aware from hearsay – he was warm-hearted to a fault and completely susceptible to any highly charged emotional situation. 'She now pretended,' Plutarch writes, 'to be dying of love for Antony, dieting to make her body more slender, and opening her eyes wide with love whenever he drew near her, and seeming to languish or faint whenever he left. She took great pains often to be seen in tears, tears which she would swiftly wipe away as if she did not want Antony to notice them.'

Her courtiers and friends also did all that they could to plead the Queen's cause. They pointed out that Octavia had only married him as a political act, urged to it by her brother, whereas Cleopatra had become his mistress out of love. She would die if he left her, they told him, and she, who was the Queen of so many people, must surely love him since she had even been prepared to be called his mistress rather than his wife. This account of the events, which comes from Plutarch, is often quoted to prove that Cleopatra and Antony were never married, but it means no more than that in Roman eyes they never were. It was the intention of all writers after the victory of Octavian to portray Egypt's Queen as a dissembling, conniving courtesan. This was something she never was. Dissembling and conniving perhaps, but in the interests of her country and her children; there is no evidence whatsoever that she was sexually promiscuous. She had four children – one by Caesar and three by Antony. If she had had children by other men or if there was any evidence that she was licentious in her private life we can be sure that we would have heard about it from Roman historians and poets.

Cleopatra realized only too well that she could not afford to let Antony out of her sight whether to Greece or to Armenia and the north. All her efforts, and those of her friends, were bent on preventing Antony from beginning his Parthian campaign that year. In this endeavour – however much their policy was influenced by Cleopatra's – they were almost certainly correct. The reorganization of the legions and their equipment could certainly not have been completed in time, and Antony had learned by bitter experience that the autumn was no season to be caught in that cold and mountainous region. Besides, by postponing the campaign he was in effect saying to Octavia and her brother: 'I do not need your troops and supplies at this moment'. Octavia returned to Rome and despite Octavian's determination to capitalize on the situation she put a bold front on the whole affair.

> She refused to leave the house of her husband [as Octavian had ordered her to do] and she even begged him to ignore Antony's treatment of her, saying that it would be infamous if the two rulers of the world should plunge it into civil war for the sake of a woman. She confirmed her words by her deeds, and lived in her home just as if her husband were still there, caring not only for her own children, but also for those that Fulvia had borne him. Beyond this, she even received in Rome such friends as Antony sent to the capital, and helped them obtain audience with her brother. However, she was inadvertently damaging Antony by her conduct, since he now became hated for wronging such a fine woman. (Plutarch.)

The words one must suspect here are 'inadvertently damaging'. Octavia, however noble and good-hearted a woman she really was, undoubtedly took her cue from her brother. Roman matrons of that time whatever their class did what their menfolk told them to do – but especially in the ruling classes, where the politics of

188

Reconstruction of the Acropolis, Athens

power were so well understood. Octavia's behaviour must therefore be seen as conditioned by her brother's instructions and policy. She may have borne Antony three children, but it is doubtful whether she still loved him – especially after his treatment of her. But by acting the saintly and forgiving wife she helped to discredit him in the eyes of all Rome. Thus by first of all allowing her to go (or sending her) to Athens, and then by accepting her back to Rome as a wronged but forgiving woman, Octavian had twice outmanoeuvred his rival. On the surface Cleopatra had won, 'queen' had taken 'queen'. In actual fact Octavian, who was playing a very cool game, had moved himself into a position of great strength.

Yielding to Cleopatra and to the advice of her friends Antony now allowed himself to be led back to Alexandria and, for this year at least, to abandon his plans. The decline in his morale is obvious. Was this the man who claimed descent from Hercules, and who had been hailed as the God of War? Antony was a simple man and Cleopatra was a very clever woman, yet even so it is astonishing that he could have been taken in by her theatrical performance. One must conclude, therefore, not only that he was fascinated by Cleopatra, but that his physical health and moral fibre had weakened through his years of self-indulgence. Like many men in their mid–forties he had been used to abusing his health and strength, and could not now believe that they were declining.

It is hardly surprising that Antony's meek withdrawal from Syria in the wake of the Queen occasioned a lot of mocking comment in Rome. As was later to be said of Nelson, what was this hero doing 'inactive in a foreign court'? The people remembered the legend of Hercules and Omphale, the Queen of Lydia who had kept the hero in bondage to her for three years, doing women's tasks about her palace. Some years later Propertius was to write an elegy on the subject, and drinking vessels found in Italy, which were produced about this time, depict the legend. They were probably propaganda against Antony. Hercules rides in a chariot drawn by centaurs, but he is in a Greek woman's dress, while a maid-servant holds a parasol over his head. Another one waves a fan, and yet others are bringing him those traditional emblems of the housewife, a spindle and a skein of wool. Omphale, for her part, is borne in a chariot wearing the hero's helmet and lion-skin. In her left hand she holds the club of Hercules, and with her right she is reaching forward to grasp the hero's vast wine bowl. Antony had often been criticized in Italy for his general behaviour and conduct, but this criticism was usually good-natured for his virtues were seen to transcend his vices. Now he was being caricatured as a man gone soft and enslaved by a woman.

While Antony was withdrawing from his projected campaign Octavian, by contrast, had managed to solve one of his major problems: that he had too large an

Herodian wall, Jerusalem

army to keep inactive. He decided to use them in a large scale exercise and pacifying operation against the tribesmen of Illyria. This was a clever idea, since it removed them from Italy – where they might have become troublesome, gave them some battle-training, and provided new land to resettle the veterans. In this way Octavian dealt with several problems at one blow and gave the army commanders a chance to distinguish themselves. By successful conduct of the Illyrian campaign Octavian won himself considerable political capital with all classes in Rome. It was Antony's neglect of Rome which was to be his undoing, for only in Rome was political power to be found. Alexandria might be a finer city, but politically it meant nothing at all.

Antony spent the winter of 35–34 B.C. quietly in Alexandria. There are no more references to the 'Club of Inimitable Livers', or to any of the drunken escapades that had characterized his first winter in the city. He was seriously engaged in administering the affairs of the Eastern Empire. In this he showed that however much he had been influenced by Cleopatra to abandon both Octavia and the Parthian campaign, he was still very far from being entirely her creature – as he was subsequently depicted by impartial historians. His major problem at this time was the state of affairs in Judaea, and he and Cleopatra were in almost direct conflict in the solution of this.

Herod had married the beautiful Mariamne of the famous Maccabees family, whom he himself had driven from the throne. His marriage was certainly influenced by politics, for he hoped by this alliance to add lustre to his name, but he was also genuinely in love with Mariamne. His mother-in-law Alexandra, however, was a typical oriental woman ambitious of power for her children. Apart from this she almost certainly detested Herod for having usurped the throne that belonged to the Maccabees; at the very least she thought that the office of High Priest, which had been occupied for generations by the family, should go to her son. Since this office in Judaea was almost co-regnant with his own Herod naturally did not want to place Alexandra's son Aristobulus in a position where he and his mother would do all they could to unseat him. Alexandra, who knew Cleopatra's feelings about Herod, sent despatches to the Queen imploring her help in the matter of making Aristobulus High Priest. Cleopatra loved intrigue at all times – and intrigue that would unseat Herod and restore her friends the Maccabees was very much to her taste.

This time Antony demonstrated that he was quite capable of resisting Cleopatra's blandishments. He liked and respected Herod, and he had no intention of doing anything against him. Perhaps also he was determined to show the Queen that although he had yielded to her once it was he, and not she, who was running the Roman Empire of the East. The sequence of events as related by Josephus is as tortuous and involved as Daedalus's maze. It ended with Antony asking Herod to send Aristobulus to Alexandria; presumably to state his side of the case. This was something that Herod was unwilling to do, for he was sure that the combination of Cleopatra and Aristobulus could not possibly bode him any good, and thought that Antony might change his mind and restore the Maccabees. He yielded, therefore, to the pressure exerted by Cleopatra and his mother-in-law, and installed the young man in the office of High Priest. Aristobulus was not to hold it for long.

Disturbed by the concession that he had to make, Herod was determined that Aristobulus and Alexandra should be held as palace prisoners and not allowed to escape to Egypt where they might make common cause with Cleopatra against him. However (possibly at Cleopatra's instigation), they tried to have themselves smuggled out of Judaea into Egypt in two coffins. These were to be taken out of Herod's palace and then transferred to a waiting merchant ship. The whole episode smacks so much of the Queen's first visit to Julius Caesar that one cannot help but wonder whether she was not at the bottom of this audacious plan. Herod, whose intelligence service was one of the best in the world, got wind of the plot and had the 'bodies' removed before they could leave his kingdom. Probably only his regard for Antony and his fear of Cleopatra prevented him sending them to rejoin their coffins as genuine corpses.

Herod proceeded with apparent magnanimity to forgive both of them for the whole episode, and Aristobulus was confirmed as High Priest. It seemed that the Maccabees aided by the Queen of Egypt had won the day. Then a most mysterious accident occurred. At the Feast of the Tabernacles in Jerusalem the young High Priest (he was only seventeen) offered sacrifice, and was loudly acclaimed by the people as the descendant of the Maccabees and the rightful holder of his office. Immediately afterwards Herod and his family gave a banquet to celebrate the occasion; Aristobulus was naturally invited. During the course of the festivities, Herod, who was known to be fond of Greek gymnastics, asked Aristobulus to show him his prowess in this field. Complimenting him later he led the new High Priest to the fish-ponds in the palace gardens where a number of other youths were swimming. Aristobulus, naturally enough after his exercise, jumped in to cool off and the young men began playing games and ducking one another in the water. Suddenly – and to the greatest consternation of Herod – it was discovered that Aristobulus had not surfaced from this simple horseplay. He was later hauled out drowned. Perhaps it was not intentional, as was commonly said, but it was certainly more than convenient for Herod. In view of his record it is difficult not to suspect that the whole episode was a very carefully planned murder.

Alexandra was determined to be revenged for what she was quite convinced was murder. She sent urgent despatches to Cleopatra, imploring her to exert her influence and have Herod brought to trial. Antony, who was already making arrangements for a further campaign in the north, did no more than tell Herod that he wanted to meet him at Apamaea in Syria as soon as he arrived with his troops. It would seem that he never at any time intended to try his client, and Herod, after giving his explanation that the whole affair was an accident, was acquitted.

Antony's spring campaign was carried out with considerably less bluster and self-confidence than his previous expedition against the Parthians. He let it be known that it was against the Parthians that the troops would be marching, but he had in fact decided on a more limited objective, the kingdom of Armenia. That King

Artavasdes had let him down and failed to report to Alexandria when told to do so still rankled. Antony first tried to get the King into his hands by a ruse, but Artavasdes was too cunning to be taken. Accordingly Antony led the legions into Armenia, a large but relatively undefended country, and took the King prisoner. The Romans now indulged in an orgy of looting – desecrating ancient temples, melting down the statues of the gods for their gold and silver, as well as carrying off the royal treasure. Armenia henceforth was no longer to be a client-state, but a Roman province. It was not much of a victory, but at least it was something – and Antony badly needed a victory at this moment in his career.

He now managed to confirm his new alliance with the King of Media by the betrothal of his son Alexander Helios to the King's only daughter. This was a diplomatic success of the first order, for the King had no sons. It meant that Antony's son would become King of Media, uniting this very important piece of territory to the Eastern Empire. Despatches were sent to Rome announcing the successful conclusion of the campaign and the news that the Empire now had another province. To some extent this compensated for Octavian's victory over Pompey and his excursion into Illyria. But the truth was that campaigns in the distant East meant very little to the citizens of Rome. They could readily appreciate the effects of the elimination of Pompey's fleet, and the solution of the resettlement of veteran legionaries. However, they looked forward to Antony's return to Rome. They expected that he would celebrate his triumph over Armenia with the usual lavish spectacles, free banquets, games and public entertainments. Octavia may have hoped that after his return he would resume his life with her and the children. Octavian certainly cannot have been pleased by the news, but he had by now established himself so firmly in the seat of government and in public estimation that his position, in Italy at least, was unassailable.

Cast from a pottery mould manufactured at Arretium, Etruria. The subject matter, inspired by the notoriety of Antony and Cleopatra, is Hercules ensnared by Omphale.

EMPIRE OF THE EAST

Antony now committed the most impolitic act of his life. In the autumn of 34 B.C., having returned with the legions, the slaves and the loot of Armenia (together with the whole of the royal family), he set about celebrating a Triumph in Alexandria. This was something that had never happened before in Roman history. A Triumph was decreed by the Senate, after an investigation of the records of the campaign. It was the highest honour that the state could confer upon any man, and it was a uniquely Roman institution. To decree oneself a Triumph out of hand and to hold it in the capital of a foreign country was to insult Rome, the Roman people, and the whole of the nation.

What could possibly excuse such conduct? To the Romans Antony's behaviour merely confirmed the tale that he was infatuated with this eastern Queen. To the rich and influential class it was seen as an unforgivable slight, while to the general public it was infuriating since it deprived them of the free feasts and festivals that were by right inalienably theirs on such occasions. It is interesting to speculate on the reasons for Antony's action. It was natural enough that he would wish to return to Egypt laden with the spoils of war, and to efface in the country's memory the failure of his Parthian campaign. (In his previous despatches to Octavian he had made out that it had been a success. Why had he not asked for a Triumph then?) His reasons must have been twofold: a desire to please Cleopatra and to say in effect this is my real wife, and a desire to say Alexandria is the real capital of the Empire – Rome is eclipsed.

It was probably the suspicion that this was in Julius Caesar's mind that had prompted his murder. Certainly it was always Cleopatra's wish that her beloved city should become the capital of the world with Rome demoted to second place. Alexandria, apart from its planned spaciousness and its importance as the main trading centre with the East, had many things to commend it as the capital of the Roman Empire. As the Emperor Constantine was to find several centuries later when he founded his new capital city of Constantinople at Byzantium on the Bosporos, the main wealth of the Empire derived from the East, and so did its major preoccupations. Gaul, obscure Britain, even mineral-rich Spain, let alone untamed Germany, were of comparatively little account when compared with the rich countries of the East which had been civilized for centuries. It was not only their territorial extent that gave them their value; over all of them was spread that Hellenistic culture which was the foremost in the Mediterranean world. They were rich in gold, silver, gems, and artefacts like linen and sail-cloth, Tyrian dyes, Egyptian glass and papyrus, and their systems of learning such as mathematics and astronomy were far in advance of anything to be found in Italy.

Alexandria had a further geographical advantage over Rome. As Arthur Weigall comments:

> From Alexandria, a march of six hundred or eight hundred miles brought one to Antioch or Tarsus; whereas Rome was nearly three times as far from these great centres. The southern Peloponnesus was, by way of Crete, considerably nearer to Alexandria than it was to Rome by way of Brundisium. Ephesus and other cities of Asia Minor could be reached more quickly by land or sea from Egypt than they could from Rome. Rhodes, Lycia, Bithynia, Galatia, Pamphylia, Cilicia, Cappadocia, Pontus, Armenia, Commagene, Crete, Cyprus and many other great and important lands, were all closer to Alexandria than Rome; while Thrace and Byzantium were about equidistant from either capital.

It was the evident superiority of Alexandria that made the citizens of Rome so jealous of the eastern capital. They were extremely sensitive about their rights as citizens, and indeed had not granted Roman citizenship to the other inhabitants of Italy until compelled to do so by force. The idea that their capital should become second to any other was unthinkable. (It was rather like telling a modern Londoner

Silver-gilt bowl from Boscoreale, with Africa personified as a woman (perhaps in the likeness of Cleopatra VII), end of 1st century B.C.; 9 inches in diameter

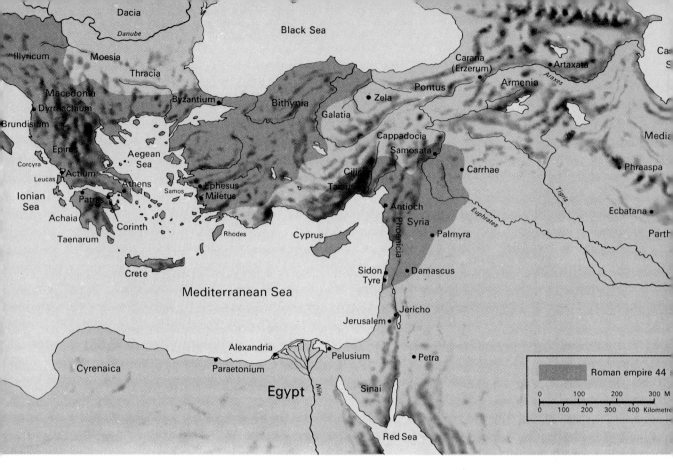

ABOVE: *The Eastern Empire in 44 B.C.*
OPPOSITE: *relief of Dionysus*

or New Yorker that Naples is now the capital of the western world.) This resentment, this detestation of the Eastern encroachment, was one of the reasons why the legions were so fervently behind Octavian in the forthcoming conflict. In his propaganda he was skilful to point out the whole non-Roman 'foreignness' of the East – all those Princes and Potentates, Kings (ever a bad word), and at their head a Woman, a Queen, followed by a dog-like, devoted Antony, a Roman who had lost all shame.

The Triumph which Antony now so rashly celebrated in Alexandria was a unique spectacle even in that ostentatious city. Leading the procession came a body of Roman legionaries bearing on their shields the large letter C, which some said stood for Cleopatra, and others for Caesar. Either of these was an offence in Roman eyes, for only Octavian, by benefit of Julius Caesar's will, had the right to bear the name of Caesar. On the other hand if it stood for Cleopatra it was unthinkable that Roman soldiers should bear the initial of a foreign monarch as though they owed allegiance to her and not to Rome. These troops were followed by units of the Egyptian army, contingents from the allies and client-states of the Empire, and then by the Armenian prisoners, among them Artavasdes in golden chains, accompanied by his wife and

196

children. Behind these again came the usual procession of carriages laden with the the spoils of war, captured insignia, and objects from the Armenian treasury. These were followed in their turn by deputies from the various vassal cities, each bearing a golden crown that their municipalities had awarded to Antony. Finally there came the victor himself in his elaborate chariot, dressed not as he would have been in Rome as a general, but in the guise of Dionysus, bearing the god's thyrsus (a reed tipped with a spear point, and with a pine cone at the top) and wearing the god's garland of ivy. Antony was celebrating an Egyptian Triumph for the Egyptian, Greek and other peoples of the East, and was appearing as he was known in Alexandria. Once again he had as it were discarded Rome.

The procession made its way through the principal areas of the city so that the majority of the inhabitants could enjoy the new splendour that Antony and his Queen were conferring upon them and Egypt. Starting most probably from the Lochias Palace it will certainly have moved through the Forum, thence into the great thoroughfare of Canopus, and past the artificial hill of Pan. Eventually it reached the Street of Serapis, at the far end of which stood the Serapeum, the elaborate temple to the principal god of the city. Serapis has been called 'the only god ever successfully made by modern man'. He was a creation of the Ptolemies. 'He became', as Sir William Tarn writes, 'the Greek god of Alexandria, whose great cult-statue, with its golden head and jewelled eyes gleaming from its darkened shrine, became one of the chief glories of that city.'

On the raised ground where the Serapeum stood were grouped Cleopatra, her

court officials and the principal dignitaries of Alexandria. The Queen was seated on a golden throne with the priests of Serapis on either side of her waiting for the moment when Antony should make his way into the temple to sacrifice to the god who had brought him victory. Antony now dismounted from his chariot and went into the temple to perform his religious duties. If this whole action in holding his Triumph in Alexandria had been designed to infuriate the Romans and to proclaim that theirs was only a second-rate city, his sacrificing to Serapis was the final insult. By long tradition just as a Triumph could only be held in Rome at the decree of the Senate so a victorious general always made a solemn procession to the temple of Jupiter Capitolinus. Consuls entering upon their office always sacrificed to Jupiter Capitolinus, who determined the course of all human affairs, and who was Imperator, Victor and Invictus. To equate this eastern god Serapis with the principal god of the Roman pantheon and the special protector of the city itself, was to say: 'Serapis is the patron of Alexandria. I have won a victory in the East. This is, therefore, in the province of Serapis. Since Alexandria is destined to be the capital city, I shall pay my respects to her titulary god – and not to Jupiter Capitolinus in secondary Rome.' Whether such were really his intentions or not, or whether this was how his action was interpreted by those who were in favour of Octavian, the fact remains that this was the way Antony's behaviour was construed by the citizens of Rome. He had deliberately insulted the capital city, the Motherland and the gods of the Italian people.

At the conclusion of a Triumph in Rome it was, as has been seen in the case of the unfortunate Vercingetorix, the custom to put the conquered monarch to death. Antony and Cleopatra were more kind towards their late enemy in their Egyptian Triumph – and this despite the fact that the royal family declined to kneel in homage before the Queen. When told by his guards to abase himself before Cleopatra Artavasdes refused to do so, but merely addressed her by her name. It might have been expected that this would have been quite enough to lead to his execution, but it seems that both Antony and Cleopatra were touched by his nobility of bearing. He and his family were not harmed, but treated with honour, only being held as state prisoners in Alexandria. Artavasdes was no barbarian king, but a man of considerable refinement, a poet and a playwright among other things. Antony, for all his faults, was never a cruel or vindictive man but, as he often demonstrated in his life, both generous and kindly. If Artavasdes had fallen into the hands of Octavian he would have received very different treatment. The latter was nicknamed by his enemies The Executioner on account of the numbers of people whom he had tortured or crucified.

Shortly afterwards an extension, as it were, of the Triumph was held in the great Gymnasium near the tomb of Alexander the Great in the presence of the city functionaries, the army and an immense crowd of Alexandrians. It was a unique spectacle, eclipsing even the Triumph. On a silver dais erected in the centre of the stadium two golden thrones had been set, with four smaller golden thrones around

Bronze statuette of Zeus–Serapis, 2nd century A.D.; *2½ inches high*

them. Antony and Cleopatra took their seats on the two thrones, while the four others were occupied by the thirteen-year-old Caesarion, Cleopatra's twins by Antony – the six-year-old Alexander Helios and his sister Cleopatra Selene, and the little two-year-old Ptolemy Philadelphus. A dynasty was being proclaimed.

Antony as Dionysus and Cleopatra as Isis were making it known, not only to the Greco-Egyptian population, but to the Roman legionaries and beyond them to Rome itself, that the Empire of the East was a separate entity. It was not governed by Rome, but ruled from Alexandria by divine god-kings and goddess-queens on the Pharaonic and Ptolemaic system. If Antony's holding the Armenian Triumph in Alexandria was a challenge to Octavian's position as co-ruler of the Roman world, the ceremony that now took place was a direct statement that Antony considered himself and his Queen-Wife Cleopatra sole rulers of the eastern half of the Empire. Where this challenge contained a certain absurdity was in the fact that it was the Roman legions, far more than the troops of the client states, that made the whole thing possible. To alienate Rome would ultimately mean to alienate the generals, officers and legionaries who represented Rome in the eastern Mediterranean.

When everybody was assembled, Antony arose to address them. If Egypt was to be his base, it was essential that he should impress the people – the Alexandrians that is, for the peasantry counted for little or nothing – as to his standing in the world and the benefits that he was about to confer upon Greco-Roman Egypt. His success in Armenia had given him 'the lever' with which, in Archimedes' phrase, 'to move the world'. Cleopatra was proclaimed Queen of Egypt, Cyprus, Libya and the southern part of Syria. Caesarion was named co-regent of these areas, and given the title (so dear in the East) of King of Kings. Caesarion, according to Suetonius, was the very image of his father, and might possibly, if things had gone differently, have made an excellent ruler of the whole Roman world. It is curious to think of Antony conferring upon Caesar's son by Cleopatra so grandiose a title, but it must be borne in mind that the whole episode was no more than a piece of statecraft, and the execution of a carefully-thought-out plan to remove from Octavian the richest part of the Empire and to give room for Antony to manoeuvre against his rival. The portions of the Empire assigned to the twins, Alexander Helios and Cleopatra Selene, were to the former Armenia and Media (on the basis of the boy's marriage to the daughter of the Median King) and all the territories beyond the Euphrates. This meant in effect the kingdom of Parthia, which still remained to be conquered. His sister Selene was given the rule of Cyrenaica and as much of Libya and other adjacent parts of North Africa as were within Antony's control. Little Ptolemy Philadelphus, the two-year-old, was proclaimed King of northern Syria and Cilicia. For the occasion Caesarion, one may assume, was in Roman or Greek dress, but Antony's children by Cleopatra were arrayed in the costume of the countries that they were one day to govern. Thus Alexander Helios was in the Persian style of clothing which was also worn in Armenia and Media: trousers, a flowing cloak over a sleeved tunic and a tiara on his head from which hung (like an Arab burnous) a cloth flap to cover the neck. His infant brother was dressed in Macedonian costume with the boots of Macedonia, a purple cloak, and the Macedonian cap with a diadem around it. Even this last was a political act, for Antony was asserting that Macedonia (a Roman province although within his sphere of influence) was going to have a king one day.

On the face of it Antony had almost eclipsed Alexander the Great and furthermore he could say that through his succession he intended to enlarge the Eastern Empire even more and to hold it through Caesar's and his children as a divine monarchy quite separate from the world of Rome. Politically the most important part of this ceremony was Antony's acceptance of Caesarion as Caesar's son by giving him precedence over his and Cleopatra's own children. Octavian had become through Caesar's will his adopted son and rightful successor to all that Caesar had achieved, and senior member of the Julian clan. But Antony by this act was declaring that Octavian was no more than a usurper, and that this child of Caesar's flesh and blood was the rightful inheritor of all the Western Empire as well as the one that Antony was holding and creating in the East. In those days, when the media of propaganda were limited, and when the bulk of the people were illiterate, it was necessary by such simple, visual exhibitions to get a message across to the public as to the policy that the ruler intended to pursue. Lampoons, poems, coins and theatrical sketches were also used throughout the ancient world to present the people with the ruler's intentions and diplomacy.

At the end of this much publicised ceremony Cleopatra's children saluted their parents, and were escorted from the stadium by bodyguards dressed in the costume of the various countries which had been assigned to them. Coins were struck to commemorate the occasion, bearing Cleopatra's head and the inscription 'Cleopatra, Queen of Kings, and of her sons the Kings'. On the other side was the head of Antony wearing the Armenian crown, with the inscription, 'Armenia is conquered'. Antony of course could not and did not want to keep this occasion secret from Rome. He sent despatches to Octavian recording the changes he had made in the distribution of the Empire. The news was received with both astonishment and indignation. Octavian made good political use out of it, having the contents of Antony's despatches made public so that the people could see for themselves what Octavian's partner was up to in the East. Not only was he calling his children, and the 'so-called' child of Julius Caesar, Kings, but he was also calling himself a King, and Cleopatra his Queen. The 'African Problem' – formerly Carthage – was once more seen to be raising its head. No doubt every means was used to equate Cleopatra with Dido, the founder of Carthage. This Eastern Queen, it was said, had suborned Antony, and Antony was portrayed as rolling in drunkenness from one orgy to another.

In the propaganda struggle that now took place, presaging the real struggle that was to follow, not all the cards were in Octavian's hands. Antony could point to the fact that he had achieved his Armenian victory without the twenty thousand men that Octavian had promised him at Tarentum, while Octavian's triumph over Sextus Pompeius was largely due to the ships that Antony, faithful to his part of the bargain, had made available to him. Then, too, Antony had never been consulted about the situation after the conquest of Sicily. 'After taking Sicily away from Pompey', writes Plutarch, 'Caesar [Octavian] had not assigned part of the island to him. Furthermore he had not returned all the ships that he had borrowed for the war; and, thirdly, after depriving Lepidus of his office and degrading him, he was keeping for himself not only the army, but the revenue and territories that had been assigned to Lepidus. . . .' All this was true enough and Antony did have genuine cause for complaint. He, in his turn, had not assigned any part of Armenia to Octavian. To this charge he could reply that he would have done so if his share of the Sicilian territory had been forthcoming.

The year 34 B.C. was an important one in Cleopatra's life. She was confirmed as the Queen of immense territories, and seen openly as Antony's wife and the mother of his children. How much of the statecraft involved in the establishment of the Eastern Empire was hers and how much was Antony's is open to question. Antony was ambitious certainly, but he rarely showed much capacity as a statesman. It seems more than likely that the woman who had successfully prevented him from seeing her rival Octavia and who had lured him back from Syria was responsible.

SHIPS AND THE MEN

In the early months of 33 B.C. it became increasingly clear that the uneasy alliance between Octavian and Antony could not last much longer. The rejection of Octavia, the Alexandrian Triumph, followed by the redistribution of the Eastern Empire (known in Rome as 'The Donations'), were evidence that Antony meant to run for power alone, and in the same way that Caesar had done. The Egyptian Queen was inevitably seen as the storm centre of this movement. She was using Antony just as she had Caesar as the basis of her claim to becoming Empress of the whole Roman world. The one great difference, and one which the Roman people almost certainly did not appreciate, was that Caesar had quite coolly 'used' her. The case of Antony was quite different. It was the ability of Octavian's propaganda to point out Cleopatra's hand in Mediterranean affairs that was so damaging to his rival. The idea of a woman manipulating Rome and the Empire was intolerable. A Roman woman would have been bad enough, but an Eastern Queen, an Egyptian, an Oriental (the fact that she was Macedonian Greek could easily be forgotten), the product of numberless incestuous unions – this was something that could not be borne.

The Roman historian Florus writing a century later perpetuated the hostile (and largely untrue) portrait of Cleopatra that had grown up over the years:

> As the price of her love she demanded from her drunken general the whole Roman Empire. Antony promised it to her, just as if Rome was easier to conquer than the Parthians. . . . Forgetful of his name, his country, his Roman toga, and the insignia of his office, he had completely degenerated in feeling, outlook, and even dress, into that monster with whom we are all familiar. A sceptre of gold was in his hand, a scimitar at his side. He wore robes of purple embellished with large jewels, and on his head a crown, so that he might be shown to be a king beside the Queen he loved.

Octavian was steadily consolidating his hold upon the Roman people. Between 35 and 33 B.C. he conducted a series of campaigns in Illyria in the course of which he extended the frontiers of the Empire and planted several new garrison towns. All this was good both strategically and politically. Strategically because he was barring Antony from the coastline from which he could invade Italy, and politically because the results of his success were immediately evident to the Romans. In January 33 B.C., in the annual Senate debate on 'The State of the Republic', for the first time he openly took the initiative against Antony. He criticized him for his conduct of affairs in the East and particularly for his manner of recognizing these areas which were so important to the Empire. He further increased his standing in Rome by returning to the city standards that had been lost in earlier campaigns in Illyria, housing them in a large hall which he erected on the site of one that had been built by his ancestors. New aqueducts were constructed, public buildings renovated, and streets and squares which had become dilapidated during the civil wars were restored and improved. His clear intention of making Rome not only the equal, but superior to any other city in the world, was a sign to the people – and to Antony – that the claims of Alexandria were discounted.

The news of Octavian's public attack upon him reached Antony in Alexandria, and he immediately retorted in a letter, part of which is quoted by Suetonius: 'Why this change of attitude? Because I sleep with the Queen? But she's my wife. Besides, what's new about it? This all started nine years ago. Do you only sleep with Livia? By the time you read this letter I'd be surprised if you haven't slept with Tertulla and Terentilla and Rufilla and Salvia Titisenia, or the lot of them together. In any case, does it really matter with whom one copulates?' Even if the rest of his life were not evidence enough, this fragment would be quite sufficient to expunge any idea that Antony was 'the great romantic lover'.

After this exchange it was plain to all in the know that it was only a matter of time before the two rivals came into open conflict. From 34 B.C. onwards the whole Mediterranean world stirred uneasily and, as always when a war was impending, the rumour of it was first heard in the shipyards. Caulkers and ropemakers, ship-wrights and carpenters, sailmakers and riggers, all by their increased activity revealed that the battle for the world would soon be joined. As has been seen Octavian had acquired, largely through the brilliant activities of Agrippa, a sizeable and efficient fleet. The Egyptian navy, however, was still second to none and Antony had within his sphere of influence the sailors of Greece and in particular of the island of Rhodes. Since the struggle between Octavian and Antony would largely be decided upon the sea it is important to have some idea of the types of ships and of the men who manned them.

The Romans themselves were never sailors at heart, as of necessity were the inhabitants of Greece. Not unlike most modern Italians they regarded the sea with considerable mistrust and, as Gibbon remarks, 'to the Romans, the ocean remained an object of terror rather than of curiosity'. In his study *The History of Roman Sea-Power* Professor Thiel observes:

> The sea as a sentimental frame, as a sounding-board for the sensations of the lonely human being on the beach is found in the poems of Catullus and others. . . . And yet, however delicately and sensitively these things may have been worded and voiced by many a Roman poet, the fact remains that their effusions are utterances of the observer on the beach, who is lonely perhaps, but at heart feels safe and comfortable, and not of the man who has conquered the sea or rather, in a continuous fearful struggle, shares his life with her.

Phoenician war-galley, clearly showing two banks of oars and the ram. Detail from the reliefs in the palace of Sennacherib at Ninevah depicting his campaigns; c. 700 B.C.

The Romans had taken to the sea by *force majeure* during their conflict with Carthage. They had based their first warships on the lines of a captured Carthaginian vessel and had evolved the technique of grappling their opponents. Unlike the Greeks, a nation of seamen who regarded service in their navy as the natural duty of the citizen, the Romans considered that legionary service was an honourable duty but that service at sea was no more than a necessary evil. To supplement this deficiency in their character the Romans relied almost entirely for their seamen, oarsmen and sailors upon their foreign allies. In fact the phrase *'socii navales'*, naval allies, came to be generally used for sailors.

Rhodes and Pergamum, both of which were important naval states, provided a great part of the Roman navy, while the Greeks who had been settled in southern Italy long before the rise of Rome supplied a contingent from the homeland. Even the defeated Carthaginians, as well as other Semites from Syria and the Lebanon, made their contribution to the Roman navy. It is an astonishing fact but, to quote Professor Thiel again: 'Up to the age of Caracalla you will find among the naval personnel of Misenum and Ravenna no Roman citizens, no Italians, and during the whole imperial age naval service was regarded as inferior to service in the land army, exactly as had been the case in republican times.'

In the age of Cleopatra the Mediterranean was regularly traversed not only by oared galleys but by large sailing vessels, some as big as one thousand tons. Among the largest were the Egyptian grain ships which made regular passages between Alexandria and Rome. It has been deduced that at least thirty different types of vessel were active upon the sea. Cleopatra will have been familiar with many of them as she gazed out from her palace on Lochias promontory. There were *Barides*, the big Egyptian cargo-carriers, and *Camarae*, small open boats that could hold about twenty-five men. *Celoces*, which were fast cutters, were used as despatch boats for fleet communications. *Cercuri*, which possibly hailed from Corcyra, were oared vessels that could be used either for cargo-carrying or as war galleys. *Corbitae* were large Roman vessels almost entirely dependent upon sail. One of these is on record as having carried as many as six hundred passengers. From Syria and ancient Phoenicia there came the cargo-carrying *Gauloi* (literally, tubs) and from the Adriatic the *Lembi*, small swift warships, but unlike war galleys in having no ram on their bows. Light, fast vessels used for scouting and shadowing duties were known as *Speculatoriae* (spies). The Roman author Vegetius in a treatise on warfare describes how these were carefully painted so as to be inconspicuous – an early example of warship camouflage. 'Their sails and ropes are dyed blue, the colour of sea-water; and even the wax with which the hull is painted is similarly coloured, while the soldiers and sailors aboard them likewise dye their clothes.'

The principal warship was the bireme, propelled by two banks of oars. It had changed little since its evolution in Greece during the great days of Salamis and the war against the Persians. For a time the trireme with three banks of oars had super-seded it, but it was found that in the long run the bireme was just as fast and a great deal more manoeuvrable. To quote Gibbon again: 'Experience seems at length to have convinced the ancients that as soon as their galleys exceeded two, or rather at the most three, ranks of oars, they were suited rather for vain pomp than for real service.'

Some of the ships in Cleopatra's navy were, as has been seen, designed for 'vain pomp', but the warships which she was to contribute to Antony's cause were very far from being ineffective. Indeed, with their Greek crews, the Alexandrian contin-gent was probably one of the best afloat. They were large, heavily timbered biremes, equipped with fighting castles from which arrows and other projectiles could be hurled at the enemy while grapnels could be cast by catapults to secure the opposing ship alongside. Agrippa, who was mainly responsible for Octavian's ultimate success, had decided after his victory over Pompey to invest in a lighter type of warship. These were known as Liburnians after a district in Illyria on the Adriatic where they had been evolved over the centuries by the local seamen who were famous for their skill in seamanship and navigation. They were also built with two banks of oars, but were designed for speed and manoeuvrability whether under oar or canvas. Having been built for the stormy Adriatic where the north wind, the Bora, can sometimes blow at one hundred knots, and manned by the natives of that rugged coastline, the Liburnian was probably the finest warship of its time.

ABOVE: *head of Agrippa*
OPPOSITE: *geometric representation of a Greek galley showing the underwater ram, from a vase, 8th century* B.C.

Indeed, the term *Liburna* ultimately became standard throughout the Roman world for any two-banked vessel. Although triremes and even quinquiremes continued to be used it was the light bireme of the *Liburna* type that formed the backbone of the navy. Imperial Rome, which was unchallenged on the Mediterranean sea, needed chiefly a navy of 'frigates' and the Liburnian supplied the answer.

Sea battles were still, as in the days of classical Greece, fought by biremes which had a long underwater ram constructed at the bows for punching a hole in the enemy's side. At the same time the Romans, because of their disinclination for sea warfare always tended to try and grapple their opponent and use the fighting power of their legionaries. (Similar in later centuries were the men of the Spanish Empire who were soldiers first and foremost and who, when confronted by the English or the Dutch, tried to redress the balance by fighting something akin to a land action.) The bireme was not only an oared vessel but when on passage stepped a mast on which was set a square sail. This, while of no use if the wind came from anywhere forward of the beam, was quite efficient when the wind came from any points aft. It enabled the galley to be driven at a speed of six knots or more, while at the same time giving the oarsmen a chance to take a rest. Most sea travel was still confined to the months between spring and autumn, all the galleys being hauled ashore for repair and refit over the winter months. In the case of the war galley it was still customary to unstep the mast and remove the sails and sailing gear before going into battle, since they tended to get in the way of the fighting men. This was the main reason why practically all ancient sea battles took place within a few miles of the coast. The galley was there to cover the transhipment of troops, who were themselves carried in heavy and somewhat unwieldy transports. Time and again one reads how the sailors landed the sailing equipment on some adjacent beach before action was commenced. As will be seen, the curious factor in the Battle of Actium was that Antony's and Cleopatra's warships put to sea to engage those of Octavian with their masts, spars and sails on board.

When it came to military operations the basic unit of the Roman army anywhere in the world was the legion. This was generally a division of about four thousand five hundred men, some three thousand of whom were heavily armed infantry while the remainder was made up of lightly armed infantry, slingers and cavalry. The legionary, who was to dominate the world for so many centuries, was originally recruited from those Roman citizens who had some private means. To quote F. J. Haverfield: 'For battle they were divided into one thousand two hundred

207

hastati, one thousand two hundred *principes* and six hundred *triarii*: all had a large shield, metal helmet, leather cuirass, short Spanish thrusting and cutting sword, and in addition the *hastati* and the *principes* each carried two heavy throwing spears *(pila)* while the *triarii* had ordinary long spears.'

The basic principle on which the legions were operated in combat was in sub-units known as maniples, usually of about one hundred and twenty men. These were deployed somewhat in the fashion of a draughts board so that the front rank could retire when necessary through the second without disordering it, while the second in its turn advanced. The first routine part of an action was for the front rank to hurl their *pila* at the enemy. These spears were designed so that if they were caught on the opponent's shield their metal necks bent and caused the man either to fall or to discard his shield, at which point the legionary would be at him with his sword. The second rank would repeat this process if necessary, while the third rank with their long spears formed the reserve. Discipline was the basis of the Roman army and the reason for its conquest of the ancient world. Gauls, Germans and Parthians were every whit as brave but they tended to operate in a disorganized fashion which made them only too vulnerable to the cool precision of the Romans. The main weakness of the legions – as had been shown in their actions against the Parthians – was that they were particularly susceptible to the guerilla-like activities of horsemen armed with the bow and arrow.

These were the instruments with which Octavian and Antony now confronted each other across the Mediterranean. Neither had much advantage in quantity, but in quality it is probable that Octavian was superior. None of his troops had recently suffered the demoralization of a defeat as Antony's had done, and most of them were native-born Romans whereas Antony's were, apart from the Roman legions, a heterogeneous collection from provinces and client states.

In terms of the private lives of the two men who were so soon to challenge one another Antony, for all his faults, seems to emerge the better. True he was a heavy drinker, a buffoon, and had let his position go to his head, but he was also kind hearted and always generous to a fault. Octavian on the other hand had a sly and secretive nature. Sexually he was just as promiscuous as Antony had ever been. An interesting fact is that the only charge Octavian makes in his propaganda against Antony is his relationship with the Queen of Egypt. It seems as if Antony had indeed turned over a new leaf and become faithful to one woman. But Octavian was widely rumoured to have innumerable mistresses, to send emissaries into the streets of Rome to find women to amuse him, and even to take the wives of his friends out from dinner parties into his sleeping quarters if he found them attractive. Cool and dispassionate, Octavian was superior to Antony in that he knew exactly what he wanted – power. Antony, although he too wanted the dominion of the world, was a prey to ease and self-indulgence. Out of the three, Octavian, Cleopatra and Antony, the last-named emerges as the pleasantest character, but also, as is so often the case, the weakest.

'THE KING
WITH HALF THE EAST AT HEEL....'

Even though Octavian had managed to attain a considerable amount of favour with the Roman masses he was still largely unpopular among the upper classes. In the year 32 B.C. both of the consuls, Caius Sosius and Domitius Ahenobarbus, were open supporters of Antony. As was customary at the beginning of the new year, when the consuls took up their term of office, the debate in the Senate was on the general subject of the 'State of the Republic'. It might have been expected in view of his recent successes in Illyria together with his amelioration of Roman affairs and improvements in Italy generally that Octavian would have got a more than favourable reception. He knew however the strength of the opposition against him and wisely stayed away from the Senate meeting. (He would find out by report exactly who were his enemies and who his friends.) Sosius in his speech used the occasion to make an outright attack on Octavian, saying among other things that Antony was prepared to drop his office of Triumvir if Octavian would do the same. This meant nothing in effect since Antony was already lording it in the East, but it was a deliberate appeal to republican feeling in the Senate. At the end of his speech Sosius even went so far as to suggest that Octavian should be relieved of command of the army, a request that was immediately vetoed by one of the tribunes.

Octavian's response to this personal attack upon him was to appear at a subsequent meeting of the Senate surrounded by his supporters, all of whom carried weapons beneath their togas, and clearly did not bother too much about concealing them. He then began a speech of open abuse of Antony, declaring that his 'Donations' of the Eastern Empire to Cleopatra and her children were an insult to Rome. This was indeed true, and Octavian knew well that he could count upon a majority of the Senate feeling the same way. Even Sosius did not dare to reply to Octavian's accusations for he had Antony's letter and he was perfectly well aware of the way in which the East had been distributed. Octavian's authority backed by his show of arms cowed the already demoralized Senate. Caesar had treated the senators like lackeys and had paid for doing so, but it was Octavian who now proclaimed the principle that was to dominate the Roman Empire – that the Senate was no more than a rubber stamp in the hand of the supreme man. The dangerous word 'King' would be heard no more in Roman history, but the Dictator and Emperor, two concepts again deriving from Caesar, were now established. The Republic was at an end. Many of the Senators, together with the two consuls, Sosius and Domitius

Ahenobarbus, realized that their lives were in danger and that it was only a question of time before open war was declared between Octavian and Antony. All Antony's supporters including the two consuls now fled from Rome and made their way to join him in the East.

Antony and Cleopatra were at Ephesus, one of the most famous Greek cities on the coast of Asia Minor. The patron goddess of the city was Artemis, or 'Diana of the Ephesians' as she is later called, a sophisticated evolution of the primitive Mother Goddess who had long flourished in Asia and who had indeed once dominated nearly all the Mediterranean basin. The magnificent shrine, the Artemision, a Hellenistic temple erected upon the site of numerous temples before it, with its columns over sixty feet high, was one of the wonders of the ancient world comparable with the Pyramids and the Pharos of Alexandria. It was here in Ephesus that Antony was busy assembling his army and his fleet for the forthcoming contest against Octavian. It seemed likely that he would win. He had all the wealth of the East behind him, and the Queen of the richest country in that area was his wife. He had the finest sailors from the Greek archipelago and all the shipbuilding resources of Greece, Asia Minor and Egypt. He had over fifty thousand Roman legionaries and about eighty thousand infantry and cavalry from the eastern provinces. Ships were being built on the neighbouring island of Cos, and from all the East other ships and troops were assembling. Cleopatra herself had brought the Egyptian fleet, a large sum of money for paying the troops, grain, clothing and arms. The impending battle was seen as being between the East and the West: between Rome which had always exploited its provinces and threatened its client states, and Alexandria the centre of the Hellenistic civilization and culture.

The arrival of the two consuls together with over three hundred senators, out of a body of one thousand, gave Antony some judicial grounds for declaring that the Senate in Rome was not the true representative of the Roman people. Octavian and his supporters' vote to deprive Antony of his consulship and triumviral power for the year 31 B.C. was thus declared null and void. Antony formed his own 'senate' in Ephesus, intimating that the new Rome was to be established in the East. He failed to see that his actions were bound to estrange him from the Italian people, and that it was in Italy that real political power was to be found.

What caused some immediate consternation among the self-exiled consuls and senators was the discovery of the important part that Cleopatra played in the strategies of the impending war. They had thought of her as Antony's mistress or even his wife, but they had not envisaged that it was she more than Antony who was in command of the whole affair. The rulers of the East who now hastened to Antony's side were not doing so out of any love of Rome or the Italian people. The Kings of Cappadocia, Cilicia, Paphlagonia and Pontus, Amyntas of Galicia, King Mithridates of Commagene, Sadalas and Rhoemetalces of Thrace, and Bogud of Mauretania – what did they care about Roman senators or the Roman people? It was against Rome that they were taking up arms, against the dominance

Marble head of Artemis in archaic style, 1st century B.C.; 1 foot 1 inch high

imposed upon them by this distant Latin people. Antony by his association with Cleopatra represented for them a new power arisen in the East which would eventually enable them to rule the world.

On the surface the justification for the war against Octavian seems to have lain in young Caesarion. From the moment that Antony had made Caesarian co-equal with Cleopatra in the affairs of the East and had declared him Caesar's real son he had said in effect that Octavian's claim to be Caesar's heir was illegitimate and that the latter was no more than a usurper. But the kings and princes who now prepared to embark on a war against Octavian could not have cared very much about the legality of either Octavian's or Caesarion's position. What they wanted to see was the overthrow of Rome and the establishment of an eastern monarchy with its capital in Alexandria and its subsidiary administrative centres in cities like Antioch and Ephesus. Dio Cassius in his *History of Rome* confirms that the real cause of the war between Octavian and Antony was the latter's recognition of Caesarion's legitimacy and therefore of his right to Caesar's inheritance. Among all the potentates who now flocked to Antony's standard there was one notable absentee, the very man whom Antony had always favoured and who might have been expected to be the first to join him – King Herod of Judaea. The latter, who was among the most consummate politicians of his time, was at this moment engaged in a war against the neighbouring Arabs. Some historians have suggested that he may have been thus involved at the instigation of Cleopatra – anxious to deprive her enemy of any share in the forthcoming triumph. Knowing what one does about Herod it seems much more likely that he was sitting on the sidelines. He was shown to have been wise, and his absence from the gathering at Ephesus was to secure him the permanent rulership of his country.

'Eight hundred fighting ships,' says Plutarch, 'together with merchant vessels, of which Cleopatra provided two hundred, together with twenty thousand talents and supplies for the whole army during the war' were now assembling at Ephesus. Cleopatra is said to have remarked often during these days when asked for her affirmation on any subject, 'It is as sure as the fact that I shall one day administer justice from the Capitol'. She felt quite secure now that the position she had been deprived of by Caesar's assassination would shortly be hers through the victory of Antony. She and her burly soldier-husband would be Emperor and Empress of the known world, and her child by Caesar would be their inheritor, while her children by Antony would rule nearly all the East. But autocratic queens were not to the taste of the newly arrived Roman senators. Once again Antony's failure was principally a political one.

Domitius Ahenobarbus was one of the first and foremost to show that he did not recognize Cleopatra's position in the armed camp that Ephesus had now become. Ahenobarbus came of a famous old republican family and he had joined Antony largely because he thought there was more chance of the republic being restored under him than under Octavian who had so swiftly assumed Caesar's mantle. To show that he did not accept kings, queens and princes he resolutely refused to give Cleopatra her title, but when addressing her merely called her by her name. It seems he also said to Antony that Cleopatra was a serious drawback to his cause. In any case there was no place for women in military operations and she should go back to Egypt and stay there until the issue was decided. Domitius Ahenobarbus was an old friend of Antony's, and Antony's elder daughter by Octavia was betrothed to his son. He could not help but listen to his advice, especially when it was pointed out to him by Domitius and others that Octavian was making good capital out of his relationship with the Queen, and was even saying that he was ruled by a woman. Antony's cause in Rome and Italy was being seriously damaged by Cleopatra's presence at his side. Cleopatra realized quickly enough how these influential Roman senators were trying to get her out of the way, and took action accordingly. Publius Canidius was one of Antony's closest associates and a man upon whose advice he largely relied, and in the forthcoming war he was appointed general in charge of all the land forces. Knowing in what esteem Antony held him, Cleopatra put her case forcibly to Canidius and bribed him to oppose Domitius Ahenobarbus and the others who wanted her to leave. Canidius's argument to Antony in favour of the Queen staying with the army was not entirely spurious. The Egyptian fleet, he pointed out, would surely fight more readily if their ruler was with them, and they needed the Egyptian money which Cleopatra had up to now so readily supplied. 'Also,' he added, 'she is in no way inferior in intelligence to any of the Kings who have joined us. She has long been the ruler of a great country and she has had considerable experience of statecraft in your own company.'

The Queen had won. Antony, whether he had at one moment wanted to send her away or not, was probably greatly relieved at having her still by his side. Over the years he had come to rely upon her in so many ways, not least for her political sagacity. But by yielding he had made a fatal mistake, for not only was there now considerable dissension among his Roman supporters, but he had played into the hands of Octavian's propaganda. The latter would seize on the fact of this foreign Queen preparing to make war on Rome and would make Cleopatra the main issue in the war. In this he was not far wrong for it seems that at about this time Antony had even suggested a reconciliation and an agreement that he would disband his fleet and army if Octavian would do likewise. Cleopatra however was determined on war, for only by eliminating Octavian could she make sure of the claims of her son Caesarion to be Caesar's true descendant. It was true that her own personal ambition to sit on the throne as Empress of the Roman world was a driving force, but throughout her life one must recognize that her prime aims and ambitions were centred on Caesarion. Although she had been cool and calculating in her seduction of Antony and almost certainly was to end up despising him, it would seem that she had once really fallen in love in her life, and that was with the aging rake, hero, general and intellectual, Julius Caesar. She would never feel that his death was truly avenged until she saw his son as King and Emperor.

Antony was now poised on the springboard of Asia Minor ready for his invasion of the Roman world. His opponent Octavian was as usual playing a very cool and careful game. Throughout the year of 32 B.C. he allowed Antony to take up his position in Asia, encouraging him to make the first move and to declare his hand. Judging from Plutarch's account of the events Antony was too slow in moving, and had he invaded Italy during the summer of 32 B.C. he would almost certainly have found the people on his side. There were riots and general hostility against Octavian on account of the taxes which he was levying in his preparation for war.

Island of Samos

There is probably some truth in this viewpoint, but Antony had to collect his forces from so many nations that he had to enlarge his fleet in order to transport them to the contest with Octavian. This inevitably meant that he suffered more delays than his rival. Octavian's strength was that from his central base in Italy he could call upon the legions to defend the homeland and that he was not dependent upon foreign allies.

While the final preparations were being made, Antony in contrast to his quiet, dour enemy decided that the time was ripe for a massive celebration in anticipation of his victory. So, as Plutarch writes:

> they sailed to Samos and there made merry. Just as all the kings, dynasts, tetrarchs, nations and cities between Syria, the Maeotic lake, Armenia and Illyria had been ordered to send or bring their equipment for the war, so now all the dramatic artists were ordered to appear in Samos. While nearly the whole world was filled with groans and lamentations

this one island for many days resounded with the music of flutes and harps. The theatres were filled, and choruses competed against one another. Every city sent an ox for sacrifice and kings vied with one another in entertainments and gifts. Everywhere men began to ask how on earth the conquerors would celebrate their victory when their festivities at the opening of the war were so expensive.

In May, Antony and Cleopatra and their assembled forces sailed for Athens where 'once again sports and entertainments engaged him'. In Athens Cleopatra set about making herself popular with all the chief citizens, for she was well aware that Octavia had enjoyed great favour in the city and she was determined to efface her rival's memory. She was also determined that the moment had now arrived for Antony to send the formal letter of divorce to Octavia. There can be no doubt that she had long been pressing him to do this but Antony was not prepared to make a formal breach with Octavian until such time as his forces were all ready. For almost the first occasion in her life Cleopatra now allowed her feelings as a woman to override her political judgment. Octavia in Antony's Rome house had proved a rallying point for Antony's supporters and by her very presence there with Antony's children had prevented Octavian from openly breaking with his brother-in-law. But Cleopatra, confident of success, was determined to enter Rome at Antony's side as his one and only legitimate wife. She could not tolerate the thought that she might be regarded by the Romans as she had been in Caesar's day as a mistress and no more. There can be no doubt of the influence that she now exerted over her middle-aged, heavy-drinking husband. Antony, who was an honorary citizen of Athens, erected a statue to her in her role as Isis next to his own on the Acropolis, and in a public oration would seem to have heaped further honorary dignities upon her.

All these proceedings provided fresh fuel for Octavian's propaganda. He had already asked Octavia to divorce Antony but she had declined, most probably because she felt that with growing years his infatuation with this Egyptian Queen would burn itself out. It can have been no secret that Cleopatra was urging Antony to send the note of divorce to his sister, for travellers were regularly passing between Rome and Athens and the gossip of one city was heard in the other within a few days, Possibly suspecting that Antony would be too wise politically to declare an open breach, thus putting himself in the wrong – for no charges could be laid at Octavia's door – Octavian was prompted to a bold and unscrupulous move. Two defectors from Antony's cause, both of whom had been friends of his but who had fallen out with Cleopatra, arrived in Rome and informed him of the contents of Antony's will. This was lodged, as was often the case with influential Romans, with the Vestal Virgins who in their role as symbols of purity guaranteed the will's inviolability until the owner's death. Prepared though he was to believe what he was told about its contents, Octavian knew well enough that only the will itself could convince the senators and the people of Antony's future intentions. He immediately sent to the Vestal Virgins and demanded that it be handed over to him. As was only right and proper they refused, saying that they were not allowed to do so and that the only way he could get in was by the use of force. Octavian did not hesitate and went and seized it personally. He opened and read it and was more than delighted to find that it confirmed what he had been told.

He next read it aloud to the Senate, many of whose members disapproved of his action in doing so, maintaining that it had been obtained unjustly and that in any case it was not right to hold a man accountable for his dispositions after death while he was still alive. Its contents however astonished them. Antony not only confirmed the 'Donations' of the Eastern Empire but also the legitimacy of Caesarion as Caesar's rightful heir to the whole Empire. There was one other clause of which Octavian made telling use and this was that if Antony were to die in Rome his body was to be carried in solemn procession through the Forum, but that after this it was to be shipped to Cleopatra and buried in Alexandria. There could be no denying the implications of this. Rome was the burial place for its rulers and distinguished men, but Antony was now declaring that Alexandria was in future to be the burial place. He intended to be interred like a Ptolemy in this rival city of the East.

Two marble statues of Roman ladies represented as priestesses, or vestal virgins, 1st century A.D.

ROAD TO ACTIUM

Antony was now nearly fifty and Cleopatra was thirty-eight. The discrepancy in their ages however was more marked than it should have been. Antony's roistering, wenching and drinking had aged him prematurely, while from what we know of Cleopatra's cool and precise intelligence it is almost certain that she was physically younger than her years. Her ascendancy over him becomes very marked from now on and it is in the light of this that one must judge their subsequent history. Had Antony confronted Octavian only a few years earlier there can be little doubt that he would have won, for he still had powerful support in Rome and Italy generally and he was a far more able general. But Antony had squandered so many of his assets, time in particular, as well as much of the good will of the Roman people and the respect of the Italian legionaries. It was here that Cleopatra's influence was disastrous. She presented not only to Octavian but even to many of Antony's supporters a target for abuse or an object for recrimination. Perhaps she was right in thinking that without her presence the kings of the East would not have marched for the over-throw of Rome, but where she was wrong was in thinking that the Romans would willingly accept a foreign queen. Her fatal mistake was in leaving Alexandria. Cleopatra had also compounded her error by her insistence that Antony should formally divorce Octavia. Emissaries were sent to Rome with the formal letter of severance, and Octavia was forced to leave her home taking with her her children as well as Antony's son by Fulvia.

Octavian, true to his principle of 'hasten slowly', allowed Antony a whole year in which to take up his position in Greece. Unhappy Greece was destined once again to become the scene of a civil war, for geographically Greece divides Italy from the East. The pattern of events between Caesar and Pompey was to be repeated.

Antony's friends in Rome were becoming seriously disturbed. Plutarch writes: 'they sent one of their number, Geminius, to entreat Antony not to conduct himself in such a way as to be voted out of office and proclaimed an enemy of Rome'. This was prompted by the many tales that were circulating about his behaviour. It was said for instance, that on one occasion at a banquet he had even risen from his table in the presence of all his guests and rubbed the Queen's feet – the duty of a slave! Another story went that even when on official business or giving judgment in court he would receive love letters from the Queen which he would eagerly open and read. He was enslaved, they said, besotted with the woman as well as with the wine. Cleopatra had him completely in her power by means of sinister love potions from the East. Why, on another occasion when Antony had been presiding over an official assembly the Queen had chanced to pass through the forum and Antony had leapt to his feet, broken up the assembly, and followed on foot behind Cleopatra among her eunuchs. There were many other pieces of malicious gossip, most of them no doubt inventions of his detractors, but just as damaging as if they had been true. It was the mission of Geminius to inform Antony of what was being said and get him for the good of his and their cause to send the Queen back to Egypt. His advice in fact was the same as that which Domitius Ahenobarbus had given Antony in Ephesus, but since Cleopatra's ascendancy over him was now much greater it was most unlikely that it would be regarded.

Cleopatra knew at once why Geminius had been sent from Rome. She knew also that Antony was having to consider the republican feelings of many of his supporters; even on one occasion declaring that within two months of Octavian's overthrow he would have the Republic re-established. Republics were not for Cleopatra, the future Queen-Empress. The divinely-descended Ptolemies were rulers by the appointment of the gods and would pay no attention whatsoever to the wishes or advice of petty human senators. She would see that this Geminius was humbled in every possible way and not allowed at any time to have a private audience with Antony. Geminius accordingly was regularly placed in the lowest seat at any meal or banquet and the Queen's friends took every opportunity to make him the butt of their jokes and contrive to humiliate him.

Geminius endured all this with controlled persistence, waiting for the opportunity to arise for him to state his mission. This came at last at a banquet when, as was almost inevitable in Antony's camp, the wine had been circulating more than freely. It was Antony himself who provided the opportunity. One must imagine the burly but running-to-fat, aging and drunken Dionysus gazing somewhat vacantly across the hall and calling out to this man seated at the foot of the table 'What brings you here from Rome, Geminius?' 'Important matters', Geminius replied, 'require a sober head. This is no time to discuss them. However, there's one thing I'll tell you, whether drunk or sober, and that is that everything will be all right if only Cleopatra will pack her bags and go back to Egypt!' Antony was furious but the Queen merely replied in calm tones: 'Well done, Geminius. You have told your secret without having to be tortured.' A few days later Geminius slipped away from Athens and made his way back to Rome. He had seen that the basis of the tales about Antony was true. There was yet another defector to Octavian in the making. Others were to follow him, among them Marcus Silanus and the historian Dellius. The latter had offended Cleopatra at supper one night by complaining of the quality of the wine that they were drinking, and adding 'While at this moment in Rome Sarmentus will be drinking best Falernian'. This was a quip designed to wound Cleopatra for everybody present knew that her adored Julius Caesar had been homosexual in his youth and that Sarmentus had been one of his favourite boyfriends.

Although Antony still had many clients in Italy, families that is to say who were bound by long allegiance to his and whom he as patron would protect and sponsor, as well as many legionaries who had served him and loved him, Octavian had more or less won the political battle.

The return of Geminius with his report of the state of things in Athens and the subservience of Antony to the Egyptian Queen gave Octavian the perfect opportunity to act. He declared war not on Antony but on Cleopatra, on the Egyptian Queen who with all the forces of the East behind her was preparing to invade the motherland of Italy. Nothing at all was said about Antony.

Octavian's political brilliance was outstanding. He had had Antony voted out of office but he had been very careful not to declare him 'an enemy of Rome'. In this way he did not alienate any of Antony's clients and supporters, nor compel them in any way to take his side in the forthcoming struggle. Octavian as sole remaining Triumvir was declaring war, 'a just and righteous war' in the formal phrase, on a foreign sovereign who was threatening the State. He made a solemn procession to the temple of the war goddess Bellona on the Field of Mars and from there he hurled a blood-tipped lance in the direction of the enemy – the East. Octavian was later to say that 'the whole of Italy of its own accord swore loyalty to me and asked me to be the leader in the war which I won at Actium. The provinces of Gaul, Spain, Africa, Sicily and Sardinia also took the same oath.' This was certainly not entirely true, for we know that the inhabitants of Bononia (modern Bologna) who were clients of the Antony family were specifically not required to take the oath. But all this was a formality, and Octavian was a master in understanding the rituals required in Rome and the necessity for having all the legal and juristic rights on his side. Constitutionally his position was now unassailable, while Antony leagued with this foreign Queen was no more than a renegade Roman who was lending his support to the enemies of the State.

As the winter of 32 B.C. drew on the forces of the two contestants were facing each other across the narrow strip of the Ionian Sea. Antony and Cleopatra and their supporters took up their winter quarters at Patras at the entrance to the Gulf of Corinth, prepared for their move in the spring. Their fleet was sent up to the Ambracian Gulf on the west coast of Greece just north of the island of Levkas. This gulf is a giant arm of sea penetrating the land to a distance of about ten miles and about five miles wide across. Because of the heavy rainfall and the cold it could never be imagined as a good place to winter, nor indeed is it a pleasant place even in summer. True, it provides a secure enough harbour, but Antony or his advisers had made a bad mistake when they sent their ships and men to so uncongenial an area. Even today, as the British Admiralty Pilot bears witness, the gulf can hardly be called attractive:

The coast of the gulf is so indented by bays with long projecting points, that in places the dangers off the latter, on opposite sides of the gulf, are barely two miles apart. There are a few islets, some of which are covered with shrubs and verdure. . . . Within the shores of the gulf the hills are composed of rugged limestone. The northern shore of the gulf is an irregular stretch of swamp, marsh and lagoon, in many places only separated from the waters of the gulf by a narrow strip of sand and mud, which in winter is overflowed and makes the gulf appear much more extensive than it really is. Malaria is very prevalent in this locality in the summer. These marshes are infested by snakes and reptiles, some of which are venomous; the mosquitoes are troublesome in every part of the gulf. The lagoons abound in fish and enormous prawns, and are the resort of vast numbers of aquatic birds. The depths all along the northern shore are very irregular, and sounding is the only guide when in its vicinity.

Why Antony sent his ships up to the Ambracian Gulf to winter must always remain a mystery. Apart from Patras, where the army was quartered, he had many other good ports and harbours within easy reach, including the fine harbour and city of Corinth. Since there could be no question of a fleet engagement during winter when normally the galleys were all hauled ashore and refitted, his decision can only be interpreted on the basis that he feared Octavian would come down over-land from Illyria and steal a march on him. Organization was never Antony's strong point, but it was at organization that Octavian was an expert. Aided by the remarkable Agrippa he was to achieve his ultimate success not so much through superior tactics but through superior method.

Octavian, who had based his main forces at Brundisium and Taranto, ready to cross into Greece in the Spring, was in a far better position than Antony. His ships and men were in their homeland where there was better organized accommodation and their morale was consequently that much higher. He was still anxious however to bring the war to a rapid conclusion, for the burden of paying his men had caused him to raise taxes to an almost unprecedented degree. He is even said to have sent a message to Antony asking him not to protract the struggle but to come over and fight him then and there. The latter, having gone into winter quarters, was naturally not willing to risk his fleet on that iron-bound and tempestuous coast and retorted by asking Octavian to meet him in single combat. Aging though Antony was the sickly Octavian would have had no chance against him. In any case the whole proposal was ridiculous and shows Antony at his most irrational – as if the fate of the Roman Empire could be decided by two men fighting together! Octavian naturally refused, as he also refused Antony's next request that he bring his army over to Pharsalia (where Caesar had beaten Pompey) and fight him there.

BATTLE FOR THE WORLD

The fate of the Mediterranean and the Roman world was settled for centuries in the year 31 B.C. Possibly it had to some extent been settled during the late winter, for many of Antony's soldiers had died from disease and even starvation. So inefficient were the supply arrangements that the thousands of oarsmen and sailors in the cold weather of the Ambracian Gulf had even been allowed to run out of stores and compelled to forage in that bleak and unhealthy part of Greece. The result was that Antony was now compelled to conscript all and any kind of labour that he could find in order to bring the crews of the vessels up to strength. Peasant-farmers, 'harvesters, ploughboys, donkey drivers and even common travellers' were forced to man the oars of the great war galleys. These were unlikely to compare favourably with the men whom Agrippa had so carefully trained for Octavian's ships. Furthermore the morale was high in Octavian's fleet, for these were the men who had defeated Pompey off Sicily and had cleared the Roman trade-routes of all the ships of the self-styled 'Sea King'. Octavian's legions too were battle-hardened from their campaigns in Illyria – campaigns which they had won. Antony's troops, on the other hand, had been badly mauled in the Parthian war and the only success they could claim was their expedition into Armenia, which had been little more than a plundering raid. Although there was little to distinguish them in numbers, there was a great deal of difference between the fleets and the troops who now faced one another.

From the very beginning Octavian made the running, or rather his brilliant lieutenant Agrippa made it for him. A squadron of ships under Agrippa went on a daring raid into Greece and seized the important port of Methone in the south west of Messenia. This served two purposes. On the one hand Agrippa's ships managed to capture a number of cargo vessels coming up from Egypt with corn for Antony's army, and on the other it diverted Antony's attention to this corner of Greece. He imagined that this force was probably an advance guard of Octavian's army. But while he was looking uneasily over his shoulder, as it were, and preparing to march in the direction of Methone, Octavian had slipped across with his army from Brundisium and landed unopposed in Epirus near the Acroceraunian promontory at a port called Toryne. By this daring move he had cut off troops whom Antony had stationed at Corcyra to the north, and he was immediately poised above the Ambracian Gulf itself. While Antony had felt himself menaced from the occupation of Methone to the south of him he now found that the real threat was developing to the north, and in the neighbourhood of his all-important fleet. Inevitably there was some consternation in the camp at Patras, for it was seen that the initiative had passed into Octavian's hands. Such was to be the pattern of the whole campaign.

Octavian had now landed some eighty thousand men, against which it is estimated that Antony had about one hundred thousand. The latter now had to transport most of his troops across the Gulf of Patras and march north against an enemy who was already advancing in the direction of his fleet. It was upon the fleets that the final issue must be resolved for Antony could only invade Italy by destroying Octavian's ships, and the latter could only maintain himself in Greece by having command of the sea. On the face of it it might seem that Antony's ships in the security of the Ambracian gulf were in the best position, but Octavian by capturing Corcyra had given himself a good harbour, while the Ambracian gulf was not only a refuge but also a potential trap. It was true that Octavian could not storm the narrow entrance, for Antony had had large towers and catapults erected to command it. On the other hand Octavian's fleet was able to prevent any other ships from entering the gulf, with the result that all the stores for Antony's fleet and army would have to be brought up overland.

Antony now encamped on the southern peninsula at Actium facing his opponent who was on the northern side, although some miles back from the entrance itself. Part of Antony's army was also stationed on the tip of the northern peninsula so that he commanded the whole entrance to the gulf where his fleet of heavy warships rode at anchor. Most of Octavian's fleet was concentrated in Gomaros bay, an open roadstead a little to the north but secure enough unless the Bora or strong westerlies were to blow. Octavian proceeded to make a fortified camp on an eminence now known as Michalitsi Heights and sat down to await developments. Antony commanded all the surrounding countryside but Octavian could still bring in all the supplies he needed for his fleet and army from Italy. Antony's fleet was in fact blockaded, and therefore quite ineffectual at this moment in the struggle. He had only two options. One was to burst out of the gulf and defeat Octavian at sea, thus preventing his army from getting any more supplies. The other was to march round the gulf and engage Octavian in a pitched battle. In view of the strength of Octavian's camp and fortified position the latter was hardly practical. Octavian had thrown the ball into Antony's court and had only to wait and see what the other would do.

Cleopatra with all the other attendant kings and princes now joined the army. Her presence was to prove, as it had done throughout the previous months, a hindrance rather than an asset. But she was determined to stay at Antony's side, to be there when Octavian was defeated, and to sail with the conquering army for the throne that she was confident awaited her in Rome. Meanwhile the stalemate

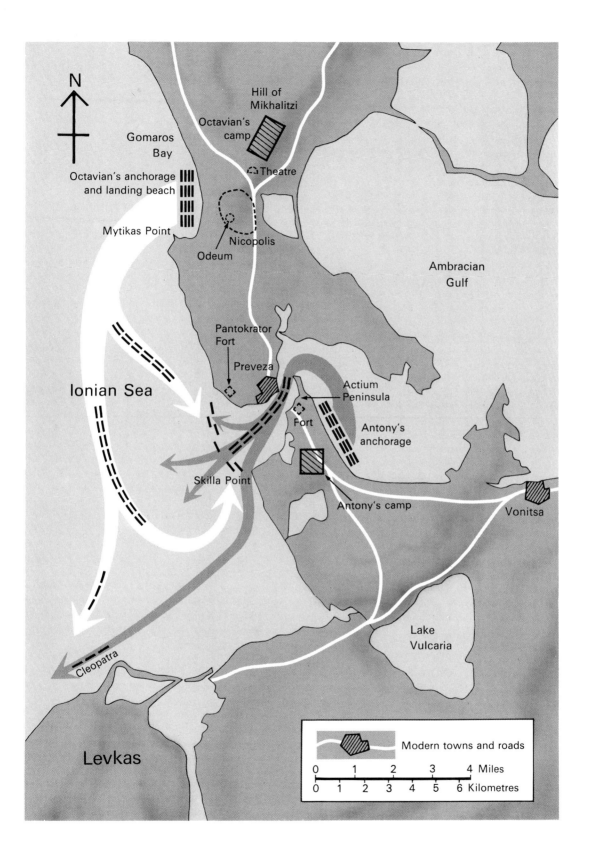

N

Hill of
Mikhalitzi

Octavian's
camp

Gomaros
Bay

Theatre

Octavian's anchorage
and landing beach

Mytikas Point

Nicopolis

Odeum

Ambracian
Gulf

Pantokrator
Fort

Preveza

Actium
Peninsula

Ionian Sea

Fort

Antony's
anchorage

Skilla Point

Antony's camp

Vonitsa

Cleopatra

Lake
Vulcaria

Levkas

Modern towns and roads

0   1   2   3   4 Miles

0   1   2   3   4   5   6 Kilometres

continued, both armies confronting one another in positions of strength that seemed unassailable. Octavian had only one weakness, the fact that he was dependent for most of his water supplies on a small river to the east of his camp and Antony's cavalry were constantly harassing his men at this point. But such minor skirmishes could have little bearing on the main issue – was it to be a land or a sea battle?

While the weeks dragged by Agrippa, using his ships with his customary skill, made a great change in the whole picture. He deployed a number of them just to the south of the Ambracian gulf and captured the towering limestone island

---

Cast of detail of the Arch of Augustus, as reconstructed by Michelangelo, dedicated to the consuls, tribunes and others who fought at Actium; 19–11 B.C.

of Levkas. This island, only separated from the western coast of Greece by a narrow channel, commands the whole area to the south of Actium. By seizing Levkas Agrippa had placed Octavian in an even stronger position, for he had deprived Antony of any chance of getting supplies up from the south by sea. Now not only was Antony's fleet blockaded but also his army. Every single requirement – clothing, weapons, food supplies – had to be transported by narrow roads and craggy cliff-paths from the south. It was hardly surprising that Antony's heterogeneous body of men began to grow dispirited and, as had happened before the death of Julius Caesar, a whole crop of unfavourable portents were later quoted as having taken place. Word came from Athens that a famous statue of Dionysus, the god whom Antony had impersonated, had been hurled to the ground in a violent thunderstorm. At the same time people recalled that a few months previously in Patras the temple of Hercules, Antony's supposed ancestor, had been struck by lightning. Even within the first few weeks there must have been some who began to think about abandoning Antony's cause and casting in their lot with Octavian.

The latter had once more shown his political astuteness by bringing with him to his camp all the Roman senators except those who had already left Italy and thrown in their lot with Antony. By this action Octavian was again clearly saying that the contest lay between the Roman senate and people and a foreign power that was attempting to invade Italy. It would not be long before the combination of the blockade, the heat of summer, and the malarial, unhealthy terrain where most of his troops were encamped, would begin to cause not only loss of morale among Antony's troops but even the defection of a number of his supporters to the other side. Octavian on his cool heights to the north, and with his ships bringing in regular supplies from Italy, was in a far better position. His opponent with his stretched lines of communication and supplies, with his blockaded ships, and with the whole of the Ionian dominated by Agrippa's fleet, would in due course have to make a move or collapse from sheer inanition.

Antony tried on several occasions by cavalry and other minor actions to try and provoke Octavian to fight a pitched battle. The latter was not to be drawn. If Octavian was not going to come out there was only one thing to do and that was to burst past Actium point with all the fleet, destroy Octavian's ships and, leaving most of the army behind, sail for Italy. There would be no opposition there even if Antony took only a few legions. The senators hostile to Antony as well as the whole of Octavian's army would then be the ones who would be blockaded. With their fleet gone and with the bulk of Antony's forces in command of the surrounding countryside they could be starved into surrender. This seems to have been the initial concept behind the battle that was to follow, and one cannot help wondering whether this plan of campaign was not Cleopatra's. Antony was a general and not a sailor, while most of his friends and advisors were also soldiers. There was no equivalent in Antony's camp to Marcus Agrippa.

As the torrid sun of summer began to shake over the gulf, warm up the marshes and cause swarms of mosquitoes to arise, the first defections began. Two thousand Galatians and their commander went over to Octavian's camp. Antony's cavalry were also defeated in a battle. Morale sank. Soon afterwards Domitius Ahenobarbus, who had always been against Cleopatra's participation in the campaign, deserted to Octavian. This was a bitter blow, one which Antony attempted to pass over with a shrug, saying that Domitius wanted to get back to his mistress in Italy. But he must have known in his heart that what Domitius and Geminius had said was true – the Queen's presence was fatal to his cause. It was not only politically fatal but it would seem that Cleopatra was also trying to dictate the actual conduct and strategy of the war. Antony was torn, as he had been for months, between his regard for Cleopatra and his regard for his friends and supporters. Inactivity never suited him and here he was being compelled by Octavian to play a waiting game. No doubt he continued to drink heavily as usual and the combination of wine, the summer heat, the continual friction between Cleopatra and his other advisers, seem to have led to violent quarrels between him and the Queen. At this moment Canidius, who was in command of the land forces, approached him and said that he was convinced that Cleopatra should go back to Egypt. But the latter, whose fleet lay in the gulf below and who was in any case providing a great deal of the finances for the campaign, was adamant.

A story that was later circulated, but which was probably quite untrue, suggests that during these weeks the relations between Antony and Cleopatra became so bad that he even believed that she was prepared to poison him. It was said that he had become so suspicious of her that he had his food and drink tasted before he would touch it. Cleopatra, so that tale goes, in order to show him that she could get rid of him whenever she wanted, one day took some flowers from a garland she was wearing and threw them into his wine cup and bade him drink. Antony was about to raise the cup to his lips when the Queen stopped him and ordered a condemned criminal to be brought in. The latter was given the cup of wine, drank it, and immediately fell dead. The improbability of this and other tales lies in the fact that Cleopatra needed Antony. Whatever she may now have felt about him and the obvious degeneration in his character and faculties, she must have Antony at her side in order to enter Rome. The people of Rome would not accept a foreign Queen entering their city as its mistress, and it was most unlikely that the legions would follow her. In order to achieve her ambitions for herself, and particularly for Caesarion, she must be with Antony when the victorious army marched into the imperial city. What became of him afterwards, when Caesarion was an adult and ready to take over the reins of office, was possibly immaterial to her. All her actions in the meantime must be gauged by the fact that she was determined not to let Antony out of her sight until their victory was established.

It was high summer and Antony's forces had now been blockaded for four months. He could not bring Octavian to battle and it was unthinkable in view of the current supply problem that the fleet and the army could stay in place once the

Bow of a Roman warship, from a relief in the temple of Fortune at Praeneste, Italy, of the type that would have been employed at Actium, 2nd half of 1st century B.C.

rains of autumn began to fall – followed so quickly in that part of the world by the cold of winter. Something must be done, and done swiftly. The dissensions in Antony's camp contrasted with the harmony in Octavian's. There one, or two men, if one accepts the important part that Agrippa played in the campaign, were in complete agreement as to the nature and necessity of the war.

At the end of August a council of war was held by Antony. It reached the conclusion that the only solution was for the fleet to make a break-out. Many hotly opposed this, saying that they were soldiers first and foremost and had not come all this way to do battle on the sea. The situation was deteriorating rapidly. About this time the King of Paphlagonia deserted to Octavian, to be followed shortly afterwards by a Roman senator and a chieftain from Arabia. The two latter were caught and executed as a deterrent to any other potential defectors. It is significant however, even though the history of events was written later by protagonists of

227

Octavian and the subsequent emperors, that we hear nothing of senators or anyone of importance leaving his lines and crossing to Antony's. Morale in the Caesarian camp was obviously high. On one occasion when Antony was walking down to the harbour accompanied by a staff officer a small band of Octavian's men who had penetrated their enemy's lines jumped over the defensive wall and attempted to capture him. By mistake they seized upon his junior officer, enabling Antony to make his escape down the road – no doubt considerably out of breath.

As Plutarch puts it:

> There were defections among the kings, and Amyntas and Deiotarus also went over to Caesar [Octavian]. Quite apart from this, since Antony's naval forces seemed to be of little use, and always too slow to be of much help, the best thing would have been for him to turn his attention to his army. . . . Canidius urged him to abandon the sea to Caesar, who had gained considerable knowledge of naval affairs in the Sicilian war. It would be far best for Antony, who was so experienced in military terms, to make use of his many legionaries and not to distribute them among the fleet and thus fritter away their strength.

All this was true enough, but since Octavian would not be lured into a land battle, Antony had little option.

Plutarch, who was writing about one hundred years later in the reigns of the emperors Trajan and Hadrian, naturally enough puts the blame for the events of Actium entirely upon the shoulders of Cleopatra: 'She prevailed with her opinion that the war should be decided with ships'. But the fact of the matter was that so long as Octavian refused to accept a land engagement Antony was powerless. The decision was accordingly taken to prepare for a break-out by sea and preparations were set afoot for the ships to be manned by the legionaries and for all the vessels which were redundant or unserviceable to be burned. It has to be borne in mind that Antony's fleet had been many months in the Ambracian gulf and there can be little doubt that in those warm waters, especially in mid-summer, many of them must have become not only foul from weed and barnacles but also attacked by the *Teredo navalis*, the wood-devouring worm which is the greatest enemy of wooden ships in the Mediterranean. Agrippa's fleet on the other hand had crossed from Italy in the spring, no doubt having been hauled ashore and carefully waxed and tarred over the winter in their home ports.

The exact circumstances of the battle of Actium will always be a matter for conjecture, but there seems little doubt that from the very beginning it was planned that the Egyptian squadron which consisted of about sixty ships should, if the battle went against Antony's forces, make a dash for home. It must have been clear by now that the land army, sickened and demoralized as it was, would probably have to be abandoned. If the action at sea were successful then of course the tables would be turned on Octavian, the morale of Antony's troops would be immensely reinforced, while his fleet would cut off his enemies from their vital sea-route with

Italy. Even so there were still many ignorant of the true state of affairs who were eager to conclude the whole issue by one large set-piece land battle. One veteran centurion, we are told, came up to Antony and pointing to the many scars that he had earned in the latter's service burst out: 'General, look at these wounds! Why have you now decided to put your trust in miserable pieces of timber rather than in our swords? Let Egyptians and Phoenicians, if you will, fight upon the sea, but give us the land where we know how to stand and fight, and either conquer or die.'

By 29 August 31 B.C. all was ready for the great engagement. Antony, after disposing of his unserviceable warships, had four squadrons consisting of about three hundred vessels against which Octavian opposed some four hundred, all of which were smaller but were almost certainly in better sea-going condition. At this moment a westerly gale blew up. It lasted for four days, completely preventing Antony's fleet from leaving the gulf since its mouth faces practically due west. No ancient writers make any reference to the ability of Agrippa's ships to survive this gale which put them on a bad lee shore, but one can only suppose that they put out to sea and kept themselves head to wind under their oars. It is a tribute not only to the construction of his ships but to the training of his sailors that, when the gale finally blew itself out, Octavian's blockading vessels were still at sea off Actium and in sufficiently good condition to do battle. 'Lying in harbour,' Nelson was to remark centuries later, 'rots ships and rots men.' Antony's ships and men had lain in harbour for far too long and neither were in fit state to tackle the salt-hardened sailors nor the fine ships that were waiting outside to meet them.

On the morning of 2 September the weather had cleared, the swell subsided and the time arrived. What is most astounding is that all of Antony's fleet, not only the Egyptian squadron, put out to sea for a naval engagement with their masts, spars, sails and all their rigging aboard. They were thus, as has been said, putting themselves at a grave disadvantage. The only conclusion one can draw is that Antony had either abandoned hope and was already prepared for flight, or that he had come to an arrangement with Cleopatra that, if things went against them, she and her ships should make their way to Egypt. There they could continue to run the Eastern Empire and prepare themselves for a second round with Octavian.

The fact that the rest of the ships also went into battle with their sailing gear on board is easily explicable. It could hardly fail to be remarked by all the seamen, sea-captains and even those soldiers who were at all familiar with naval warfare, that the Egyptian ships were prepared for a long sea passage. Antony had a glib but unconvincing explanation: 'When his shipmasters asked him to let them leave their sails behind he ordered that they should be put aboard, saying that he did not want a single one of the enemy to be allowed to make his escape'. This was absurd. Sea battles of that period were entirely dependent upon the strength of the rowers to bring their vessels into action. No one fought under sail. The fight was either determined by the rams of the galleys or by a 'land-battle' fought by the

ABOVE: *Roman galley on a coin issued 32–31 B.C.* OPPOSITE: *casts of fragments of a marble relief thought to represent Augustus giving thanks to Apollo for the victory at Actium; time of Tiberius*

legionaries in ship-to-ship boarding actions. Flight was clearly in the wind, and the subsequent collapse and demoralization of Antony's fleet must be attributed to the fact that only too many were aware that even if he had not already given up hope he was at least prepared for failure and ready to make a dash for safety. A further indication that he was either despondent about the outcome or that he had at last determined on Cleopatra's withdrawal from the scene of the struggle was that all her private treasure, jewels and plate had been shipped aboard before the fleet got under way. It is just possible that this could have been done in secret, but such preparations combined with the order to have the sailing gear on board the ships could not have failed to arouse the suspicions of all but the simplest soldier.

On that morning, under the eyes of the opposed armies, the ships of Antony and Cleopatra headed for the narrow mouth of the Ambracian gulf. Octavian's fleet was waiting to meet them. Twenty thousand legionaries and two thousand archers, according to Plutarch's account, were embarked in Antony's ships, presumably in his three main squadrons. Cleopatra's squadron, which also included merchant ships, formed the fourth. Canidius was left behind in command of the land forces, together with the rest of the troops who must have amounted, counting for deaths from disease as well as desertion, to less than fifty thousand men. His orders were to fall back through Greece after Antony's break out and then make his way to Asia. It seems clear that the battle of Actium, whatever Antony may have said at the time, was never really an offensive operation on his part. He might possibly have succeeded against Octavian, but with his undermanned and demoralized fleet against the confident men on the opposite side it was always extremely unlikely. From the very beginning the battle of Actium was the flight of Antony.

Octavian seems to have considered letting Antony get well out into the open sea and then cutting him to pieces at leisure with his faster and more manoeuvrable ships. Agrippa pointed out however that there would be a risk of the enemy escaping, and that the best tactic would be to lay off just far enough to prevent their opponents from getting away and at the same time to lure them from the narrows where they were assembling. After all his preparations Antony had to come out, and it was he who was once again committed to making a move. Plutarch gives a vivid account of the opening phases:

> As for the leaders, Antony visited all his ships in a rowing boat and encouraged the soldiers, telling them that since they were in very heavy ships they should fight just as though they were on land. He also told the captains of the ships to receive the enemy's attacks as if they were lying at anchor [i.e. not to attempt to out-manoeuvre the Liburnians] and to hold their position at the mouth of the gulf since it was narrow and difficult.

This suggests that Antony hoped to provoke Octavian's fleet into entering the gulf itself, where the weight of his vessels would have told and where the greater speed and manoeuvrability of Agrippa's ships would have been of no asset. The latter was not to be drawn. He knew exactly what his ships could do and he knew also that Antony was now committed.

Octavian had had a happy omen. 'He had left his tent while it was still dark and was going round to visit his ships when he was met by a man driving an ass. He asked him what was his name and the man replied "Fortunate, and my ass's name is Victor".' At a later date when Octavian built the new town of Nicopolis to celebrate his victory, decorating it with the beaks of the captured ships, he had a statue of a man and an ass placed in the forum.

Antony disposed his four squadrons of ships with three of them in a double line ahead. The fourth, the Egyptians, were set behind them. The latter were to take no part in the fighting, and it is quite clear that Cleopatra's squadron was always designed to make off for Egypt if at any moment it should be seen that the battle was going against them. Approximately one hundred and seventy ships therefore were stretched in two columns between Skilla Point to the south and the northern

point of Pandokrator. Antony thus had both his wings well protected as he waited and invited his opponents to attack him. About a mile to seaward some four hundred of Octavian's ships also rested on their oars.

On that bright summer day, with the two armies drawn up in their camps and watching the encounter that was to decide all their fates, the sun itself took a hand. Many years later Propertius in his poem on the battle was to ascribe Octavian's success to the intervention of the sun god Phoebus Apollo: 'Phoebus keeps faith: Rome wins, and all the sea is strewn with the doomed whore's sovereignty'.

In this part of the western coast of Greece, as indeed in many Mediterranean areas in summer, there is a regular pattern of land and sea breezes induced by the sun, 'le brise soleil'. The mornings are often calm and still, and one may assume that this was the case when Antony's ships took up their battle-position off the entrance to the gulf. As the sun rises however, the land begins to warm up. While the sea temperature in early September may be as high as 80 degrees Fahrenheit the land temperature may be 90 degrees or more by noon. Since hot air rises, and 'nature abhors a vacuum', the cooler air over the sea floods in to take the place of the rising air over the land. Plutarch specifically comments on this: 'It was now the sixth hour [noon] and since a wind was blowing off the sea Antony's men became impatient and, relying on the size and height of their ships, put their left wing into motion.' With a wind drawing onshore, which would increase throughout the afternoon only to die away at nightfall, Antony had to get to sea or be embayed. Furthermore, since the wind in this area usually shifts around from west to north west before it declines, Antony needed to get several miles out to sea before he could hoist his sails and make off round the island of Levkas to the south.

Plutarch writes:

> When they were engaged there was no ramming or charging of one ship into another because Antony's great vessels were incapable of the speed to make such a tactic effectual. Octavian's ships on the other hand dared not charge prow to prow against Antony's which were all protected with hard bronze and spikes, nor did they feel confident to attack the sides of his ships for they were so strongly constructed of huge timbers that the attackers' rams would have broken off on impact. The struggle came therefore to resemble a land battle, or rather the struggle around a fortified town; for there were always three or four of Octavian's vessels around each one of Antony's pressing upon them with spears and poles and fiery missiles. Antony's men for their part responded with catapults from their high wooden towers.

Agrippa's men were better trained, they were battle-hardened, and they had spent months at sea during the campaign. Antony's crews had been port-bound for far too long, and many of them were not seamen at all but unwilling conscripts.

Ships on Roman medallion and coins. LEFT: *trireme, A.D. 238–244;* CENTRE: *galley A.D. 119–138;* RIGHT: *the harbour of Ostia, A.D. 64–68.* BELOW: *relief from Beirut of a merchantman, 2nd century A.D.* OVERLEAF: *Gulf of Actium.*

Octavian had packed into his four hundred ships almost twice the number of legionaries that Antony had embarked. The latter had also the dead-weight of his 'tail', the Egyptian squadron with Cleopatra aboard, serving women, eunuchs, courtiers, and useless furniture, as well as invaluable treasure. Soon each of his large and ungainly galleys were beset by groups of Agrippa's vessels like hounds around a stag. Agrippa's ships seem to have worked around Antony's line to the north, but, since it was clearly always Antony's intention to let Cleopatra's squadron escape, this suited him very well. After about two hours of ship-to-ship fighting, with the battle going steadily in Octavian's favour, the Egyptian vessels which were now well out to the west of Levkas Island suddenly hoisted their sails and made off to the south.

This action which has puzzled so many writers from ancient times to this day is quite explicable if one accepts the fact that from the very beginning Antony had prepared for it. He had no doubt hoped that he had a chance of defeating the enemy but, greatly outnumbered as he was, he can never have been too sanguine about his prospects. Cleopatra fled, as Virgil wrote, 'with the wind called Iapyx', that is to say that she had a north-westerly in her sails – something which Antony and all his advisers must have known was the usual direction to expect a breeze at that time on a late summer afternoon. If one sees Antony's whole action at Actium as designed to extricate Cleopatra and himself from a hopeless situation then there is no mystery about the battle. He had instructed his army commander to withdraw the troops to Asia and his intention was to get the Queen and her ships safely away to Egypt. He had been outmanoeuvred by Octavian and Agrippa from the very moment when the latter had captured Methone and the former had landed unopposed in Greece. His position throughout the summer had been hopeless, with his fleet trapped and his army dying in malarial marshes. Actium was later celebrated by all the poets and historians of the Roman Empire as the triumph of Octavian which had established their world. It was indeed a victory for Octavian. It was also a victory for Antony, even if a limited one.

The romantic version as projected first by Plutarch and then by Shakespeare is clearly not true. Antony did not fly 'like a doting mallard' after Cleopatra. Once he had seen that the Egyptian squadron had escaped and that the battle was quite lost, he transferred from his flagship to a lighter, faster vessel, and followed Cleopatra to the south. His other ships were left behind to fight a rearguard action. This they continued to do with great gallantry throughout the night and into the following morning. Antony's conduct can hardly be considered very noble, but it was practical. He had lost the battle of Actium months before, but he still had a chance to fight another day.

Roman anchors, Bay of Actium

THE LAST YEAR

Antony's galley quickly drew up with the retreating Egyptian squadron and he and two companions transferred into Cleopatra's flagship. Whatever his expectations may have been regarding the battle – and from all the indications they were never very sanguine – he now abandoned himself to despair. He could not conceal from himself the fact that he had lost the whole campaign of the summer, and now he had lost the bulk of his fleet. It was true that his army might still rejoin him in Asia and that he could build another fleet over the coming autumn and winter, but he could never regain the self-confidence which had been his when he had been mustering his forces for the contest with Octavian.

'So Antony came up with Cleopatra's flagship,' as Plutarch writes, 'and was taken on board, but he did not see her nor was seen by her. Instead he went forward into the bows and sat down by himself in silence, holding his head in both hands.' Not long afterwards some Liburnians were seen coming up in hot pursuit and Antony had the flagship put about to face them. All of them were driven off with the exception of one which was commanded by Eurycles of Sparta, who had fitted out his galley at his own expense. He waged a personal vendetta against Antony because the latter had had his father executed on a charge of robbery. As the Liburnian came on at him Antony called out from the bows 'Who is this that pursues Antony?' Eurycles called back his name, adding that he had come to avenge his father's death. In the confused action that followed Eurycles's vessel collided with another flagship – probably one that had got away from Antony's centre – and then swept into a smaller galley which he captured. Antony's vessel turned about and the whole squadron resumed their flight to the south.

They were headed for Taenarum, the southerly point of the Peloponnese where there was a small harbour and roadstead, which had clearly been designated as the rendezvous point in the event of defeat. It took them three days to get down there, during all of which time Antony refused to move from his solitary vigil in the bows, sitting in total dejection like a statue to failure. It would have been better to have died in battle than to fly with the Queen. Whatever he may have thought before Actium, however much he may have anticipated failure and been prepared to escape in order to have another chance of beating Octavian, he must now have felt that everything was over. Even if his army got away, even if he built a new fleet, he had lost faith in himself.

When the ships dropped anchor at Taenarum, Charmion, Iras and others of

Cleopatra's serving women at last induced Antony to come aft to the Queen's quarters and 'then persuaded them to eat and sleep together'. While the vessels were watering and making ready for the voyage to Egypt a number of others came up with them. Some of these were survivors from the fleet while some were probably galleys and merchant ships that had been at ports on the west coast of Greece or in the Gulf of Patras. They brought news that the fleet was indeed defeated and all the ships either captured or burned, but that the land army was still intact. It might have seemed then that there was still a ray of hope. This was soon to be extinguished.

Canidius had indeed begun the withdrawal, marching east towards Macedonia. But Octavian's forces, exhilarated by the victory at sea, were in no mood to let any of the Antonians make their escape. They caught up with them and the two armies once again faced one another – but not, as it turned out, to fight. Antony's commanders as well as his men were completely demoralized, especially at the news that he had not gone down in battle but had escaped with the Queen of Egypt. Cleopatra! Once again it was seen that his dependence upon her was fatal

Ships of the type that fought at Actium, from Trajan's column, Rome

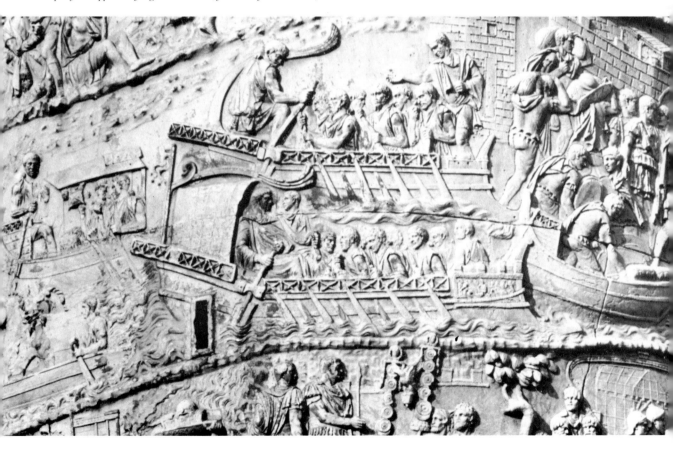

239

and that he was no longer the Antony they had known in earlier days. It was not difficult for the astute Octavian to get them to lay down their arms, especially when he promised the veterans that in the distribution of land now that the war was over he would ensure that they received the same treatment as his own men. The bargaining went on for some days, Octavian even conceding that he would keep on six of Antony's legions and amalgamate them with his own. When it was quite clear that the men were going to accept Octavian's terms Canidius and some of the other commanders escaped overnight. However generous the victor might be to junior officers, centurions and soldiers, they knew well enough that his generosity would not be extended to them.

Antony meanwhile, ignorant as yet of the situation of his troops in Greece, was concerned about the fate of the friends who had followed him. He pointed out that he and the Queen were headed for Egypt, that it seemed as if his cause was lost, and that he did not want his friends to suffer on his account. 'He selected one of the transport ships which carried a great deal of money as well as very valuable gold and silver objects from the royal treasury and made them a present of it, telling them to divide it up and look after their own safety. They refused his gift and were in tears for him. . . .' Even at this moment, when most of his friends hated Cleopatra and despised Antony for his dependence on her, even after he had sought safety in flight rather than die in battle, they still could not dislike Antony. Warm-hearted and generous, he always had charm. Antony sent them away to Corinth with a message to his steward there to look after them and keep them in safe hiding until such time as they could make their peace with Octavian.

Cleopatra and Antony and what remained of their fleet set sail for Egypt. The Queen must go to her capital, Alexandria, and it might have been thought that Antony would accompany her in order to make plans for the future, organize his affairs in the East, and set about a large-scale ship-building programme. But it seems that he could not face the idea of returning to the palace and the court, to the crowds in the streets, to his friends and fellow soldiers, as the man who had just been defeated by the sickly Octavian. Was it conceivable that he, Antony, who had been one of Caesar's greatest generals, who had avenged the latter's murder on the battlefield of Philippi, the descendant of Hercules, should be stared at and possibly even mocked as a ruined runaway? While the Queen went to Alexandria Antony with two companions stayed on at the small garrison town of Paraetonium where the fleet had made its landfall. The place lies about one hundred and sixty miles west of Alexandria on that barren coast which is backed by the Libyan plateau. In those days there can have been little more than a small fort overlooking the headland where a narrow inlet of the sea runs in through high limestone cliffs. The desert is all around, and in September the heat will have been oppressive, especially when the *khamsin* wind blew up from the south with all Africa on its breath. The two companions who stayed with Antony in his self-imposed exile give some indication of the varying range of men to whom he appealed. One was an intellectual, a Greek rhetorician called Aristocrates. The other was a Roman soldier, Lucilius, whom Antony had pardoned on the field of Philippi. Lucilius had been fighting on the side of Brutus and when it was clear that the battle was lost, had pretended to be Brutus in order that the latter could make his escape. Antony admired his gallantry and forgave him for the deception. Lucilius was to remain faithful to Antony until the end of his life.

During the weeks when Antony was brooding forlornly in this barren outpost, even threatening to commit suicide when he heard that the legions in Cyrenaica had gone over to Octavian, the latter was busy in Greece. Having achieved the peaceful demobilization of Antony's army the victor was busy eliminating Antony's former supporters. All the cities of Greece with the exception of Corinth swore allegiance to Octavian. The very people who only a few months before had been hailing Antony as Dionysus and Cleopatra as Isis, now threw down their statues and heaped honours upon Octavian. The news of Actium had spread throughout the Mediterranean world as fast as ships and horsemen could carry it. It could only be a matter of time before the eastern provinces and client states declared themselves for Octavian. Nothing would then be left but Egypt.

While Antony was trying to summon up the courage to kill himself and Octavian was busily making arrangements for the new order in Greece and the East, Cleopatra was far from idle. For the second time she had played for the highest stakes and lost. But one thing she had not lost was her courage and perseverance. She knew by now (and had probably known for a long time) that Antony was not only a drunkard but a failure. She had had three children by him and she had originally seen him as the man most likely to inherit the Roman Empire and establish with her the Greco-

---

Silver denarius with portrait of Mark Antony, c. 39 B.C.

241

Roman dynasty that would rule the world. But after the long months of summer and the battle of Actium she could have had little or no faith in his capabilities. She may well have hoped that like many another defeated general of that time he would fall upon his sword and kill himself. It was a hard world and, as Arthur Weigall comments:

> The many wars conducted in recent years, and the numerous political murders and massacres had made people very familiar with violent death. The case of Arria, the wife of Paetus, is an illustration of the light manner in which the termination of life was regarded. Her husband having been condemned to death, Arria determined to anticipate the executioner; and therefore, having driven a dagger into her breast, she coolly handed the weapon to him, with the casual words, 'It isn't painful'.

But men who might casually throw away their lives when they are young are increasingly reluctant to do so as they grow older, and Antony's addiction to the wine god and self-indulgence in general had sapped his willpower. One may suppose that it was without too much of a struggle that he allowed his friends Aristocrates and Lucilius to prevail upon him not to commit suicide after the defection of the legions in Cyrenaica but to go quietly back to Alexandria.

Here in the city where he had once been so happy Antony fell into even deeper despair. Perhaps it was the memories of his first visit as a young cavalry officer, and then of that first Alexandrian winter, and then of the plans that they had made together for the destruction of Octavian, which completed his physical and mental collapse.

> Antony forsook the city and the company of his friends and built a dwelling for himself near Pharos on a mole which he had specially constructed out into the water. He lived here an exile from humankind. He said that he was emulating the example of Timon since his experiences had been similar to his, for he had been wronged and ill-treated by his friends and therefore had come to the conclusion that all mankind should be shunned and mistrusted.

All this of course was nonsense. Antony's friends had stood by him throughout the campaign in Greece and many of them had died for him after he had fled with Cleopatra. The Timon upon whom he now pretended to model himself was a noted misanthrope who had lived in Athens during the period of the Peloponnesian war. He is said to have been very fond of Alcibiades and, when asked why, to have replied 'Because he will do a great deal of harm to Athens'. It is said that he once entered the assembly in Athens, something which caused a considerable stir since he was known to loathe such meetings, and called out: 'Athenians! I have a small building plot on which a fig-tree grows – a tree from which many fellow citizens

Temples in the sanctuary of Apollo, partially reconstructed, at Cyrene, Libya

have hanged themselves from time to time. But now that I intend to build a house there I give you all fair warning that any of you who also desire to hang yourselves should do so quickly before I have it cut down.' An epitaph he composed for himself, and which is reported to have been inscribed upon his tomb, reads:

> Timon, who hated men, lies here below
> Revile me if you will – but only go!

It was upon this obscure and singularly unattractive figure that the descendant of Hercules and the New Dionysus now decided to model himself. Antony had always had a paranoiac streak and he seems never at any time to have had control of his emotions. When he abandoned himself to despair he was determined to do it as thoroughly as when he abandoned himself to wine.

Cleopatra can have had absolutely no sympathy with his current mood. She was a fighter to the last and she was determined to salvage what she could from the ashes of Actium. It was now that, in Plutarch's words,

> she entered upon a hazardous but great undertaking. The isthmus which separates the Red Sea [the gulf of Suez] from the Mediterranean Sea off Egypt is considered to be the boundary between Asia and Libya, and in the part where it is narrowest it measures three hundred furlongs. Here Cleopatra determined to drag her ships ashore and transport them across the land and then launch them into the Gulf. She would take with her as much money and men as possible and would settle in some area outside of Egypt, thus escaping either war or servitude.

Cleopatra realized well enough that the West was now forever closed to her, and that the provinces and client states of Asia Minor would soon acknowledge Octavian. After that it would be only a matter of time before he would strike at Egypt and all would be over. There was one route left open to her and that was to the East. In pursuance of her new policy she determined to consolidate her relations with the King of Media. Artavasdes the imprisoned Armenian King had been an enemy of his and it is possible also that he was caught trying to communicate with Octavian. Cleopatra accordingly had him executed and sent his head to the King of Media. By executing his enemy as a token of good faith she achieved another purpose, for she prevented Octavian from using Artavasdes's name as the real claimant to the throne of Armenia. It was probably at about this time that she sent her child Alexander Helios and the King of Media's young daughter to whom he was betrothed to the King's court. They at least would be safe there and out of Octavian's reach.

At the same time as she was preparing for the transport of her ships to the Gulf of Suez she embarked on a large shipbuilding programme in the region of modern Suez, clearly with the intention of making herself mistress of the Red Sea and the

Statue of Augustus

Arabian Gulf. Allied to the King of Media – an alliance now cemented by ties of blood – she might well build up a new kingdom in the East, where she would be shielded from the Romans by Media and the fierce Parthians. Caesarion would finally come into his own and there might yet be a chance that when he was a man he would be able to march 'with all the East at heel' and claim his rightful inheritance of the whole Roman Empire. But once again implacable fate dealt Cleopatra a further blow. The Nabataean Arabs whose capital was the mountain fortress of Petra, and who had long been on bad terms with the Egyptians, got wind of Cleopatra's intentions. They were naturally hostile to the idea of the Egyptians extending their kingdom or establishing themselves anywhere in their area. They staged a massive raid on the docks where Cleopatra's new fleet was building and burned everything to the ground including the first of the ships which had just been transported from the Mediterranean. It was the end of Cleopatra's dream. From now on nothing was left her but Egypt, and that for only so long as Octavian cared to leave her alone.

The reason the latter did not follow up his victory at Actium was that first of all he had to secure Greece and make his provisions for the East, and then that he had a great deal of trouble in Italy. The resettlement of the veterans was always a grave problem at the end of any war and there were also plots against Octavian, one of which his friend Maecenas uncovered. The author of it, Marcus Lepidus, son of the former triumvir, was put to death. Octavian had intended to winter in the island of Samos, the very place where Antony and Cleopatra had celebrated their forthcoming victory the year before. From here he intended to make the disposition of the legions for the forthcoming campaign, ensure his control of the provinces and client states of Asia Minor, and march down to Egypt in the spring. But the state of affairs in Italy forced him to take ship and hasten back to Brundisium, for many of the demobilized legionaries were in a state of mutiny. Even Agrippa could not cope with the situation and it was he who had requested Octavian to return. Although it was now mid-winter and the normal sailing season was long over Octavian did not hesitate. It is clear enough evidence of the power and personality of this young man that he had settled the whole affair within a month of his arrival, distributing land to those who had been with him throughout his campaigns and money to those who had joined him later. This was no Timon of Athens moping on the seashore.

With the failure of her plans for building a new state in the East Cleopatra did not lapse into fatal gloom. She knew now that both she and he were doomed, but she was determined that they should end their lives in a manner befitting those who had been among the great ones of the earth and who had very nearly ruled the world. If Empire was no longer attainable at least they should go down in laughter and flowers just as they had celebrated the first month of their relationship together.

Detail from Trajan's Column showing the Emperor haranguing his troops

247

Her feelings at this moment are probably best expressed by the Victorian poet Ernest Dowson writing many centuries later, but aware that he too was destined very soon to die:

> They are not long, the weeping and the laughter,
> Love and desire and hate:
> I think we have no portion in them after
> We pass the gate.
>
> They are not long the days of wine and roses:
> Out of a misty dream
> Our path emerges for a while, then closes
> Within a dream.

Cleopatra inveigled Antony out of his solitary and pointless seclusion. From the moment of her arrival in Alexandria she had acted with all the commendable authority of a great leader. There had been riots and opposition to her, all of which she had suppressed with a heavy hand. She was determined to make sure that the people knew that she, Cleopatra, the Queen and Isis incarnate, the descendant of the Ptolemies, was still firmly in command of her country. When Antony had been on the verge of suicide at the news that the legions in Cyrenaica had gone over to Octavian Cleopatra had kept her nerve. Even when it was known that the governor of Syria had also defected, Cleopatra did not collapse or lose her moral courage. She realized that she and her soldier-husband as well as her country were now finished – unless she could pull off some last diplomatic coup. Her old enemy Herod threw in his lot with Octavian but even this did not break the Queen's spirit. She came from a long line of survivors. She felt that if only she could revive Antony's morale there was still the remotest chance that she could come to some conclusion with Octavian and possibly ensure the throne of Egypt for her son Caesarion.

The 'Club of Inimitable Livers' was revived, only it was given the new name of the 'Club of those who Die Together'. Cleopatra had been familiar with death in all its forms since she was a child. She now sensed death very close on the shadowy horizons to the east and west of Alexandria. Alexander lay dead in the city itself and the Pyramids and innumerable other tombs and objects had constantly reminded her of the darkness that falls after the sun goes down. If Antony was afraid of it she must revive his spirits so that he could face the last enemy as he had once faced so many others.

Petra, Jordan

THE GOD DESERTS ANTONY

An elaborate ceremony was staged in Alexandria in April 30 B.C., a ceremony designed to secure the throne of Egypt for the descendants of Cleopatra. This was the coming of age of Caesarion. He was now seventeen and, since he was the son of a Roman, the Roman traditions were followed and he adopted the *toga virilis*, the sign of manhood. Cleopatra was in effect saying to her people that they now had a man as a ruler and that in future she would gradually efface herself from the scene. Antony's eldest son by Fulvia, Antyllus, although he was two years younger, was also made to put on the Roman toga and declared an adult. This affair which was conducted with great formality was Cleopatra's last significant political act. It was also the greatest mistake of her career. By declaring the two youths adults – in particular by declaring that Caesar's son and heir was now a man – she had condemned them both to death. When Octavian arrived in Egypt he would never allow these two claimants to the leadership of Rome to stay alive.

Cleopatra knew that she herself was almost certainly doomed and she prepared for death in her usual methodical way. As was customary with the Egyptian rulers she had had an impressive mausoleum built to house her remains. The Pharaohs had established the tradition of monuments to death centuries before, and the tomb of Alexander in the centre of the city was yet another memorial to the mighty dead. Cleopatra now set about testing methods for killing herself, for she was determined never to walk as her sister had done, a defeated and chained victim at a Roman Triumph. 'So she began collecting all sorts of deadly poisons and testing them out on prisoners who were under sentence of death to see whether they were painless or not.' This is the story according to Plutarch, but it is extremely unlikely that this was necessary. The use of poisons was widely known in the East and there can be little doubt that the Egyptians, who were among the foremost pharmaceutists of the ancient world, were completely familiar with every drug and poison then available.

However this is the tradition, and Plutarch is still our best authority.

> She saw that the speedier poisons made death more painful while the milder poisons were not quick enough. Accordingly she had experiments made with venomous animals and watched as they were set upon one another. . . . She found that the bite of an asp alone induced a quiet sleep without any spasms or pain, with only a little perspiration on the face, while the mind was gently relaxed. The victims could not be aroused or restored, but were just like people who were sound asleep.

The Greek 'asp' is probably the hooded cobra (*Naja haje*), which is the ancient royal symbol, the uraeus. This distinctive emblem of the Pharaohs is shown on royal crowns threatening the enemies of the King.

It is incredible that even at this moment Cleopatra, and Antony too it appears, thought that it might be possible to effect some *modus vivendi* with Octavian. An ambassador was sent to him with the proposal that Cleopatra should resign the throne if he would allow her children to inherit. Antony hoped for the same destiny as Lepidus, the third triumvir, who had been permitted after his failure against Octavian in Sicily to retire to his country house at Circeii. He accordingly asked that he might be permitted to live as a private citizen, if not in Egypt then in Athens. But the only reason that Octavian had spared Lepidus was that he was a spent force and no challenge to his authority. It had also suited him at that moment to be clement and not to antagonize any of Lepidus's friends and supporters. He knew how to be magnanimous when it would redound to his credit. Antony and Cleopatra were quite another matter. As long as they were alive his position would be insecure. He could never be certain that, whilst he was in Rome or in other parts of the Empire, they would not be preparing for another bid for power. Far more than that, there was the question of Caesarion. Despite the fact that some ancient writers declared that Caesarion was not Caesar's child there can be little doubt that Octavian believed, or knew, that he was. As the adopted head of the Julian clan, as 'Caesar', which he had styled himself ever since the contents of the Dictator's will had been publicly approved, he could never permit another Caesar to rule in the East and one day make a claim for the whole Empire.

But Octavian was always cautious and he was not going to reject the proposals outright. He would see whether he could not play one of his enemies off against the other. He made no reply to Antony's request, but sent word to Cleopatra that she would receive reasonable treatment on the condition that she either expelled Antony from her kingdom or had him put to death. But there can be little doubt that even if Cleopatra had been willing to accede to his suggestion he would still have marched against Egypt and taken her back to Rome in chains when he celebrated his Egyptian Triumph.

No one will ever know whether Cleopatra seriously considered Octavian's proposal. It seems improbable. She may well have hoped after Actium – or even now – that Antony would fall on his sword in the traditional manner of defeated Roman generals. But Antony, that great lover of life, clung to it resolutely to the end. When Octavian made his suggestion he was probably a victim of his own propaganda, and prepared to believe that this monstrous eastern Queen would stoop to anything. He was to be disillusioned. Although later Roman historians were to make great play with suggestions of Cleopatra's treachery or attempted treachery throughout the coming months, there is no evidence that she ever did anything but try to keep Egypt independent of Rome and secure the throne for Caesar's son.

Octavian in his attempt to drive a wedge between Antony and Cleopatra sent one of his freedmen, Thyrsus, who is described as 'a very personable man', to the court at Alexandria to have secret discussions with the Queen. These were probably about having Antony either exiled or killed. Cleopatra treated this emissary with extreme politeness and appears to have been quite willing to have long and private discussions with him, discussions to which Antony was not invited. The latter finally lost his temper and had Thyrsus hung up and flogged. He then sent him back to Octavian with the message that if he did not like what had been done he had Antony's permission to have his own freedman Hipparchus dealt with in the same way. This was a joke, for Hipparchus had betrayed him and gone over to Octavian. The Queen was probably amused by Antony's action, for it is extremely doubtful if she had been doing any more than play for time. To quote Plutarch:

> After this Cleopatra did her best to relieve Antony of any causes for complaint or suspicion, paying elaborate court to him. While she kept her own birthday in a modest manner as was suitable in view of the circumstances, Antony's was celebrated in a most luxurious and splendid way. Many of those who came to the banquet arrived poor and went away rich.

This was hardly the behaviour of a woman who was trying to betray Antony to Octavian.

In late spring, when it was known that Octavian was in Asia Minor and preparing for the *coup de grâce*, Cleopatra sent Caesarion away from the capital. To the very end she was determined that her son by Caesar should survive whatever happened to her, to Antony, or to her other children. Caesarion travelled south with his tutor, by ship up the Nile as far as Coptos and from there he was to go on across the desert to the Red Sea port of Berenice. This was one of the main trading centres with Arabia and India, and it was Cleopatra's intention that he should stay there until the forthcoming campaign was over. There was still a chance that Antony would out-general Octavian in a pitched battle in which case everything would be changed overnight. If Antony lost Caesarion could make his way by sea to Arabia or India, where he was certain to be well received as the son of Egypt's ruler. There would still be hope for his future.

In May 30 B.C. Octavian came down with the legions from Asia Minor and marched into Syria where all the garrisons surrendered to him. Since Herod of Judaea had already deserted Antony's cause the road lay open into Egypt from the north. Octavian's general Gallus who was advancing from the west now seized the garrison town of Paraetonium, where Antony had gone into miserable retreat after Actium. Egypt was about to be attacked on both sides. Even if Antony's legions and Cleopatra's fleet had the heart to fight, the situation was critical in the extreme. Cleopatra had already anticipated the worst and had all the royal treasure taken into her mausoleum – 'gold, silver, emeralds, pearls, ebony, and ivory'. Large quantities of inflammable materials were stacked round about, for she was determined that the ancient treasures of the Ptolemies should not fall into the hands of this upstart Octavian. She could be almost certain that she had lost, and that she would never see Caesarion again. All that remained to her was the prospect of dying in a manner befitting a queen.

Octavian now advanced on Pelusium, the garrison town on the eastern branch of the Nile, which had been the scene of innumerable battles and sieges in the course of Egypt's long history. Once Pelusium fell the road was clear to Alexandria. Octavian said later that he 'took Pelusium by storm' and there is no reason to doubt his words, but both Plutarch and Dio Cassius suggest that it was deliberately handed over on the orders of Cleopatra who was being treacherous to Antony. But what had Cleopatra to gain by letting Octavian advance unscathed into Egypt? She had already spurned his offer to have Antony banished or murdered and she had sent her son away to keep him safe. As all her preparations make clear she knew well enough that the end was in sight. She had been vanquished by Octavian – and Octavian had instituted the Principate. It was in the interests of every emperor therefore to capitalize on the events of these years and to say, as it were, 'Look what happened last time when you did not have one man, and one man alone, ruling the

Relief of a ceremonial cavalry parade on the marble base for a column erected in memory of Emperor Antoninus Pius, who died 161 A.D.

Empire!' Horace, Virgil, Propertius and others were all in what might be called 'the conspiracy' to blacken Cleopatra.

With Pelusium in their hands Octavian's troops advanced steadily into Egypt. It was late July, when the desert road and all the area to the north of the city wavers with heat and only the Meltemi wind that blows down from the north, from Crete and the Aegean, makes life supportable. When Octavian's legions arrived to pitch camp against Alexandria they were dusty and desert-stained, thirsty and exhausted. Antony knew that his only chance was to catch them before they had time to regroup, refresh themselves, and assault the city. If he could defeat Octavian, the legions advancing from the west might possibly be discounted. It was a forlorn hope, but at least at this very last hour Antony showed something of his old dash and leadership. As the legions began to encamp he led out his cavalry and fell upon Octavian's advance guard when it came up towards the outskirts of the city. In Plutarch's words, 'He put them to flight in a brilliant action and pursued them back as far as their own camp.' He then made his archers fire arrows into Octavian's lines bearing messages offering large rewards to any who would defect. Many of the soldiers knew Antony and had once admired and followed him, but after Actium nothing could ever be the same. His flight with Cleopatra had ruined him in the eyes of the troops, let alone of the officers. Octavian once more showed his perspicacity and, far from concealing his knowledge of the rewards offered, called the troops together and read out one of Antony's messages. He then carefully pointed out that there to the west of them lay Alexandria, all shimmering with marble and filled with treasures. It was theirs for the taking and nothing that Antony could offer could ever equal the city that was within their grasp. (He had no intention of letting them plunder and despoil Alexandria, but was to keep the city as one of the glories of the Empire, though secondary to Rome.)

Antony rode back to the palace after his cavalry action. Still wearing his dusty armour, he flung himself into Cleopatra's arms proclaiming the success of the encounter. He then presented one of his men who had conducted himself gallantly during the day. As a reward the Queen made him the gift of a golden helmet and breastplate. The same night this soldier slipped out of Alexandria and made his way to Octavian's lines. It was plain to everyone, plain even to Antony one suspects, that to win a cavalry action is not to win a battle, let alone a war.

Once again, as he had done at Actium, Antony strove to reduce the whole contest to the level of the ancient days of Rome or the Homeric encounters of the far distant Trojan war. He sent Octavian a challenge to single combat. Octavian replied that he could see little point in the suggestion: if Antony wanted to die, he said, there were many ways open to him.

Clearly Antony must now prepare for a protracted siege of Alexandria or make one last desperate effort in a general engagement by land and sea. Alexandria was strongly fortified and capable of resisting a siege, but a besieged city can hold out only so long as the soldiers and the citizens within it are prepared to endure the hunger, harship and discomfort that such a state entails. The citizens of Alexandria, a notoriously easy-going, dissident and dissolute mélange of nationalities, would never undergo all these deprivations for the sake of a Roman general who was losing a war. When he was the all-conquering Hercules and the riotous Dionysus they had acclaimed him. But now things were altogether different. They had everything to gain by throwing in their lot with the man who already held the whole of the Roman world, with the exception of their own country, within his grasp. It was doubtful whether Antony's four legions, who knew themselves about to be attacked by superior forces on both sides of the city, would be prepared to fight. Why should they fight for a general who had fled from Actium while others died for him, saving his own skin and following a woman?

On the night before the last engagement, while the fires and flares burned brightly in Octavian's lines, Antony ordered a banquet in the palace. It was the last ever given by the leader of the 'Society of the Inimitable Livers' or of 'The Diers Together'. He told the servants to make sure that he was better fed and had more wine than usual, for it was quite likely that they would be serving a new master by the following day. As for his friends, who were openly crying at his words, he told them that he had no intention of leading them into battle. What he sought was death for himself and he saw no reason why they should have to follow him. As always, Appian writes, 'he showed a character and spirit that was decent, straight-forward, and without malice'. There is no mention of Cleopatra being present at this last dinner-party, but this is no indication that there was any rift between them for it would have been natural for the historians to assume that she was with him. One can be sure that if there was any tale to the contrary it would have been widely reported in order to demonstrate how, even at this late hour, the Queen was trying to betray him and make her peace with Octavian.

Antony's last night on earth was marked by a strange phenomenon:

> It is said that round about the middle of this night when the city was all quiet and everyone fearful of the outcome of the next day, suddenly there was heard the noise of music and a sweet harmony from many musical instruments, together with the shouts of a great group of people. There were Bacchic cries and the sound of satyrs leaping. It seemed as if a great troop of boisterous revellers was leaving the city, and it sounded as though they were making their way down the centre of Alexandria and heading for the gate against which the enemy was encamped. It was at this point that the tumult became loudest. Then suddenly it all died away into silence. It appeared to those who sought some explanation of this strange event that the god to whom Antony had always likened himself, and to whom he was most attached, was at last deserting him. (Plutarch)

It was this passage which inspired Cavafy, the great twentieth-century Alexandrian poet, with the theme for his poem *The God abandons Antony*:

> When at the hour of midnight
> An invisible choir is suddenly heard passing

With exquisite music, with voices –
Do not lament your freedom that at last subsides,
Your life's work that has failed, your schemes
That have proved illusions.
But like a man prepared, like a brave man,
Bid farewell to her, to Alexandria who is departing.
Above all, do not delude yourself, do not say that
It is a dream,
That your ear was mistaken.
Do not condescend to such empty hopes.
Like a brave man for long prepared, like a brave man,
Like to the man who is worthy of such a city,
Go to the window firmly,
And listen with emotion.
But not with the prayers and complaints of the coward.
(Ah! Supreme rapture!)
Listen to the notes, to the exquisite instruments
Of the mystic choir,
And bid farewell to her,
To Alexandria whom you are losing.

(Trans. George Valassopoulo)

On the morning of 1 August 30 B.C. Antony made his last attempt to escape from the stranglehold of his young and relentless enemy. It was a forlorn hope, and he had known it as such the night before, but he was determined at least to die 'with harness on my back'. Even in this he was to be disappointed, for his troops saw no reason to lose their lives. Later Roman historians made out that it was Cleopatra who betrayed Antony in order to try and save her kingdom for herself and her son, but the defection of Antony's troops required no bribery or conspiracy on the part of the Queen. They were men familiar with war and they knew well enough when a situation was hopeless.

Antony's intention was for the fleet to sail out from the Great Harbour on the east and attack Octavian's fleet while at the same time his cavalry and legions were to make a frontal assault against the enemy. The latter, although greater in numbers, had still had little more than a night's sleep under canvas after their long desert march. Proudly the Egyptian navy moved out, the survivors of Actium, ships that had long been on guard at Alexandria, and new vessels built over that winter. Antony watched them from a hillock where he stood with his staff officers, his legionaries drawn up for the attack. The ships slid forward across the quiet summer sea, only two or three miles separating them from Octavian's blockading fleet. It is very quiet at that hour, very still in the early Egyptian morning before the north wind starts to blow, and before the life of the town begins to murmur and vibrate with cart-wheels, the voices of working people, and the cries of tradesmen. No doubt on that morning there was an especial stillness, since those who were in the know waited in expectation, and those who were in ignorance waited in fear. The Egyptian ships were now closing with their opponents and at any moment it might have been expected that the first evidences of action would be seen: the discharge of great stones, grapnels, and fire-baskets from the assailants prior to a general engagement and the ensuing ship-to-ship encounters. Then all Antony's and Cleopatra's ships suddenly 'boated their oars' – lifted them out of the water – as an indication that they were not coming in to ram or to attack but that they came as friends.

At almost the same moment, and whether the event was prearranged or whether inspired by the action of the fleet no one can ever say, the whole of Antony's cavalry dashed out from their positions – not to charge the enemy but to join him. Only the legionaries for a time stood firm, but they were no match for their opponents, reinforced as these were by Antony's cavalry. Finally the sight of all Octavian's ships, together with the Egyptians, making their way in ordered lines towards the eastern harbour convinced even those who were most devoted to Antony that all was over. The soldiers broke and ran; their commander retreated with them into the city. He was heard to cry out that Cleopatra, for whose cause he was fighting, had betrayed him. In his bitterness and despair his words are understandable, but they were the words of a weak man who even at this moment was not prepared to concede that his defeat at Actium and now in Egypt was largely his own fault.

Cleopatra, seeing the turn that events had taken, rushed down the corridors of the palace accompanied by her serving women Iras and Charmion and made her way to the mausoleum which adjoined the temple of Isis. Once inside the women dropped the bolts on the great door and resigned themselves to despair. According to Plutarch, Cleopatra now sent a messenger to Antony to tell him that she had killed herself. Whether this was really the message that she sent, or if she merely said that she *intended* to kill herself, will never be known. It may well be that Cleopatra, knowing Antony's weakness and irresolution, despatched a messenger to say that she was dead in order to prompt him to suicide. There was nothing else for him to do. It was Antony's duty as a defeated Roman general and as the forsaken of Dionysus to kill himself. He owed it to the soldiers and sailors who had died for him at Actium to close his life with dignity.

The messenger reached Antony in the palace, where he was raving about the desertion of his fleet and cavalry, and complaining of the treachery of Cleopatra. Those simple words 'The Queen has killed herself' shattered his whole world. 'Why delay any longer, Antony?' he cried. 'Fate has taken away the last and only reason for your clinging to life.' He unfastened his breastplate and laid it aside and was overheard by bystanders to say, 'I am not sad to be parted from you Cleopatra for I shall soon be with you. The only thing that troubles me is that a general such as I should have been found inferior in courage to a woman.'

He turned to his faithful slave Eros, whom he had earlier made promise to kill him if all should be lost, and ordered him to draw his sword and fulfil his oath. Eros drew it from Antony's scabbard, raised it as if to obey, and then fell upon the sword himself. As he lay at his master's feet Antony was finally shamed into doing for himself what another, and a slave, had shown him how to do. 'Well done, Eros, well done!' he said to the dying man, 'Although you did not do it for me, yet you have taught me what I must do for myself.' With these words he fell upon his sword, driving it in below his ribs. Even now he was not destined to make as easy an exit as his slave. The sword failed to pierce his heart but went into his stomach. As he dropped face downward upon a couch he fainted. No doubt the servants who had crept in to witness their master's end thought that Antony was dead. After a time however the blood ceased to flow and he recovered consciousness. He begged the bystanders to give him the finishing stroke, but they were all too terrified when they realized that he was still alive and fled from the room. So Antony lay there groaning in agony while the servants rushed to Cleopatra's mausoleum to tell her that Antony had tried to commit suicide but was not yet dead.

She had expected to hear that he had killed himself. She immediately sent off her secretary Diomedes with orders to bring him to her tomb. Diomedes rounded up some slaves and told them to place Antony upon a litter and carry him to Cleopatra. It is hot in Alexandria in August (that month which was to be named after the victorious Octavian/Augustus). Only the wind from the north will have been stirring across the gardens and the courtyards that lay between the palace and the mausoleum as the slaves, accompanied by Diomedes, carried the dying Dionysus to Isis, his Queen and his wife.

Cleopatra was determined not to be taken alive by any advance guard of the troops who were now preparing to march into Alexandria, nor let any potential looters into the tomb, and she refused to unbolt the great doors. Her face and those of her two companions were seen by onlookers peering down from a window high up in the building as Antony was brought on his litter up to the main door. Soon ropes were seen snaking down from the window and, as Plutarch tells it, 'Antony was fastened to these and the Queen herself, aided by her two women, slowly drew him up to the window. Never, so those who were present tell me, was there seen a more tragic sight as, covered with blood and struggling in the grip of death he was drawn up, stretching out his hands to her even as he hung there in mid-air.' Antony was a big and heavily built man, and he had run to fat in recent years. 'The task was not an easy one for women. Cleopatra with her hands to the rope and her face strained with the effort could hardly pull him up to her. Meanwhile those who were standing below called out encouragements, mentally sharing all her efforts and anguish.' At long last, leaving a pattern of blood-stains on the hot stonework of the mausoleum's side, Antony was drawn into the window and rejoined the woman whom he loved, who had brought him to disaster.

Unless there was some pulley erected above the window it seems a little unlikely that three women could have drawn up Antony's body by the strength of their arms alone. The fact that Plutarch continues his history with what sounds like an eyewitness's account suggests that the slaves or bystanders below laid ladders against the side of the mausoleum to assist Antony's ascent, and that some of them subsequently peered through the window to watch the culmination of the tragedy. 'Once Cleopatra and her attendants had got Antony inside the building and laid him down to rest the Queen abandoned herself to grief. She beat and tore her breasts, wiping off some of his blood upon her face, and calling him her lord, her husband, and her emperor. In her pity for him in his agony she forgot all about her own terrible misfortunes.' No longer Isis, no longer even Queen of Egypt, she was Woman incarnate, bewailing the death of her lover, her husband, the father of her children. The tears of Cleopatra are written forever on the memory of the world.

After a short time Antony rallied and begged Cleopatra to desist from her grief. Even though the god had deserted him he remained faithful to the last to Dionysus, asking the women to get him some wine, 'either because he was thirsty or because he thought it would hasten his death'. He lay back again after he had drunk. No doubt his internal haemorrhage soon increased, for the passage of any liquid would promote the flow of blood while alcohol, by raising the pulse rate, would almost certainly prove fatal. But before he died he was still strong enough and sufficiently in his senses to tell the Queen that she must try and make terms with Octavian. The only man among the latter's advisers whom she could trust, he said, was a certain Proculeius. His last words according to Plutarch were that she must not pity him for this turn of Fate. 'Be happy with me,' he said, 'in the remembrance of the good times we shared in the past. I have been among the most powerful and illustrious of men, and now I am not ignobly conquered, but a Roman by a Roman overthrown.' He died in her arms, the gold Egyptian sunlight pouring in through the window embrasure, and the sea-wind stirring the dust along the marble floor.

DEATH AND THE VICTOR

The news that Antony had killed himself was brought to Octavian in his camp by one of Antony's bodyguard. Shortly afterwards a further messenger despatched by Cleopatra confirmed the fact that his enemy was dead. Octavian was triumphant, but even at this moment he knew how to play his part. No doubt he remembered the story of how Julius Caesar had greeted the news that Pompey was dead with tears, and he felt that the occasions were so similar that he should emulate his great ancestor by a similar display of emotion. After a suitable length of time – he had no need to hurry for all Egypt was already his – he called several of his friends into his tent. All of them had known Antony and no doubt some of them still had real affection for him, so Octavian felt called upon to justify himself. He proceeded to read out to them copies of letters which he had sent to Antony, followed by Antony's replies. They could see, he pointed out, how he had always tried for a reconciliation with his fellow triumvir, only to be met with arrogance and insults. Perhaps he referred to Cleopatra, pointing out that it was Antony's subservience to the ambitions of Egypt's Queen that had brought him to his sad end. It was plain that he could not be blamed either for the recent war or for Antony's death. No doubt Octavian sighed.

In the meantime his friend Proculeius, the one man whom Antony had told Cleopatra that she could trust, had made his way into the city and hearing that the Queen had locked herself in her mausoleum had gone straight to the massive closed door. He called out to the Queen and waited, expecting perhaps that she would let him in. But Cleopatra, as was natural, remained suspicious and would speak to him only through the door. All that was left to her now were the children and it was of them that she spoke, begging that whatever happened to her they at least should be allowed to inherit her kingdom. Proculeius certainly could make no promises on that score so he temporized, merely telling her to be of good heart and assuring her that she could trust Octavian in everything. This can have been of little comfort to Cleopatra for she knew well enough that it was against her that Octavian had declared war and that it was she, not Antony, who had been branded as the enemy of the Roman people. Cornelius Gallus, the general who had invaded Egypt from the west by way of Paraetonium, was now sent by Octavian

Statue of the Emperor Augustus, from Spain

to engage the Queen in conversation. While she was talking with him Proculeius accompanied by two other officers went round to the back of the mausoleum. They swiftly placed ladders against it and swarmed up through a window at the top into the very room where the body of Antony lay in a welter of blood. Running down the stairs to the ground floor they saw Cleopatra and her two serving women standing against the door, the Queen engaged in talking to Cornelius Gallus on the other side. One of the women turned round at the sound of their footsteps and cried out 'Unhappy Cleopatra, you are taken prisoner!' Cleopatra swung round, saw Proculeius and snatched a dagger from her girdle. But before she could stab herself Proculeius had rushed forward, smothering her arms so that the dagger fell from her hand. Not only had she failed to take her life, but all the treasures of the Ptolemies, surrounded by the wood and combustibles which would never now be kindled, were in Octavian's hands. She had failed in everything and she knew then the bitterness of total despair.

Proculeius after reproaching Cleopatra for having attempted to take her own life and assuring her once more that she could expect only reasonable treatment from so generous a man as Octavian, ordered his men to unbolt the doors of the mausoleum and open them to the sunshine. Shortly afterwards Octavian's freedman Epaphroditus arrived, with orders for the Queen to be searched to see that she had no poison concealed on her. She and Iras and Charmion were then confined under guard to the upper room and the body of Antony was removed.

The victor entered the city shortly before sunset, when all the marble buildings and temples, the Mouseion and the palaces of Lochias promontory, were turning ruby-red as the sun went down over the desert. Octavian rode in a chariot and to the astonishment of the citizens it was seen that an Alexandrian philosopher, Areius, stood beside him and that Octavian was talking with him in a most friendly manner and had even given him his right hand to hold. The victor was demonstrating to them in the most clear and forthright way that he was no terrible conquering war-lord but a civilized and gentle man. He drove on into the great gymnasium where all the principal citizens and local magnates had been told to assemble. Octavian now mounted a rostrum that had been prepared for him and proceeded to address the Alexandrians. As he stood up everyone immediately prostrated themselves, but he told them to rise saying that he did not hold the people of Alexandria in any way to blame for the recent war. He had already given strict orders to his officers to ensure that there was to be no looting, and he now assured all the people present that he had no intention of harming their city, firstly in honour of the memory of its great founder, secondly because it was so grand and beautiful, and thirdly to gratify his dear friend the philosopher Areius. Once again Octavian adorned his triumph by his political sagacity, showing himself familiar with the

The Gemma Augustea: sardonyx cameo, Augustus seated at the side of an image of Rome, being crowned by a female figure, the personification of the civilized world

pride they took in their history and architecture, as well as proving himself an admirer of philosophy and the arts.

Immediately on entering the palace and taking up his quarters in those halls where Cleopatra had reigned as Queen and Antony had revelled as Dionysus he revealed the implacable side of his nature. A party was despatched to catch up with Caesarion and make sure that he did not manage to make his escape via the port of Berenice. At the same time, informed by Theodorus, the tutor of Antony's eldest son Antyllus, that the latter had taken refuge in the temple which Cleopatra had erected to Julius Caesar he gave orders for him to be killed. The wretched youth was dragged from the altar and out of the temple and his head was cut off. In the general struggle and confusion Theodorus managed to steal a very valuable gem which Antyllus had worn on a chain around his neck. His theft was discovered and reported to Octavian who gave orders for the tutor to be crucified. Meanwhile, acting on the advice of Areius who knew about the dispositions and attitudes of the various members of the court, he had all those who had been fervent adherents of Antony and Cleopatra put to death. Areius hardly needed to remind him that 'Not a good thing were a Caesar too many', for the horsemen were already speeding across the desert in hot pursuit of Caesar's only son. But where clemency could be politically useful to him, and where there was no danger to his interests, Octavian could be clement. Antony's two youngest children were to be spared and taken back to Rome and raised as if they were his own.

What to do with Antony's body and then what to do with the Queen? Again a public display of magnanimity seemed called for, and Octavian gave permission for Cleopatra to have full charge of the burial rites – always of course under the strict guard of his soldiers. So Antony was buried close to the mausoleum in a place no doubt already set aside for him, Cleopatra, her two serving maids and other women of the court accompanying the cortège. The Queen abandoned herself to that violent and tempestuous display of grief which was and still is expected of a widow in the land of Egypt. 'In consequence of so much grief as well as pain,' says Plutarch, 'for she beat her breasts so much that they were wounded and inflamed, she subsequently relapsed into a high fever.' She was lamenting not only Antony whom she had lost, but Egypt.

The last days of the last Ptolemaic Queen of Egypt are well documented, for Plutarch had access to a record of them, now unfortunately lost, which was written by her personal physician, Olympus. It seems that she used the fever from which she was suffering as an excuse to take no food at all, for she had every intention of starving herself to death rather than walk in chains to grace Octavian's triumph. This was not at all to the victor's liking. To complete his victory and to satisfy his ambition he must at all costs keep the Queen alive. Whether or not she knew that Antyllus was dead, and whether or not she knew that Octavian's men were in pursuit of Caesarion, she did indeed know that her two youngest children were in Octavian's power. To complete her misery, but to ensure her staying alive, he sent word that if she persisted in her present conduct he would have both young Ptolemy and her daughter Cleopatra Selene put to death.

It is doubtful whether up to this moment Cleopatra had ever seen Octavian or he her. At some time during this period, probably at the onset of her illness, Octavian had permitted her to return to the palace at Lochias and here, where she had once been so powerful and so happy, she listened from her quarters to the tramp of officers, centurions and soldiers – but Octavian's not Antony's. For the first, last, and only time the two opponents met face to face. Octavian decided to visit the Queen who was now, he was assured by her physician, on the road to recovery. He decided to give her no opportunity to prepare herself for the meeting, to array herself perhaps in her royal robes as Queen of Egypt and Isis incarnate, but arrived unannounced saying to Iras and Charmion that he had come to congratulate the Queen on the restoration of her health. The world was in Octavian's hand, for here he was as Caesar, sole ruler of the whole Empire, condescending to visit the woman who all those years ago had been his uncle's mistress and had born his only son. Cleopatra, according to Plutarch's account, 'was lying on a pallet-bed wearing nothing but a shift. She sprang up as he entered and threw herself at his feet, her face disfigured and her hair in disarray, her eyes sunken, and her voice trembling. Through the thin dress the marks and scars of the bruises and lacerations that she had inflicted on her breasts were clearly visible.' Octavian, a cool man and a cold lecher, cannot have been impressed but embarrassed rather. So this was the great enemy, this the monstrous Queen of Egypt, this shaking, aging and ruined woman who knelt at his feet! 'But despite all this,' we read, 'the charm for which she was so famous and the boldness of her beauty had not entirely left her. They seemed to shine out from within and revealed themselves in all the expressions of her features.' Octavian raised her up and bade her rest herself again upon the couch.

There seems little doubt that her physician Olympus either was present throughout this famous interview, or learned all about it from one of her serving women, for there is an authenticity in Plutarch's description that defies any fictitious reconstruction. The later Roman stories that even at this moment she tried to seduce Octavian must certainly be discounted. She was sick, vanquished, and growing old. Antony had been fifty-three when he had killed himself and Cleopatra was now thirty-nine. It was only by playing upon sentiment – something that Octavian rarely permitted himself to indulge in – that she had any chance at all of securing her childrens' interest. Accordingly she showed him letters that Caesar had written to her, pointing out that it was Caesar himself who had conferred the crown of Egypt upon her, and handed him his uncle's letters so that Octavian could see for himself what had been written to her by the great conqueror in the days when she had been young, beautiful, and 'the ally of the Roman people'.

A gold coin of Augustus, from Lyon, 2 B.C.–A.D. 11; RIGHT: *coin minted in Asia Minor 29–27 B.C. with arch surmounted by a statue of the triumphant Augustus in a chariot*

Octavian glanced at them briefly but he was not to be caught. It was essential however that Cleopatra should be lulled into a false sense of security and he assured her that he had no ill intentions. At this moment comedy intruded. Cleopatra had sent a messenger to her steward Seleucus telling him to bring to Octavian a list of her personal treasures and jewelry which she had set aside. Seleucus arrived and, while Octavian was looking through the inventory, pointed out that a number of articles of great value were not recorded. At this point Cleopatra leapt up, seized the man by his hair and struck him repeated blows on the face. 'Caesar,' she cried, 'is it not vile when I am in this wretched plight that a slave should have the temerity to accuse me of seeking to keep behind a few articles of women's jewelry – designed indeed not for me but for Octavia and your wife Livia?' She had hoped, she said, that by these presents she might secure the intercession of Antony's former wife and Octavian's on her behalf. Octavian seems to have been convinced by this episode that, whatever else, Cleopatra was determined to live – something which suited his plans entirely. Cleopatra, however, by the end of the interview had undoubtedly assessed the nature of the man who confronted her and realized what plans he had in store for her. She was one of the greatest politicians of all time: she had understood Caesar, and she had controlled Antony. She was not to be deceived by this pale young man with his remarkable luminous eyes and his air of quiet authority. At last she had met her match, and she prepared for the end. 'So Octavian went away, supposing that he had deceived her, but in reality having been deceived *by* her.'

Among the officers and soldiers who had been detailed to guard Cleopatra and to keep an eye on all her actions was a close friend of Octavian, Cornelius Dolabella, who was moved by her plight and had developed a great affection for her. He felt no doubt that, whatever her faults, she was a woman of considerable distinction, and that Octavian's cat-and-mouse game was despicable way to treat this Queen who had done no more than try to preserve her country and her dynasty. He kept her constantly informed of what passed in Octavian's councils and finally brought her the news that the latter had decided to march back with his legions through Syria before returning to Rome. He also told her that Octavian had decided to ship her and the two young children off to the capital in less than three days' time, so that she might be ready to take part in the Egyptian triumph which he was planning to celebrate. She remembered her earlier boast that she would one day sit and give judgment in the Capitol. She remembered too that either as Caesar's or as Antony's wife she had always intended to rule there as Empress, a triumphant Greek Ptolemy dispensing law and order to a rough and vulgar people. She also realized now that, unless Caesarion had already made his escape, he would certainly be killed and that the kingdom of Egypt would come under Octavian's control. She had tried to temporize and she had tried to secure the rights of her children, but she understood that, if there was to be any future at all for them it could be achieved only by the elimination of herself.

Cleopatra now sent a message to Octavian asking him if she might be allowed to visit Antony's grave in order to make the usual offerings for the dead man's soul. Octavian, convinced that at last she was completely overcome and broken in spirit, was kind enough to permit her this normal ritual – one that showed him in the most favourable and clement light. So at the end of August, nearly a month after the defeat that had sealed her fate, Cleopatra visited the site where her dead husband lay interred. 'Dearest Antony,' she cried, 'only so recently I buried you with free hands, and now I pour libations for you with hands that are those of a slave. I am so closely guarded that I cannot disfigure this body of mine any more either with blows or with tears. I am so closely watched in order that I may grace the victor's triumph over you. Expect from me no more libations and honours, for these are the last from captive Cleopatra. Nothing could part us in life, but now in death we are likely to change places, you the Roman lying here in Egyptian soil, and I, helpless woman that I am, being buried in Italy.' Even these last words show that she was determined to give Octavian's soldiers the idea that she had resigned herself to this Roman triumph and to being executed at the end of it, just as Vercingetorix had been. She fell upon Antony's gravestone kissing it passionately, placed some wreaths of his flowers upon it in his memory, and was then carried back to her mausoleum. There can be no doubt that this expedition, during which she had drawn so heavily upon the simple emotions of the Roman soldiers who escorted her, was carefully planned to give her the necessary freedom of movement to accomplish her end.

She and Iras and Charmion now entered the mausoleum, a guard being mounted outside, and Cleopatra made her way into the main chamber from which the treasures of her fathers had long since been removed. Here, in this monument to

Stela with figure of Isis holding a torch between two snakes, one wearing the double crown of Egypt and holding the staff of Hermes

death where her husband had already died, she had determined to end her life. She ordered a bath to be prepared, had her hair washed, scented and dressed, and then had herself arrayed in her formal robes as Queen of Egypt and the goddess Isis. 'A sumptuous meal' was prepared and Cleopatra reclined on a couch to eat, remembering no doubt all those many banquets with Antony and the 'Society of the Inimitable Livers', when it had seemed that the whole world was theirs and all the pleasures in it. Antyllus, she must have known by now, was dead, but her two youngest children were alive in the palace and there was every hope that her beloved Caesarion had reached Berenice and escaped from Egypt. It was at about this time that 'there came a man from the country and approached the mausoleum and when the guards outside asked him what he had in the basket over his arm he took off the leaves that were on top and showed them that it contained only figs. The guards were amazed at the size and beauty of them, whereupon he smiled and invited them to take some for themselves. Naturally they were disarmed by his approach and, suspecting nothing, allowed him to take them in to the Queen.' Almost certainly beneath these green-and-purple sweet-smelling fruits was the serpent with which Cleopatra intended to end her life.

'The Queen now took a tablet and wrote a message which she sealed and gave to Epaphroditus, who was among her guards, asking him to take it to his master Octavian.' After he had gone she dismissed all her other attendants, leaving only Iras and Charmion alone with her in that sun- and wind-filled building. It will never be known how her two faithful maid servants killed themselves, but there were many poisons in ancient Egypt, drugs that could be concealed in such things as combs or jewellery.

Immediately on receiving her message, in which Cleopatra asked that she might be buried with Antony, Octavian realized what had happened and sent some officers on ahead of him to try and prevent the Queen killing herself. They arrived to find the sentries oblivious of any calamity standing on guard outside the sunlit door. They burst in to the presence of Old Egypt, of death seen and arranged as the natural culmination of life and as a spectacle which even those still living could appreciate. Cleopatra was laid out upon a golden bedstead dressed in all her royal robes. Iras lay dead across her feet, and Charmion who was in the throes of death was trying to adjust the Queen's diadem. 'A fine deed, Charmion!' one of the Romans cried out. 'Yes, it is, most fine indeed', she replied, 'and befitting the descendant of so many kings.' Those were her last words as she too fell to the ground beside the couch of her mistress and her Queen. The snake itself was never found, 'although people said that they saw some traces left behind by it on the beach, where the windows of the chamber looked out upon the sea'. Two small marks were observed on one of Cleopatra's arms and in Octavian's subsequent triumph one of the main features was a portrait of Cleopatra with a serpent clinging to her arm.

The world was now Octavian's. There were no more threats to his supreme position. He had achieved by political brilliance, by knowing how to enlist the best men on his side, and by 'hastening slowly', the very objective which the aging and more impetuous Caesar had failed to attain. His last opponent, the only one who had ever really threatened him, was dead. He contemplated her as she lay there in her royal robes. Even now in a kind of way she had defeated him. Cleopatra was not going to be led as the chained but golden ornament to his Triumph when he rode as Emperor through the streets of Rome. With the diadem on her head, with the snake-bite on her arm, she had removed herself from the sordid mortal world. She had taken refuge with those impenetrable gods and goddesses whose stony faces smiled inscrutably at him all over this strange, frightening, ancient land.

In her last letter to him Cleopatra had requested that she might be buried not in her masoleum but by the side of Antony. Octavian honourably and out of respect for the dead Queen saw that her wished were observed and she was interred with full royal honours next to her husband. The site of their graves, like even the great tomb of Alexander, has long since been lost, but somewhere beneath the tortuous streets of Arabic Alexandria there lies the dust of Antony and Cleopatra, not ignoble victims of ambition and the struggle for the world. One thing she was spared, the knowledge that her son Caesarion would never inherit Egypt. A short time after her death Caesarion, acting on the advice of his tutor that he would do best to put his trust in Octavian, returned to Alexandria where he was immediately put to death.

The treasure of the Ptolemies, heavy taxation of the wealthy citizens, the possession of fertile Egypt itself, all these enabled Octavian to rid himself of the burden of debt to his legionaries and to establish the basis of a private fortune which gave him the financial security he needed in the years to come. As for the country itself he was determined not to make it a Roman province for, quite apart from any Egyptian feelings on that subject, it was too rich a land to be put under a senatorial governor who might once again revive the dream of an empire ruled from the East. Octavian took it over as a kind of personal possession and he and all subsequent Emperors, although never formally crowned, were recognized as Kings of Egypt. In hieroglyphics inscribed on the walls of temples one finds Octavian described as 'The King of Upper and Lower Egypt, Son of the Sun, Caesar, living for ever, the beloved of Ptah and of Isis.' Near Actium, which he rightly recognized as the place where he had seized 'the lever that moves the world', he gave orders to build Nicopolis, the City of Victory. 'Look on my works ye mighty and despair' – its ruins still haunt the slopes above the mosquito-ridden gulf where Antony's hopes perished.

Cleopatra, the last Ptolemaic Queen, passed into legend, and history traduced and maligned her as an infamous woman, given to sexual excess and capable of every perfidy. The truth was quite different. She was a woman of infinite courage and political resource. From the age of eighteen until her death she had fought to free her country from the iron dominance of Rome and to secure its inheritance for the son of her first lover Julius Caesar. It was right that she should be buried in Alexandria, for in her spirit and in her ambition she was worthy of Alexander himself.

Painted funerary slab showing the Egyptian ba, an aspect of the soul which could enter or leave the body and was commonly represented as a human-headed bird; 2nd century A.D.

SELECT BIBLIOGRAPHY

ANCIENT LITERATURE

*Prime sources relating to Cleopatra, her life and times,
and the Ptolemies:*

ARRIAN · POLYBIUS · DIO CASSIUS · DIODORUS · APPIAN
JULIUS CAESAR · CICERO · STRABO · PLUTARCH · SUETONIUS
JOSEPHUS · NICOLAUS OF DAMASCUS · LUCAN

*Historians and poets who also contribute information
on the period, although less reliable:*

ATHENAEUS · VELLEIUS PATERCULUS · SALLUST · OVID
PLINY · JUVENAL · HORACE · FLORUS

MODERN LITERATURE

BALSDON, J. P. *The Romans* [LONDON 1965]

Cambridge Ancient History, Vol. X [CAMBRIDGE 1934]

CARTER, J. M. *The Battle of Actium* [LONDON 1970]

FORSTER, E. M. *Alexandria* [NEW YORK 1961]

GRANT, M. *From Imperium to Auctoritas* [CAMBRIDGE 1946]

HADAS, M. *Sextus Pompey* [NEW YORK 1930]

SYME, R. *The Roman Revolution* [OXFORD 1939]

VOLKMANN, H. *Cleopatra. A Study in Politics and Propaganda* [LONDON 1958]

WEIGALL, A. *The Life and Times of Cleopatra* [LONDON 1926]

WERTHEIMER, OSKAR VON. *Cleopatra* [LONDON 1931]

ACKNOWLEDGMENTS

The author and producers of this book are very grateful to Dr A. F. Shore, Assistant Keeper of the Department of Egyptian Antiquities, British Museum, for his help and advice on the text, pictures and captions in this book.

PICTURE ACKNOWLEDGMENTS

273

Page 13: left from Alexandria Museum, photograph Alistair Duncan, Middle East Archive; right by courtesy of the Trustees of the British Museum.
Page 14: Metropolitan Museum of Art, New York, photograph Mansell Collection.
Page 15: Cairo Museum, photograph Griffith Institute, by courtesy of the Ashmolean Museum.
Page 16: from the Mansell Collection.
Page 17: from the British Museum, photograph Mansell Collection.
Page 23: photograph Ny Carlsberg Glyptothek, Copenhagen.
Page 24: Kunsthistorisches Museum, Vienna, Photo Meyer.
Page 27: photograph Ronald Sheridan.
Page 34: photograph Ny Carlsberg Glyptothek, Copenhagen.
Page 36: both by courtesy of the Trustees of the British Museum.
Page 38: George Rainbird Limited.
Page 45: from the Mansell Collection.
Page 48: left photograph Peter Clayton; right George Rainbird Limited.
Page 50: from the Mansell Collection.
Page 51: photograph Ronald Sheridan.
Page 52: from the Mansell Collection.
Page 57: photograph Roger Viollet.
Page 62: photograph Fototeca Unione.
Page 64: photograph Oscar Savio.
Pages 67, 68: from the Mansell Collection.
Page 72: Vienna Kunstmuseum.
Page 75: left photograph Werner Forman; right Cabinet des Médailles, Paris, photograph Jean Roubier.
Page 80: from the Mansell Collection.
Page 82: photograph Lala Aufsberg.
Page 83: left photograph Alistair Duncan, Middle East Archive; right Staatliche Museen zu Berlin.
Page 84: by courtesy of the Oriental Institute, University of Chicago.
Page 85: photograph A. Mekhitarian, Fondation Egyptologique.
Page 92: from the Cliché du service des antiquités du Maroc.
Page 93: by courtesy of the Bibliothèque Nationale, Paris.
Page 94: from the Mansell Collection.
Page 97: Cabinet des Médailles, Paris, photograph Jean Roubier.
Page 98: photograph Fototeca Unione.
Page 102: photograph Lala Aufsberg.
Page 103: left George Rainbird Limited; right from the Mansell Collection.
Page 104: photograph Mario Carrieri.
Page 107: photograph Adolfo Tomeucci.
Page 108: from the Mansell Collection.
Page 110: from the Anderson Collection.
Page 111: by courtesy of the Trustees of the British Museum.
Page 113: photograph Alinari from the Mansell Collection.
Page 114: by courtesy of the Trustees of the British Museum.
Page 121: photograph Alinari from the Mansell Collection.
Page 123: from Gabinetto fotografico della soprintendenza piazzale degli galleria Uffizi.
Page 126: photograph Alistair Duncan, Middle East Archive.
Pages 128, 131: from the Mansell Collection.

INDEX